D0898792

67

WEST RIVER

STORIES FROM THE
GREAT SIOUX RESERVATION

JOHN SIMPSON

Jno. J. Simpson
Oct 2000

WEST RIVER

Copyright © 2000 John Simpson

ALL RIGHTS RESERVED
This work may not be used in any form, or reproduced by any means, in whole or in part, without written permission from the publisher.

LCCN: 99-93875

ISBN: 1-57579-156-0

Cover Painting:
Elijah Eagle Feather, 1972

Publisher
Rattlesnake Butte Press
HCR 89 Box 19
Hamill, SD 57534
Fax 605-842-3220

Printed in the United States of America
PINE HILL PRESS, INC.
4000 West 57th Street
Sioux Falls, S.D. 57106

ABOUT THE AUTHOR

John J. Simpson has practiced law in West River for nearly 45 years. He has been an Assistant Attorney General, States Attorney of Tripp and Todd Counties, taught history, law and government at Sinte Gleska University, Mission, South Dakota and was a gifted and talented instructor and administrator at St Francis Indian School, St Francis, South Dakota. He is presently an associate judge at the Lower Brule Sioux Reservation.

A special thanks to Mike and Bob Simpson for proof reading and editing.

CONTENTS

FOREWORD

These "West River" Dakota Territory stories are filled with Sicangu, Poncas, Brules, Oglalas, Minniconjous, and a host of other tribes, buffalo hunters, princes, paupers, settlers, ranchers, squawmen, racists, rustlers, murderers, soldiers, do gooders, preachers, priests, big money, foreigners, dreamers, honyockers, homesteaders, hired guns, hit men, violence, fraud, cheats, love, hate, success and failure.

The tales chronicle the development of West River country as not only a time and place, but a culture of its own. The stories are told the way they happened. There is little majesty, much hatred, greed, adventure and violence, all of the faults and few of the virtues. The view is kaleidoscopic, ever changing, and has a different appearance depending upon one's point of view.

The intent of the stories is to present the various conflicting cultures and values involved in early Territorial and Great Sioux reservation times as short, well documented history demanded by white culture modified by the oral history, tradition and culture of the Native American.

Oral history gives life and often enlightenment to the historian's written word. It also raises some interesting questions. Were the early rustlers "scapegoats" or "scoundrels"? Did the big cattlemen make secret "hit lists"? Did the Government conspire to rid the Indian people of their leaders? Did it have a "hit list" too?

SECTION ONE

CHAPTER ONE
EARLY HISTORY

In the early 1800s the Sicangu band of the Lakota inhabited the headwaters of the White River and the Niobrara ranging to the Bad Lands and the Little Missouri or Teton River. During the late 1790s and early 1800s the Sicangu were headed by a chief known as Mau-Ka'u-to-jan-jo or Clear Blue Earth.

He governed wisely and well and few leaders had his power and dignity. He was a great role model for future leaders. The band was well provided, having an abundance of meat and wild horses. Its main enemies were the Arikaras, Pawnees and Omahas.

Death of Logan Fontenelle

Most battles are subject to the interpretation placed on them by the person recording the events. A typical example is the account of the killing of the noted Omaha chief, Logan Fontenelle, by White Thunder of the Sicangu.

A newspaper report of February 6th, 1856 gives the following account of the death of Fontenelle:

"Logan Fontenelle, chief of the Omahas, has just been slain and scalped at Loup Fork, by a band of Sicangu.

Logan was a noble fellow, and in this last mortal conflict he dispatched several of the enemy to the spirit land before, to herald the coming of his own soul, he fought long, desperately, and with great effect; but numbers finally overcame him and his life departed through a hundred wounds. He died a martyr to his people, and his name should be carved upon fame's brightest tablet . . .."

The tribe was on its annual hunt on the Loup River and so were the Sicangu. When Fontenelle was notified of the approach of a larger band of Sicangu, he ordered his hunting party straight home while he tried to delay and confuse the Sicangu.

"Logan dashed away at full speed at right angles with the route his tribe had taken, and about eight miles . . . (away) . . . struck a fire . . . where the Sicangu (Lakota) could see it"

The Sicangu, seeing the fire, all rode in its direction and Logan proceeded to attempt to fool them in the same manner a second time.

They charged after the second fire spot as well. However their suspicions now were aroused and they split into different groups to find the true trail of the Omahas.

Logan was hidden by a young Omaha girl, who took his horse and rode in a circle, to further confuse the Sicangu.

When he thought he was free of the Sicangu a party of fifty appeared in front of him and the fight was on. Logan was killed, but not before he had inflicted mortal blows on some of his pursuers.

"Thus Logan Fontenelle departed, and his noble spirit was followed to the spirit land by the sighs and lamentations of his nation and the sympathies and aspirations of the brave of every land."[1]

In the early 1900s when a group of Omahas attended a Sicangu pow-wow at Rosebud the visiting between the two bands determined White Thunder of the Sicangu had killed Logan Fontenelle.[2]

The Sicangu account differed from the reported newspaper account of the battle. The Sicangu account includes the killing of Logan by White Thunder. The other Sicangu on the raid were Big Turkey, Yellow Hair, Left Hand Bull, and Brown Blanket. This account also states the Sicangu hunting party had stolen the Omahas' horses and they were pursued. In the fight that followed two of the Sicangu were wounded and Logan Fontenelle was killed.[3]

THE GRATTAN MASSACRE

Most histories of the early fights between the United States Army and the Lakota accept the army version of what happened. To be sure, the Indians killed and mutilated Lt. Grattan and all of his soldiers. The Army's and the Lakota account offer differing versions. Where does the truth lie?

Army Version

Following the Grattan massacre Lewis B. Dougherty, a common soldier, wrote his father on August 29th as follows:

". . . A Lakota chief named Bear that Scatters came up from his village . . . where. . . he was encamped, waiting for the division of annuities. . . (He) (told) Lt. Fleming that one of his Lakota warriors had killed a cow belonging to a Mormon . . . and requested him to send down his soldiers to punish the offender . . . (Lt. Grattan's command of twenty nine men). . . with two pieces of artillery arrived outside their village . . . (The chief) made his appearance . . . (and said the offender had answered) "I am alone; last fall, the soldiers killed my two brothers; this spring my only remaining relation died. I have a gun with plenty of powder and balls, a bow and quiver full of arrows and the soldiers will have to kill and then take me." Lt. Grattan . . . told the Indians he had come for the offender and would have him or all would die . . .. The two pieces of the Army's artillery were fired . . .. Before the guns could be reloaded Lt. Grattan and two men were shot down at the cannons, and then a retreat commenced, the Indians in pursuit. The whites were all killed and the bodies were horribly mutilated. The bodies could not be buried for two days because of the Indians . . . the morning after the slaughter the Lakota made a rush for the store of the American Fur Company . . . and took all . . .."[4]

The Lakota version

Susan Bettelyon, daughter of the early trader James Bordeau and a Sicangu mother, related her father's version of the affair.

She stated that the cow was killed by Iteywoga (Bad or Broken Face), a Minniconjou who was with the Sicangu. They claim that Mato wa yuhi (Scattering Bear) told Grattan that they would pay for the old cow.

The Indian annuities were stored at the Bovey place and the Indians had been waiting a long time for the agent, who was taking his sweet time, to arrive. After they killed all the soldiers they broke into the warehouse and took the annuities that had been stored for distribution to them.

All Indian accounts indicate that Lt. Grattan brought on the fight through his rash actions. James Bordeau maintained that the Indians were forced to fight and that Scattering Bear had always been friendly to the whites.[5]

The Army Investigation

Colonel Wm. Hoffman was ordered to investigate the Grattan affair. His report received a sharp rebuke from the Adjutant General, who wrote from his Washington office on August 20 1855: that the report had done "injury to . . . the gallant dead . . . (and) I have to discharge a plain duty in defending a brother officer (Grattan) against what I conceived to be undeserved attack. . . .."[6]

Hoffman's report included letters from Captain Ed. Johnson, investigating officer; James Bordeau, trader at whose place the incident occurred; the assistant Surgeon; Chaplain; and Grattan's roommate, J.H. Reed. The most important aspects of the investigation are in Captain Johnson's and Bordeau's accounts:

Bordeau, who was an eyewitness, and had been privy to the events leading up to the incident, gave the following report:

". . . Grattan . . . told me he had come down to take prisoner an Indian who had killed a cow belonging to a Mormon, and asked me to assist him."

Bordeau sent for the chief of the Brule band (Mato wa yuhi) and Bordeau told the chief that Indian who had killed the cow should go with Grattan to the Fort and await the arrival of the Indian agent.

The chief left and returned with three other chiefs. While they were talking a messenger from the Indian camp arrived and told them that the man refused to surrender. Grattan sought directions to the man's lodge. Grattan left stating: "He would have him dead or alive."

A second messenger arrived with the same report. Bordeau states that Grattan then placed his men in readiness and told them that on his command they must shoot every non white in sight.

Mato wa yuhi told Grattan that it was their custom to ask four times for the man to surrender and that they should honor this custom. Grattan persisted and marched toward the man's lodge.

Bordeau continued: "I then turned back and got up on a robe press where I could see him til he halted. During this time his interpreter was in the Camp mocking the Indians and imitating them. I told Grattan he would make trouble, and that if he would put the interpreter in my house, I would settle the difficulty in thirty minutes . . . .." The Lt. would not follow Bordeau's advice. He ordered his troops forward. He would have the Indian culprit dead or alive.

When Grattan entered the Camp he was immediately surrounded. Bordeau continued:

". . . when I got within 150 yards I saw that it was too late. The excitement was too great. At this moment the first gun was fired by the soldiers on the right." Bordeau fled from the scene to his trading post and watched the rest of the incident from his roof top.

"Little Thunder, a chief, came and told me that since the Indians had killed all the soldiers at this camp they were going to kill all at the fort and burn it up."[7]

Captain Johnson's report

(Johnson was Spotted Tail's escort when the chief surrendered to Harney the following year)

Johnson stated: "Grattan was detailed to bring in the Indian who had stolen the cow without unnecessary risks." Volunteers were requested. Johnson states: . . . "the Ordnance Sergeant, an old and faithful soldier was requested by Lt. Grattan to go along; which he declined doing, because, as he says, "he believed the Lieutenant to be rash; that there would be a difficulty, and he had no confidence in his judgment."

Johnson continued; "There is a matter connected with, and bearing in some degree upon this affair, which has not been mentioned. The summer before, a Mineconjou had fired at a soldier who was crossing the Platte in a boat. Lt. Fleming was sent at night with a detachment across the river to bring in the offender, or some others as hostages. He went to their encampment and made the demand, but the offender and nearly everyone else was gone." The troops fired on the remaining Indians, and later the band came in and the matter was amicably settled. Since Fleming had received honors for his actions Grattan wanted the same opportunity to earn glory.[8]

On the day he left he was in a state of unusual excitement. A Mr. Allen and Man That Is Afraid Of His Horses, head chief of the Oglalas, went with him. The interpreter who accompanied them was drunk.[9]

When they first saw the Indian's camp Mr. Allen remarked, "Lt. do you see how many lodges there are?"

"Yes," was his reply, "but I don't care how many there are; with thirty men I can whip all the Indians this side of the Missouri."[10]

Allen corroborates Bordeau's comments that the interpreter was baiting the Indians. He agreed that Bordeau could settle the matter in half an hour.

Johnson continued: ". . . Man That Is Afraid Of His Horses. . . says that the Bear That Scatters urged the Lt. to go home and defer the matter until the arrival of the Agent. . .(and) . . . that Mato wa yuhi (Bear That Scatters) offered the Lt. a mule in place of the cow. . . .."

Man That Is Afraid of His Horses twice came to Bordeau asking him to come quick as the interpreter was causing trouble. The chief also went twice to the lodge of the cow killer to see if he would give himself up, he replied, "tell the white chief I am ready to die."

In his report, Captain Johnson wrote: "This affair has been labeled an ambuscade -a deeply laid scheme to entrap the troops, and massacre them, in consequence of the weakness of the garrison of Fort Laramie . . . You, Sir, are aware that repeated calls had been made for more troops at the frontier posts. But there is not a shadow of evidence to show that the Indians desired a difficulty. . . .."

He concluded, "Yes, let justice be done, though the heavens may fall."[11]

The Chaplain's Opinion

The most damning testimony was given by Chaplain William Naux. He wrote:

"W. Grattan . . . had an unwarrantable contempt of Indian character, which frequently manifested itself in my presence...and I have reproved him for acts which I conceived highly improper—such as thrusting his clenched fist in their faces, and threatening terrible things. . . .."

"The awful consequences of the whole occurrences, with the existing state of things, and the unknown future results, I conceive to be the effects and not the cause of culpability. That cause is to be traced to the fact of the garrison being left under the command of an inexperienced and rash boy. "'Behold, how great a matter a little fire kindleth.'"[12]

After the massacre the Indians broke into their supplies that had been waiting for the agent to come and distribute. Bordeau gave away his goods upon the advice of the chiefs, who stated they could not control their bands.

Battle of the Blue Water

In September of the following year the Army sent General Harney in the field to punish the Sicangu for the Grattan massacre. The Sicangu had returned for their fall buffalo hunt and were camped on the Little Blue River. This was a buffalo hunting camp and they needed time to dry and cure their meat. They had no desire to move their camp.

The Indian's account of the battle states that Little Thunder, Iron Shell and another went out to meet Harney with a white flag. Harney had ordered his troops forward despite the white flag. The army charged and killed dozens of Indians the majority women and children. From then on General Harney would be known to the Sicangu as "Squaw Killer Harney." In this fight, Spotted Tail unhorsed 13 soldiers.[13]

Two Strikes' account

Two Strikes gave the following account:

"We were camped on a wide bend of the Blue River on one of our usual buffalo hunts. One afternoon, a group of soldiers appeared on a ridge west of the village.

From the men congregated on the hill a lone rider advanced at a slow gallop. When he arrived, we recognized him as Wica-Ya-Shipahe's (Squaw Killer Harney's) interpreter. After greeting us with a pretense of friendliness, that we did not suspect at the time he advised Iron Shell and Little Thunder leaders of our band that General Harney wished for a conference with them. The two chiefs signified their acceptance upon which the interpreter waved a signal with his hat. The troops without further delay advanced slowly in military formation. Upon reaching a point . . . they suddenly charged where we had gathered for the conference and proceeded to slaughter us . . . ."

The year of the Ash Hollow massacre is recorded in the Lakota winter count as Sicon-Go-Tiapaha-Wica-Ktepe (When Brules were massacred in their own village).[14]

The bugler's account

John M. Sullivan, chief bugler, gave the following account of the battle:

"On the night of the third of September we encamped at the mouth of Ash Hollow. Soon afterward our guides went up on the mountain to take a look at the country and beheld, about eight miles north of us, an Indian encampment . . . .. Col. Cook gave orders for us to leave at three o'clock the next morning–R and C Company of the 2nd Dragoons, Company G of the 4th Artillery and 3rd mounted infantry, Col. Cook and his staff consisting of two officers, Sergeant major Spear, Sergeant Kitlass, and myself, in all 200 men."

"We commenced the battle at sunrise and fought for four and a half hours-by the watch–We killed as near as we could count, one hundred Sioux's–a few above or below–Our loss was four killed, thirteen wounded, one missing . . . When our boys saw their comrades fall they fought like tigers; and when the glorious charge rang out from "my old bugle" you might have seen (them all) charge en masse, down the almost perpendicular mountain where they met the Indian warriors hand to hand. We made them bite the dust in dozens, and took fifty prisoners . . . .. All our boys now have fancy Indian war dresses, ponies, mules, etc."[15]

Indian prisoners

Lt. B.H. Robertson wrote an account of the aftermath of the battle on his arrival at Fort Leavenworth on the 18th of November 1855.

He reported: "Gen. Harney is at Fort Pierre, and . . . ready to commence an early and vigorous campaign against the Sioux in the spring. In which event he will attach to his sleigh a large number of dogs. Having captured a large number of dogs and squaws at Ash Hollow . . . .."[16]

One of Chief Iron Shell's wives was taken prisoner and went back east with her soldier captor. Others were "thrown away" by their army "lovers". When they returned to their people, they were treated with contempt because they did not escape, while at Fort Pierre.[17]

Spotted Tail's heroics

Spotted Tail, who would become a legendary chief of the Sicangu, gained early fame in the Battle of Blue Water. His exploits at Blue Water earned him praise not only from the U.S. Army, but the local press as well.

Jacob Harmon, a young Missouri runaway, who had come west in 1859, joined the 1st. Colorado cavalry and rode guard along the Platte river road in the 1860s, held this enlisted man's view of Spotted Tail: "The bravest chief that ever rode a horse was old Spotted Tail. He was a heavy set Indian who weighed about 180 lbs. and was a good fighter."[23]

After Harney surrounded the Indian village on the Little Blue, Little Thunder, Iron Shell and another together with Sam Smith, James Bordeaux's agent, went with a flag of truce to talk to Harney. Harney, however, was in no mood to talk and attacked the village. Spotted Tail gave his horse to his wife and told her to escape. Spotted Tail unhorsed the first dragoon who bore down on him. He took the dragoons' sword and mounted the soldier's horse. The Lakota tradition states that Spotted Tail then fought a delaying action and counted coup on thirteen dragoons. As each soldier fell or was unhorsed by him, his wife, who had stationed herself on a nearby hill would encourage him with an Indian war trill. She refused to leave until he joined her and together they made their escape.[18]

The aftermath

During the same year Spotted Tail and others held up the Kincade mail stage, killing the driver and passengers and stealing the U.S. Army paymaster's gold shipment. The Army sought out the killers.

Thereafter Harney held talks with the Oglala and Brule bands of the Lakota in which they agreed to surrender killers of the mail party. As bargaining chips Harney held fifty hostages he had taken as prisoners at the Blue Water battle.[19]

Harney told Little Thunder of the Brules that if the mail party killers surrendered, the rest of the tribe would not be molested.

Spotted Tail was involved and the raiding party spent the gold at Bordeau's and Bovey's trading posts.[20] The Liberty Tribune (Mo.) of November 2 1855 reported: "One of the Indians concerned in the massacre of the mail party, called Spotted Tail, was in the battle of Blue Water, and received four wounds-two pistol shots passing through him, and receiving two saber cuts, and still he escaped on the horse of a Dragoon . . . .."[21]

Harney demanded the surrender of those involved in the mail party massacre. In 1855, Spotted Tail surrendered. Spotted Tail, Red Leaf, Long Chin, Standing Elk and Red Plume surrendered to the Army in 1855. They were imprisoned at Fort Leavenworth, pardoned on January 16th, 1856, but not released until November of 1856. In all, seven warriors surrendered to Harney.[22]

From 1855 to 1865 Spotted Tail kept out of the army's hair. However local Indian lore indicates that he and Two Strike made raids along the Platte Valley in the 1860s.[24]

In 1864, the Sicangu elected Spotted Tail as spokesman for his band. He immediately told the Government straight out that the Platte Valley was the Sicangu hunting ground and they intended to keep it.[25]

Lakota Legend

The Battle of the Blue Water resulted in a Sicangu legend of mother love. The legend has been orally transmitted and represents the deep sense of family love that is part of the Lakota culture.

Little Cheyenne Woman was married to a warrior of Little Thunder's band. She was a Northern Cheyenne and was a favorite of the Sicangu camp. She had four children by her Sicangu husband, who was a great hunter.

In the month of August the band moved on the Blue Water and camped at Ash Hollow. Here the Sicangu pitched their tents and large buffalo lodges and their children played and fished along the beautiful stream while the elders prepared buffalo meat for the fall. They were in the midst of the "golden time" of their tribe, for they lived in the abundance and in the beauty of nature.

The Sicangu legend continues: General Harney attacked the camp without warning. When the fighting started Little Cheyenne Woman and her husband ran to the trees with their children. She carried the youngest, a daughter, in her arms. A Trooper cut down their oldest child with a saber, and soon all were dead except Little Cheyenne woman and the babe in her arms.

Escaping from the battle, Little Cheyenne Woman carried her baby until she arrived at the camp of Swift Bear, a Lakota chief. When she recovered from the butchery of her family she lavished all her love and attention on the baby girl.

Years passed and she never married. She was content to live alone with her daughter. When the girl was fifteen years old she took deathly sick and died.

Swift Bear's camp was plunged into grief by the death. At that time it was customary for the Lakota in times of mourning to cut their hair and cut deep gashes in their bodies. It is said that this Sicangu camp, in sympathy for Little Cheyenne Woman, literally cut their bodies to pieces.

The customary burial was to wrap and place the body of the dead in "burial trees." Little Cheyenne Woman refused to bury her child but kept the body, then the bones with her wherever the camp moved. The Lakota prepared a tree scaffold, but the mother was prepared to fight to keep the body of her child.

None of the Lakota would camp near her, but they would bring her portions of the meat that was killed by the hunters and she kept herself separate from the main camp.

She carried the bones of her deceased daughter with her for many years. There came a time when a great Lakota camp was made on a beautiful stream in northern Nebraska. The stream was called Wazi Hanska Wakpa by the Lakota. The whitemen called it Long Pine Creek.

The mother was now old and sick and had struggled to reach this camp with her people. That night after the women of the camp erected her lodge, as she was too feeble to make her own camp, she died alone.

The Lakota placed her body and the bones of her daughter on a scaffold tree near Long Pine Creek and the mother and daughter were united in death.[26]

The Council of 1864

In 1864, General Mitchell met with the Brule and Sicangu band to discuss travel and surveys being made across Nebraska.

Lt. Ware reported that Spotted Tail was there and that he was regarded as the greatest warrior of the Sicangu band of the Lakota nation, past or present and that he had counted 28 couz.[27]

Mitchell informed them that they must stay out of the Platte valley. He issued and ultimatum that if the chiefs did not restrain their men from fighting back he would hold them responsible.

Spotted Tail replied:

"The Lakota nation is a great people, and we do not wish to be dictated to by the whites or anybody else. We do not care particularly about the Platte valley, because there is no game in it . . . .. (You have driven it all out) . . . but we want to come and trade on (there) whenever we please . . . .. The Platte valley is ours and we do not intend to give it away . . . .. Besides this we will not give up the Platte valley to you until we have a regular treaty, and until we have agreed to it, and have been paid for it. It will soon be that you will want other roads to the west, If we give you this you will want another, and if we give you that you will want a third . . . .."

Spotted Tail objected to the survey of the Niobrara and stated the Smokey Hill route should be closed.[28] The Army and the Brules and Sicangu "Counciled" several more times, the Army being adamant in its demands that the Indians vacate the Platte river valley and the Indians were adamant that they stay where they were. At last in 1865 the army took matters into its own hands . . . and so did Spotted Tail's band.

Revolt at Horsehead creek

In 1865 the Army rounded up Spotted Tail's band and hired James Bordeaux and 40 other whites who had married Indian women to transport the Lakota and their possessions to a reservation next to their old enemies, the Pawnees. These traders were often used to toll the full bloods to the location desired by the government.

The Indian memory for promises made and not kept is demonstrated by the following letter written on July 17, 1878 to Major Pollock by Yellow Breast, a sub chief of the Sicangu:

"My complaint is that he (James Bordeau) . . . since 1868 . . . owed me . . . three hundred and thirty five 335) dollars . . . for . . . 87 days worked in persuading and inducing these Dakotans to come to the Whetstone Agency . . . .. which the Generals, Sherman, Harney (and others) promised me . . . $5 per day . . . (to be paid) through agent Bordeau . . . for which he has paid me nothing.".[29]

At that time there were about 200 lodges in Spotted Tail's camp. While enroute some of the northern band broke off and escaped. The remaining members led by Spotted Tail, Two Strike and others planned a surprise for the army and the civilians at Horse Creek, in Nebraska.

A select band of the Sicangu leaders plotted the surprise the night before they were to leave. On May 16, 1865 the Sicangu rebelled. White Thunder killed an officer. Four enlisted men died in the skirmish. Soap, one of the Indians who had been prisoner, was murdered after the fight was over. The Sicangu scattered themselves to the winds and escaped, to later gather at a pre-arranged site that fall at Bear Butte in the northern Black Hills.[30]

The Liberty Missouri Tribune of June 23, 1865 reported:

"About 500 Lakota Indians in camp 15 miles west of Fort Mitchell, supposed to be friendly, this morning attacked a guard of 100 men under Captain Foulkes, of the 11th Ohio Veteran Cavalry, killing Foulkes and four men and wounding seven."[31]

White atrocities

The Sicangu revolt had been sparked by the government's removal order to the Missouri River and the cruel hanging of a Cheyenne and Blackfoot at Fort Laramie in May 1865. The Indians were left dangling in the wind. The Cheyenne was hung with the ball and chain on one foot. Soon the leg pulled loose and he was left hanging for two months with just one limb.[32]

Jacob Harmon of Company D of the First Colorado Cavalry as well as Susan Bettleyon were present at the hanging. Harmon states the Indians had brought in the Eubanks captives to be returned to their families. As a cruel reward they were hung on the orders of the Captain in charge and the men were to watch them "kick their way to the happy hunting ground."[33]

This cruel treatment did not serve its intended purpose but only fostered more violence and resentment on the part of the Lakota. It would erupt at Horsehead Creek.

The killing of individual and small groups of innocent Indians was never reported. The Indians were scalped and the settlers and soldiers wore these bloody scalps for all to see. Such was the terror of the Indians toward the soldiers and the depredations that they did not even whisper about these outrages for fear of the retaliation such as that taken by the Army at Ash Hollow after the affair with Lt. Grattan.[34]

Chapter One End Notes

1. Susan Bettleyon MS., SDHC Pierre, SD.
2. *Kansas Weekly Herald*, Feb., 1856.
3. Ibid.
4. *Missouri Liberty Tribune*, October 6, 1854.
5. Susan Bettelyon Ms, South Dakota Heritage Center Archives.
6. National Archives Microfilm Records M567 #546 Sinte Gleska University Library, Mission, South Dakota Letter from Adjutant General to Col. Hoffman.
7. Ibid. James Bordeau's accounts.
8. Ibid. Captain Johnson's investigation.
9. Ibid.
10. Ibid.
11. Ibid.
12. Ibid.
13. Susan Bettleyon Ms. South Dakota Heritage Center Archives, Pierre S.D.
14. William Bordeau Ms, St. Francis Indian School Library, St. Francis, S.D.
15. *Kansas City Weekly Herald*, September 22, 1855.
16. *Kansas City Weekly Herald*, November 24, 1855.
17. MS8 Ricker, Eli Seavey, Box 4, reel #3, #1655, Tablet #11 pp. 103 to 137.
18. Jacob Harmon Ms, author's collection.
19. Susan Bettelyon Ms, South Dakota Heritage Center Archives.
20. *Missouri Liberty Tribune*, November 2, 1855.
21. Susan Bettelyon Ms, South Dakota Heritage Center Archives.
22. *Missouri Liberty Tribune*, November 2, 1855.
23. Susan Bettelyon Ms, South Dakota Heritage Center Archives.
24. Interview, Tony Black Spotted Horse, SFIS Bilingual staff, 1992.
25. Eugene F. Ware, *The Indian war of 1864*, St. Marten's Press, NY, 1960, pp. 114-115, 142, 143.
26. Eddie Herman column, *Rapid City Daily Journal*, Sunday, January 28, 1951.
27. Eugene F. Ware, *The Indian war of 1864*, p 107.
28. Ibid, pp 114-115, 142, 143.
29. Kansas City Regional Archives, Letter from Yellow Breast to Agent Pollock, dated July, 17, 1876
30. Susan Bettelyon Ms. South Dakota Heritage Center Archives.
31. *Missouri Liberty Tribune*, June 23, 1865.
32. Susan Bettelyon Ms. South Dakota Heritage Center Archives.
33. Jacob Harmon Ms. authors collection.
34. Susan Bettelyon Ms.

CHAPTER TWO
WE LOVE THEM—WE LOVE THEM NOT

Have you ever noticed that most of the foreigners or easterners who have traveled to the west, have in the main, claimed "distinguished ancestry", are of the "noble blood", or were of the "highest moral quality". Somehow all were related to some king or prince or something somehow.

Lord Metcalf, a Scottish nobleman, came to Fort Laramie in 1846, looking for adventure. He was young, handsome, and as the Scots would say of the American soldier in World War Two, "over-sexed and over-here."

While hunting buffalo with the Indians, he met and fell in love with a beautiful Indian girl. He was wealthy, so he bought her. She was a Brule and part Cheyenne. He lived with her in his lodge, slept between two buffalo robes, ate dried meat, and when winter came, left for California alone.

The following spring this beautiful girl gave birth to a handsome boy. The boy was enrolled at the Pine Ridge agency by the name of Metcalf. He stayed with his mother, never to see his real father, and later married and raised eight children.

Many of these children of love became torn betwixt and between. Their loyalties were questioned by both cultures. During the Civil war many half breed Indians became "guides or wolves for the blue soldiers." Joe Bralto was one such guide. The Army was always fearful that these guides would lead them into a trap. Here is what happened to Joe Bralto.

Good Bye Joe

Joe Bralto was a half Mexican-half Oglala Sioux Indian guide for the Colorado cavalry during the Civil War on the plains. The ruggedness of early cavalry life and a soldier's ability to "get even" is demonstrated by the following story as related by Jacob Harmon. In 1863, Company D of the 1st Colorado cavalry was dispatched and ordered to carry thirty days rations, three hundred rounds of ammunition each and start southeast of Denver toward the headwaters of the Republican and Smoky Hill rivers. After two days on the trail the following took place: "Say, George Wiggly, I smell the smoke of an Indian camp." "What was that?", said Mike Ivory. "Why Harmon says he smells Indians."

Over the next hill they encountered an Indian camp that was being hastily evacuated. On going through the camp they found buffalo robes, moccasins and squaw's dresses made of buckskin and covered with elk's teeth. They also found white scalps and a large quantity of dried buffalo meat that they confiscated to their own use.

Returning they stopped at a "whiskey ranch" owned by the Beauvais family where many of the soldiers traded Indian articles for whisky.

On returning to Denver they picked up a guide from Pueblo by the name of Joe Bralto and were ordered to go to old Fort Larnard (Larned) on the Arkansas river in Kansas.

After several days the company came across about 15 Indians in the distance. Bralto secured permission from Lieutenant Ayers (Eayre) and Phillips to take some men and talk to the Indians. Harmon and seven others rode out with Bralto to parley with the Indians. Joe Bralto talked to the Indians for about an hour. None of the soldiers understood Cheyenne so they were at the mercy of Bralto.

When they returned to the company Bralto told Lieutenant Eayre that the Indians were camped about fifteen miles ahead and that the company should come to the Indian camp and talk. The Indians would go to Fort Larned with them.

They traveled to the Indian camp but it was deserted and then the Lieutenant and Bralto discussed the best way for the unit to get to Fort Larned. Bralto advised him that four miles down stream on the Smoky Hill river there was a buffalo crossing they should use.

The company proceeded down the river to the buffalo crossing. Harmon and 15 others were in the advance guard. Bralto led them into a draw with high hills on each side. The draw was about three miles long and fifty to seventy five yards wide.

Just as they broke out on the prairie, they were attacked by a horde of Indians. Lieutenant Phillips ordered the advance troop to wheel and join the wagons coming up the draw.

The Indians were so thick that they could not reach the wagons. They dismounted, fighting on foot and then mounted making a break for the wagons.

George Wiggly (Weegly), Jacob Harmon's bunkmate, was killed and seven others were left on the prairie. Harmon and eight others made it to the wagons, where many others had been killed. The fight lasted about another three hours. Joe Bralto was not among the survivors and it was assumed that he had been killed.

Lieutenant Phillip's troop fought back up the canyon, witnessing along the way, the screams and final agony of Harmon's bunkmate, George Weegly.

"You have often heard it related that a person could whip ten or fifteen Indians. Well, I will tell you from my own experience that one Indian is as good if not better than a white man," Harmon states.

With their guide presumably killed the remnants of the company set out to try and find Fort Larned. In the party were Lieutenant Phillips, Sergeant Mike Ivory and Corporal Bill Dermint.

As the contingent traveled a large Indian force shadowed them. They loaded their ammunition and whisky in one wagon and left the others for the Indians. The Indians, however, did attack again. When they finally left, remaining in Jacob Harmon's group were Mike Ivory, Bill Dermint, James McDonald, Benjamin "Husky" Mainard, Raymond Snider and Charles Markles.

With knowledge of stars such as Job's coffin, the Big Dipper, and the north, evening and morning stars, the group was able to set their directions for travel. The group made its way to Fort Larned, where they were greeted by the Eleventh Missouri cavalry, commanded by Major Kelley.

Later while escorting the Indians who had returned the Eubanks hostages the company met up with Joe Bralto. The Eubanks hostages were a group of white women and children who had been taken in an Indian raid on early settlers and had been returned by friendly Cheyennes. Let Jacob Harmon tell his story of what happened:

"But at last we went into camp and on the second day I spied an Indian I thought I knew, and after getting a good look at him I found him to be Joe Bralto, the old guide who led us into the trap on Smoky Hill river. So I spied him out and I told Bill Dermint that I saw Joe Bralto out there in the Indian camp, and he said I was crazier than ever. I said "Bill I can show him to you."

"So we started out and soon came onto Joe. "Haven't I got a right to put a hole through his heart?" said Mike.

That evening the remaining eight soldiers from the Smoky Hill fight had a talk with their Major about Joe Bralto.

When the unit, which was escorting the Indians, arrived at the Fort, Major Winecoop (Wyncoop) had the Indians camp just outside the fort and were given rations by Wyncoop. (These are the same Indians who were massacred at Sand Creek).

While the Indians camped the eight survivors plotted for revenge against Joe Bralto. Captain Sola (Soule) joined their plot and secured two canteens of whiskey and had Harmon seek out Joe Bralto and get him rip roaring drunk. This was not the first time that the daring Soule would use intoxication to get his way.

Harmon showed Bralto the canteens of whiskey he had hidden under his coat and said they would go up the river a ways and have a party. Every so often Harmon would let Bralto have a good slug of the whisky. When they reached their destination Harmon let Bralto have all he wanted to drink until Bralto passed out.

Thereafter Mike Ivory, Bill Dermint, Benjamin "Husky" Mainard, Ruben McDaniels, James McDonald, Raymond Snider and Charles Markles appeared. McDaniels and McDonald were carrying a large log and Dermint had a long rope in his hand.

The remains of the old squad picked Joe Bralto up and laid him with his back upon the log and tied him fast. Then, McDaniels and McDonald stripped and lifted the log, Bralto and all, into the Arkansas river. The two boys waded out as far as they could pushing the log into the main stream where they turned Joe Bralto loose. The members of Company D happily cheered as Bralto floated to the happy hunting ground. Goodbye Joe.[1]

The roster of the First Cavalry of Colorado as they were mustered for pay of February 28th, l863 listed:

Field and staff: Edward W. Wyncoop, Major, Charles E Phillips, 2nd Lieut. Michael Ivory, lst duty Sg't Charles Hepple, Bugler

Privates: William Dermint; McDonough, James; Markle, Charles and Weagley, G.W.

A Jo Barraldo appears in a report by William Bent to Indian Agent Colley on August 7th 1864. At the conclusion of his report, Bent states: "I am not in a very good humor as my old squaw ran off a few days ago . . . with Jo Barraldo, as she liked him better than she did me! If I ever get sight of the young man it will go hard with him".

Captain Sola appears to be Captain Silas S. Soule of the 1st Colorado regiment of volunteers. Soule was an original Kansas jayhawker, who had helped his father establish an underground railroad. A violent abolitionist, he had himself jailed for intoxication at Charleston in order to help John Brown escape. Brown, however preferred to be a martyr and would not cooperate in the escape attempt.

A soldier of the Colorado Second named Squiers later murdered Soule because Soule had testified against Chivington when the Sand Creek massacre was investigated.

Harmon's suspicions that their guide had double crossed the unit were not uncommon. Many other misfortunes of the Army were blamed on the duplicity of the Indian guides.

White—Indian marriages

In the 1850s and 60s, Fort Laramie was garrisoned by the 11th Ohio cavalry. This unit was notorious for its "Indian marriages." Its commanding officer, Richard Garnett was the father of breed scout William Garnett. During the Civil War Richard Garnett joined the Confederacy and rose to the rank of General.[2]

Many Indian girls, after being "bought" by an officer made their escape and returned to their tiospaye. Lt. Ware in his book, *The Indian War of 1864*, states that after the Indian father ran off with the horse that was given for the bride, she soon followed. During one such escape the officer was scratched by the Indian tigress in such parts of his body that he kept to his quarters, pretending to be sick. The young tigress broke through the window and escaped.[3]

Baron E Mandat-Grancey states in his book, *Buffalo Gap, A French Ranch in Dakota, 1887*, after a white trader had physically abused his Indian wife, she got him drunk, bound and tied him to a tree, beat him with all manner of sticks, and left with his horses and cattle, leaving him their children.[4]

The whites were also quick to adopt the Indian custom of plural wives. Elbridge Gerry Ward, whose ancestor had signed the Declaration of Independence and had been responsible for "gerrymandering" had many wives.[5]

Ward had married a beautiful woman of the Wajaji band. When he spent too much time in Nebraska City on business she met her old Indian lover and ran off with him. Ward was so angered he hired her family to find and bring her back. Indian legends say she was returned, but was never the same and died of a broken heart.[6]

The 11th Ohio was noted for its fraternization with Indian women. Most of their women were of the Cut off or Loafer band of the Oglalas. The 11th also had much to do with keeping track of Spotted Tail and the Sicangu.

Double Standards

White society has always had difficulty accepting interracial unions. Until the 1960s it was illegal for a Caucasian to intermarry with another race in South Dakota. The law was archaic and honored in the breach; nevertheless it was evidence of the prevailing attitude of the governing white Anglo Saxon Protestant society of the time.

The clash between the white marriage norms and those of the Lakota was evident right from the start. The Indian Agents fought the Lakota culture at every turn. This "forcing" of white norms on Lakota society continued into the early 1950's when Rosebud Sioux Tribal President Robert Burnette launched a campaign to make all Rosebud Indian marriages "legal or else."

The whites may have won a few battles, but believe me, the Indians have won this war. "Traditional" unions are still recognized by tribal courts. In a recent conversation with a Lakota friend I asked about the status of a particular family. She told me that the mother and father had been happily married "Indian style" for many years. When the wife's sister died and left children homeless, the couple petitioned to adopt them. They were told they must first be legally married.

After their marriage, she said: "well you know everybody says that caused the end of that relationship."

C.P. Jordan wrote his hometown paper in Piqua Ohio. "It is well known. . . that some very prominent government officials and army officers of high rank, as well as their subordinates, ought to have joined the "squaw men" contingent, but they lacked the manhood to own and protect their Indian women and offspring." (This letter was particularly searing since the offending unit was from his hometown in Ohio and had been stationed at Fort Laramie when it was first established.)

"Famous men have been fascinated by Indian women and have married them in accordance with Indian customs. But some had not the moral courage to properly marry . . . fearing the punishment which immaculate society would decree. Yet the . . . Indian woman considers the alliance as binding as if performed by a clergyman."

Typically these Indian women and "their" children were left by their "husbands" and fathers to survive by the charity of her tiospaye. Just who was putting whom away? Just which society was more immaculate?

Among the persons who kept their Indian wives or were products of such marriages, Jordan listed the following:

First Lieutenant McIntosh, who was killed with Custer, Colonel Elsy Parker, General Grant's secretary, John Rolfe, Sam Houston, Kit Carson, Generals Sibley, Sully, and Patterson, Commodore Kittson, Marquis Fontanelle, Pierre Choteau,

Major Forbes, first postmaster of St. Paul, Col. James McLaughlin and C.P. Jordan, himself.

Jordan concludes his letter by stating that the term "squaw man" itself was probably originated by some thieving, incompetent Indian agent who was removed from office on account of crookedness or incompetency, or else by some embryonic, would-be philanthropist, who had no knowledge of men and affairs.

Charles Philander Jordan

Charles Philander Jordan was born at Piqua, Ohio on May 12, 1851 and died at Pierre, South Dakota on Sunday, January 10th, 1924. His life and times parallels Jacob Harmon, Jack Sully, John Kincaid, Spotted Tail, Crazy Horse, Scotty Phillip and others mentioned in this story of the west.

At the age of eleven he enlisted with the 11th Ohio Volunteer infantry and served as a drummer boy for the 110th and 94th Volunteer infantry.

In the fall of 1872 he came to Dakota Territory and was quartermaster clerk at Cedar Creek south of Fort George. In the spring of 1873 he was transferred to Camp Robinson on the Pine Ridge and remained there until 1879 when he accompanied the removal of the agency to the mouth of Landing Creek at Spotted Tail's warehouses on the Missouri River. He was chief issue clerk there until 1882, when he was transferred to Rosebud Agency where he was appointed Post trader.

On December 11th he married Julia Walks First, and they produced 9 children. Jordan's lineage included George Armstrong Custer, while his wife's included many prominent Indians.[7]

Many of Jordan's relatives were in the military service and one, Major William H. Jordan, who had been stationed at Fort Robinson, testified in Congress as to the conditions at Red Cloud Agency at the time of the arrival of the Cheyenne and Arapahoe and prior to the Sioux outbreak.

He testified that the tobacco issued to the Indians was of extremely poor quality; that the flour was inferior and the beef would not have been accepted by the army.

The Cheyenne and Arapahoe had arrived at the agency following their defeat by General R.S. McKenzie at the head of Willow creek, a tributary of the Powder River, in the fall of 1876. C.P. Jordan states that 525 Cheyenne were counted and were sent south the following spring.

Current Indian oral accounts indicate that many Cheyenne married into the Lakota and large numbers of Cheyenne were buried on the Pine Ridge reservation.

Jake Harmon's love affair

For every trail cowboy and immigrant like Utterbach, Phillip, Sully, Kincade, Quigley, and other white cowboys who married Indian girls and settled down to raise a family, there were hundreds who, when they left the Indian camp, left their offspring to be cared for by the generosity of the Sioux.

Others, like Jake Harmon, were young teenage boys, who had run away from home, met beautiful young Indian girls and fell in love. This is Jake's tribulation.

While working for Bill Whitcomb, following his discharge from the Colorado Cavalry in 1865, Jake became "best friend" with one of Whitcomb's daughters, Laura. Elias or "Bill" Whitcomb was an early adventurer in the west. He married an Indian girl and produced three lovely girls. Their daughter, Laura, is the subject of this story. Here is Laura and Jake's story, as told by Jake, some fifty years later.

"I recall to memory one night as Jack Sully and I were talking I told him: "Now Jack, I am going to Ft. Laramie, Wyoming and I might stay there all winter and I want you to see that no young buck goes to courting Laura, while I'm gone. "All right, Jake but what about me?"

Sully promised to look after Laura for Jake. He and Charles Elgin, Chet Dubrey and Chet's squaw left for Fort Laramie with a load of potatoes to sell to the Army.

When they returned Laura was waiting for him. "Oh say Laura, I think I will get ready and pull for my home in the states." Laura replied: "Look here, you can't do it its too far for you to travel alone, and I can't get along without you."

Jake told Laura that it would be lonesome without her and that he would return if he couldn't find a better girl.

"Well do you think you could find a more affectionate girl than I am, Jake?" she said. Jake agreed that she was the best but advised her to go out with Charley Elgin. Laura told him that she didn't like Charley and that he was set on her sister. "So you see Jake I would be all alone in this world and would never speak to an Indian boy because all of my love is for you and I will die, if you leave me."

Jake told her he would come back for her. Laura replied: "Look here Jake I can't believe you ever will. You know if you get down to the states among white girls you will never come back to see your own true love." Laura assured him that she was only one-fourth Indian and that they could live among the whites and no one would ever know that she was part Indian.

The conflict was left unresolved but Jake decided to talk to her father and agreed to stay another month.

The following day Jake and Laura packed their grub and bedrolls and started out on the range to catch and brand young colts. They were by themselves, as they had worked together for the past year and a half. Laura had worked her will on her father and he had let her take Jake off by Willow Creek to look for colts alone.

Laura told her father that she was going to try to keep him and asked him what he would give them if they were to marry. Whitcomb promised her that if she could get him to stay he would give them enough horses and cows to get started ranching.

Along the way to Willow Creek, Laura told him of what had transpired with her father. She told him how her father wanted to sell out and move to Montana and that he should come along and they would get all the horses and cattle they wanted from her father.

Jake was surely on the horns of a dilemma. He was in love with an Indian girl who had a rich, kind father. Here is how Jake explained his problem fifty years later when he wrote his story in 1922.

"My dear reader, you may see that my folks were all white people and if I got a "breed" I wouldn't have wanted to take her home. And if I had a wife I would want to take her home. You see it was hard for me to say no because I had been with her so long and I really loved her. She was good looking and fair complexioned and was a lady in every respect."

They spent six days and nights branding at Willow Creek.

Jake admits, "We surely had all kinds of fun." They had spent two days getting to Willow Creek, six days there, and two days to return. In all they had spent ten days together camped out on the plains of western Nebraska.

When they returned the whole Whitcomb family descended on Jake. All of them were hell bent on finding a way to induce him to stay with Laura. The next day Jake asked the father to settle up, and he would be on his way home.

The father told him that if he would stay he would give him 100 cows and 75 horses and he could marry Laura and that they could pick out the stock that they wanted and put their own brand on them. Laura begged him to stay with her.

Jake told them that he just had to go home. That he was thirteen when he left and now he was twenty and he wanted to see his folks at home.

Laura told him that her father would give them $2000.00 cash and that would pay his way down and back and she could go with him. Jake realized what a problem he had. He decided the only way out was to lie.

"Laura, I have made up my mind that I will come back as soon as I can go and see my folks," he told them. The next morning Whitcomb and his wife bade him good-bye and reminded him what would be his when he returned. All of the girls saddled their horses and rode out with him to start his return journey.

Jake and the girls rode to the South Platte River and camped for the night. The next day he continued on and the girls started back to the Whitcomb ranch.

Jake had started to feel sad and lonesome over his leaving when he heard a horse galloping up and Laura saying " wait up, Jake, I'm going with you."

Laura rode with him for two days and nights. They talked of everything. As Jake says "Well of all the nonsense we talked about words cannot express it. The another thing, I shall not tell the particulars—it was too good to give away".

Laura told him that she had a hunch that he would never return and that she would never see him again. He again promised her that he would return because "he could not leave her this way."

As it finally dawned on Jake what was going to happen he felt bitter pangs and cried and they parted on the plains with tears streaming down both their faces, he feeling low and his heart aching for the Laura who had told him of a thing that "was too good to be true."

The next morning after their good-byes Jake awoke with the same dull feeling he had felt when they said good-bye the day before. "Poor Laura had to ride home by herself. Good bye to Laura Whitcomb, he said, good bye forever".

Jake never returned for Laura. He did exactly as she had thought he would do. "Then the other thing, I shall not tell the particulars—It was to good to give away" remained Jake's secret to the end.[9]

Chapter Two End Notes

1. Harmon Ms.
2. Jordan files, South Dakota Heritage Center Archives.
3. Eugene F. Ware, *The Indian war of 1864*, p 213
4. Baron E. Mandat-Grancey, *Buffalo Gap*, Lame Johnny Press, 1981, pp 38-39.
5. Susan Bettelyon Ms, South Dakota Heritage Center Archives.
6. Ibid.
7. Jordan files, infra.
8. Denig, Edwin Thompson, *Five Indian Tribes of the Upper Missouri*, pp. 28-29, University of Oklahoma Press, Norman, 1961.
9. Harmon Ms.

CHAPTER THREE
THE PONCAS

Prior to 1500 the Ponca tradition places them in Virginia. They subsequently migrated to the Ohio and Wabash valleys. When the early traders came up the Missouri River they were settled at the confluence of that river and the Niobrara River in Nebraska. Their sphere of influence extended from the Platte River to the Black Hills.[1]

They are a linguistic member of the Sioux family and along with the Omaha, Osage, Kansa, and Quapaw made up the Degina (DeHeeNa) division of the Siouxan language.[2]

The Poncas signed their first treaty with the U.S. in 1817 and followed with further treaties and land sessions in 1825, 1858, and 1865, when their reservation was reduced to 96,000 acres.

By the Treaty of Fort Laramie of 1868, in a heartless and thoughtless act of pure negligence, the U.S. gave the land previously reserved for the Poncas to the Sioux.

Thereafter the Sioux considered the Poncas as trespassers and stepped up war party raids on their neighbors.

Sicangu-Ponca Troubles

The official reports of the Ponca agency stated:

"In the Months of March and April 1869 Dakota Chief Spotted Tail with a large party of his chiefs, headmen and soldiers visited the Ponca Agency . . . (to make peace) . . . between the Dakota and the Ponca . . . during the visits of the Dakota the Ponca did make presents to Chief Spotted Tail and his people to the amount of 31 horses, 10 beef cattle, 34 sacks of flour, 360 blankets, 610 yards of Indian cloth and twenty double guns and rifles . . . and for which Spotted Tail and his people invited the Chiefs of the Ponca tribe and their people to visit them . . . (and they would deliver their presents) . . . in July of 1869 the Ponca paid them a visit and received presents of 180 ponies. These the Lakota now claim they are taking back. It is evident that the Ponca made larger presents than they received from the Lakota."

The report also states that the Minniconjou had stolen 21 of the Ponca's horses that they refused to return. On September 15th the Sicangu stole more horses from within the confines of the Ponca camp.[3]

Spotted Tail's camp didn't need to steal anything. They were a fat agency. The Ponca on the other hand were dying of starvation. In fact, things were so good at

Spotted Tail's Whetstone agency that in July of 1870 D.C. Poole requested that the cattle delivered by the Bosler cattle company be held and not issued.[4]

On May 10th a party of Lakota attacked and killed a small boy and carried off a twelve year old girl at the "Bohemian settlement" near Niobrara, Nebraska. The Ponca were blamed by the white settlers for the depredations of the Lakota.

In 1877 the Ponca were given 25,000 dollars for moving expense and were sent packing from Niobrara, Nebraska to the Indian Territory in Oklahoma. By 1878, as a result of this tragic move, fully one third of the tribe had perished. In 1962 the tribe was officially terminated. On October 1990 the Northern Poncas were restored to federally recognized status.[6] On September 7th, 1863, agent Hoffman counted 864 members of the tribe.[7] At the time they were finally restored to federal status in 1990 there were 442 members.[8]

The following account is but one shameful event in the history of this small peaceful tribe's relations with the U.S.

Army Murders

On December 26th, 1863, Agent Hoffman took statements from Poncas who had survived a murderous massacre by members of Company B 7th Iowa Cavalry, stationed at Niobrara.

He reported that a party of Ponca was returning from the Omaha agency to their homes. That the party consisted of the following: One was There (1) and his wife (2), Red Leaf (3), his wife (4), a boy (5) and a girl (6), Dirty Face (7), and his wife (8), Nice White Cow (9) and his wife (10), Medicine man—a youth (11), his mother (12) and a boy (13), One Sleeps on the Way, a woman (14) and her child, a girl (15).

Here is their story.

On December 3rd, they arrived three miles below Niobrara and camped near the house of a friend, Mr. Huddleston. Near sunset two soldiers, who had been hunting, came to the camp and asked who they were. They signed that they were Ponca and the soldiers left.

After dark, when the Ponca were preparing for bed, some fifteen soldiers rode up. The soldiers tied their horses and went into the lodge. A black bearded soldier wearing a wolfskin coat offered One Was There money for his woman, clearly demonstrating by signs what he wanted. This same soldier then offered a one dollar bill with his left hand and with a cocked pistol in his right demanded that One Was There give him his woman.

Another soldier who wore a cavalry jacket with chevrons on his sleeve, a slender man with a short nose and large eyes, also demanded a woman, threatening to cut their throats if he was refused.

Another soldier wearing a wolf tail on his hat also drew his revolver, unbuttoned his pants, pulled out his penis and approached a person wrapped in a blanket he supposed to be a woman, but who was a young man.

One Was There sounded an alarm and the Poncas lifted the sides of the lodge and fled barefooted in the night with the soldiers firing shots after them. They managed to reach their horses and escape.

The soldiers cut the lodges to pieces, fired balls through the cooking kettles and pans, scattered dried corn and pumpkins on the ground and took three guns, seventeen bear skins, two buffalo robes, one three point blanket and other articles.

After the soldiers left with their booty, the Poncas returned to gather up what was left. They were scared off by an approaching wagon being driven by the soldiers. The soldiers then loaded a large lodge skin covering and several beaver traps and left. The Poncas returned a second time and gathered what remained of the scattered food and started their journey home.

They passed the town of Niobrara without incident. After traveling about seven miles past Niobrara they stopped to warm themselves and eat some parched corn they had saved. At that time several of the women and children left to search for wild beans, an Indian delicacy. At the camp the same number of soldiers again rode up and chased those who were in the camp away. The soldiers fired at them as they ran and wounded Red Leaf's wife and the child she carried on her back, with two balls passing through the child's thigh and one entering the mother's side.

The soldiers then took the Indians' ponies and what other articles the Poncas had left and started back. The women and children, who had gone after wild beans, were about a half mile below the camp. They quickly hid in the willows, but as the soldiers were passing a little dog barked exposing their hiding place and the soldiers quickly turned on them.

A young boy and his brother were a short ways off. The young boy hid himself and witnessed what took place. He stated that two soldiers dismounted and deliberately shot Nice White Cow's wife in the forehead as she was cowering in the bushes. His mother, (#12) was killed by three balls entering her forehead and cheek and the young girl (#14) was killed by a ball entering her breast. His mother also had her head nearly severed by a sabre or knife and the young girl had her clothes torn off leaving her naked.[9]

The young boy ran off and was chased by the soldiers. He escaped by hiding in the Niobrara River, diving into a hole in the ice.

The Investigation

After Agent Hoffman reported the murders he took it upon himself to go to Niobrara and investigate the matter.

On January 14th 1864, Hoffman reported that Sgt. West was in charge of the party of soldiers, but no soldier would identify any of the others. When asked about the "wolfskin coat" and "wolf tail hat" the well rehearsed response was that "why every body wore that coat and hat from time to time and it would be impossible to remember who wore it on the 3rd and 4th of December."

Hoffman interviewed Wm. Henry Sturges and William Young, who had reported that they had returned to Niobrara on the day in question because they had "seen" two or three Indians.

The townsfolk indicated that Sturges, who ran a small store and traded with the Indians, might have made up the Indian scare just to increase his business. They said he traded extensively with the Poncas and probably knew all of them and that his report of a scare was probably a sham.

One of the soldiers said that the purpose of going to the Ponca camp was not to attack the Indians, but for a different purpose. Hoffman does not state the purpose so one may assume that the purpose was one that a gentleman of his generation would not put in writing.

Hoffman reported:

"The general opinion of the citizens at Niobrara was that the soldiers were glad of an opportunity to cover up, if possible their transactions of the previous night."

". . . I am confident", he continued, "that the Poncas were not at all in fault, They have, in my opinion, been robbed, and some of the defenseless women and children murdered-the killing of them cannot be expressed in a milder term. . . .."

The Poncas did not demand that the guilty be delivered to them for punishment, but through agent Hoffman urged he . . . "now prefer as charges against the detachment of soldiers . . . and demand that a proper and speedy investigation of all the facts and circumstances be made. . . that the soldiers who are guilty shall receive just punishment . . . and the Government indemnify the Poncas for loss of life and property."[10]

In a letter dated April 11, 1864, Hoffman reported that the only response to his charges was in a letter from General McKean who wrote Superintendent Edmunds:

"Gen'l McKean writes that a thorough investigation will be made of the whole subject and that the property taken from the Indians, so far as it can be found will be turned over to you to be returned to the Indians.

It would seem from a short conversation I had with Major Armstrong (the army investigator) that this case will not be found to vary much from the general rule to wit: "there are two sides to it". I requested Major A., if he could possibly do so, to visit you at the agency that he might have a personal interview on the subject."[11]

Armstrong, of course, never bothered to interview Hoffman, but only interviewed Sturges and Young, and continued on his way the next day. Hoffman was incensed.

Hoffman wrote: "More than three months have now elapsed since my report (he wrote) . . . from the view of the case which you derived from a short conversation with Major Armstrong when on his way up the Niobrara, "that this case would not be found to vary much from the general rule, to wit, there are two sides to it," I conclude that he must have made very different representations from those contained in my report. My impression is that his mind was made up before he reached Niobrara. . .The unanimous opinion of the citizens of Niobrara (is) that even if it was not intended to be (the investigation) was indeed, a farce."

He continued, "If a thorough investigation of the whole subject promised by Gen'l McKean has been made, is it not time that it should be known?"

"With all due respect I am constrained to say that our Government does not deal with sufficient promptness with the Indians . . . The Poncas are not only entitled to justice, but merit the respect and deserve he charity of the Government to which they are truly loyal. . . . ."[12]

The Government must have taken Hoffman's request for justice as sheer militancy.

At last Hoffman was free to speak his mind. On August 20th, 1864 he wrote:

"Having resigned the office of Indian Agent . . . I have the honor to make the following report."

Hoffman restated all of the charges of murder by the Army and identified Lt. Comstock of the 7th Iowa cavalry as one of the first two soldiers to stop the Poncas.

"This matter was presented in full to the Department by my letter dated December 27th, in which I detailed the losses of the Indians and presented their claim for six hundred dollars for each life lost, two hundred dollars for each wounded and one thousand dollars for the loss of property and their suffering . . . .."

Hoffman restated the history of events and investigations, including the Army's, and his request of April that the matter be fully investigated and that justice be done. He had finally received a promise that the army would try the soldiers. A shallow promise indeed.

Hoffman continued.

" . . . I have labored hard for three years to improve the conditions of these Indians, having in view the great object of teaching them to use tools . . . but unfortunately for the success of my efforts, they have for more than three fourths of the time been in a state of famishment. And this has not been from any fault of theirs or mine. In the summer of 1861 they made no crop. There was no land prepared for cultivation when I took charge . . . on the 1st of June . . . .. Through the winter of 1861-61 the Poncas subsisted upon the charity of the Government. In the summer of 62 a partial crop of corn was raised. From the 20th of June until the 7th of August that year we had no rain . . . .. The records of the Hospital . . . at Ft. Randall . . . show that only three tenths of an inch of rain fell there from May 1863 to the present year . . . Crops of all kinds have entirely failed. My statistical report of farming will show the number of acres of each planting. . . .."[13]

In fact starvation had become a problem in 1863. On April 29th Hoffman sent the following letter:

"I am informed there is in the commissary store at Fort Randall, a lot of between ninety and one hundred barrels of pork which have been condemned (I believe for, the second or third time.) as wholly unfit for issue to the troops. I am informed that if ordered sold, it would probably bring one dollar per barrel. I desire to obtain this pork for the Ponca Indians, and have respectfully to request, that application be made to the Commissary General of Subsistence USA for instructions to the A.A.C.S. at Fort Randall to turn it over to me, without charge . . . or for such price as he . . . may consider it worth."[15]

Hoffman concluded with a plea for the prompt settlement of the Poncas' claims. Hoffman had been denied nearly all claims for a swather, hay press and other articles of farming utility. He had been told to make the Indians work by hand.

Having failed to secure justice for the Poncas, Hoffman wrote:

"I therefore exceedingly regret not so much on my own account personally, as for the welfare of the agency, . . . the apparent lack of confidence on the part of the Department at Washington in my judgement beg most respectfully to submit that in my opinion, a man possessed of an ordinary share of common sense and residing here on the ground is best able to judge of what is and what is not needed. If I do not possess that required ordinary share of common sense, then I ought not to occupy the position I do . . . (and) as a matter of justice to the Poncas . . . I should be removed, and a better man placed in my stead."[14]

On July 29th 1864, his resignation was accepted.

Thereafter the Ponca packed up lock stock and barrel and moved in with their friends the Omahas along the Missouri River in eastern Nebraska. They told the Omaha's agent that they had moved because they were starving and they no longer had an agent who cared for them.

Students Reaction

Students in the St. Francis Indian School gifted class in 1993 were asked to read Agent Hoffman's report of the murder and write their reactions. They wrote the following:

"Some white man probably said ok it was the Indians fault and let the white soldiers go unpunished."

"The soldiers probably said that the Indian women came onto them."

"The soldiers thought the Poncas were just a bunch of stupid, dumb, and dirty Indians."

"They were not punished because they were white."

"Back then white people were very prejudiced against us Indians. That is why it takes me a while to like a white person, even when they did nothing wrong, just because of their ancestors part. I can still feel the hatred in my eyes. I know I am wrong. But they label us as dirty, poor, drunk, crazy, thieves, etc.

"We couldn't do anything about it then or now."

If Lakota students of today have such deep sense of distrust, imagine how their ancestors felt in 1864.

Students participating in the project were Johanna Quigley, Sally Beauvais, Kayleen Young, Summer Lunderman, Emma Yellow Hawk, and Nathan Night Shield.

Chapter Three End Notes

1. Joseph Jablow, *Ponca Indians: Ethnohistory of the Poncas*, Garland American Ethnohistory series (New York: Garland Publishing Co. 1974.)
2. Ibid.
3. Kansas City Regional Archives, Letter from Ponca Agent Hugo, to Commissioner of Indian affairs.
4. Kansas City Regional Archives, Letter from Agent D.C. Poole.
5. Kansas City Regional Archives, Letter from Ponca Agent Hugo, to Commissioner E.S. Parker.
6. Elizabeth S. Grobsmith and Beth Ritter Knoche: *The Ponca Tribe of Nebraska; the process of restoration of a federally terminated tribe*. University of Nebraska. November 1990 revision.
7. Report of Agent Hoffman to office of Indian affairs Sept. 7, 1863.
8. *The Ponca Tribe of Nebraska*, Grobsmith and Knoche. infra.
9. Letter from Agent Hoffman to Superintendent Edmunds dated Dec., 1863.
10. Ibid.
11. Letter from Agent Hoffman dated August 20th, 1864.
12. Ibid.
13. Letter from Commissioner of Indians affairs to Edmunds dated July 12, 1864.
14. Ibid.
15. Letter from Hoffman to Edmunds dated April 29, 1863.

Further Reading
H. H. Jackson, *A Century of Dishonor*, Boston. Roberts Bros., 1888.

CHAPTER FOUR
SPOTTED TAIL

The Sicangu escape at Horse Creek was the first of many fights with the government over moving their agency.

The government's desire to move the agency to the Missouri River would continue throughout Spotted Tail's life, and even after his death. Spotted Tail suffered set backs during his quarrels with the government over agency sites, and supplies, but in the end he selected his own agency site and remained Chief.

D.C. Poole, Indian agent at Whetstone from 1869-70, aptly described Spotted Tail as showing "true trafficking qualities"; always asking for more, settling for less, but gradually always increasing the sum total.[2] He used the same tactic in his quarrels over the agency's location. He was a genius in his dealings with a government that seldom bargained in good faith. Despite his successes, a little too much "soldiering" on his part, petty jealousy, raw use of power and many sexual exploits would cause him to suffer the fate of many other great leaders who arose in times of colossal change. His assassination would be just a matter of time.

Tribal rivalry

Quarrels between rival factions in the Lakota nation were not uncommon. Bitter "family" or tiospaye in fighting continues to this day.

In the first movement of the Sicangu to the Whetstone agency in 1868, the "loafer" Indians under Chief Big Mouth accompanied Spotted Tail's band. They were Oglalas and many of their women had married whites. They were a part of what is called the Cut Off Band.

The origin of this band grew out of a drunken brawl that occurred in the Oglala camp in the 1840-50s. During the drunken quarrel some of Red Cloud's relatives were killed. Red Cloud and others of his band sought revenge and they killed some of Bull Bear's band and Red Cloud personally killed Bull Bear.[3] Part of Bull Bear's camp then separated from the Oglalas and took up camp with the southern Cheyennes down on the Platte and Republican rivers.[4]

In 1871 the Cut Offs came to Fort Laramie to trade and reestablished contact with Red Cloud's Oglalas. A group of them, however, went with Spotted Tail to the Whetstone agency on the Missouri River. Their leader was Big Mouth.[5] Little Wound, son of Bull Bear, was made chief of the "Cut Offs". This was done at the insistence of the government as a reparation for Red Cloud's killing of his father.[6] Trouble would follow Big Mouth's band to the Whetstone. Big Mouth was well named. Both the agent and the Sicangu really wouldn't mind if he were "out of the way."

Spotted Tail kills Big Mouth

Big Mouth plotted to kill Spotted Tail. Oral history relates that one of Spotted Tail's men knew of his intentions and removed the caps from Big Mouth's six shooter, causing it to misfire.

Big Mouth got drunk and provoked an argument with Spotted Tail. He drew his revolver and "clicked" it at Spotted Tail's head. Spotted Tail calmly drew his own pistol and dispatched Big Mouth.[7]

Spotted Tail paid the appropriate amount of ponies and property and the killing was exonerated. His use of force, however, would be one of the causes of his demise. The Cheyenne Daily Leader of March 4, 1881 reported Spotted Tail's use of force to exert his will upon his people was well known and it was reported that he had killed more of his own people than any other living chief.[8]

Governing and Soldiering

On May 4th 1870, Poole reported that Spotted Tail had "soldiered" the families of several young renegades. Northern hostile Indians were constantly visiting Spotted Tail and provoking trouble.

He reports that:

"Roman Nose a Minniconjoux Lakota Chief . . . is here now having come from the Powder River country for the purpose (he says) of trading. Red Leaf, a Brule Lakota with about thirty lodges has come into "Spotted Tail's" camp from the north. . . (Roman Nose) informed me that many young warriors, Brule, Ogallalla, Minniconjoux, San Arc and others have gone on the warpath toward the Pacific Railroad. . . . ."[9]

In late April of 1870 Spotted Tail's camp was some 17 miles from the agency. There agent D.C. Poole met with Spotted Tail and other chiefs and found that affairs were very unsettled, but Spotted Tail was using every effort to keep the peace. Spotted Tail stated Indians constantly visited him from the north. Spotted Tail remarked that if he could be assured of the arrival of goods as stated it would be of great assistance to him in restraining his young warriors and keeping them in camp.[10]

Restraining his camp from raiding the Ponca or the Pawnees was another matter. On the night of September 15, 1870 Spotted Tail's band stole seven ponies from the Ponca and wounded the work oxen, rendering them useless.[11]

The Big Hunt

After Spotted Tail moved from the Missouri to a new agency near Chadron Nebraska, the Government in 1871-1872 took Grand Duke Alexis of Russia on a buffalo hunt in western Nebraska. The Government gave him the whole nine yards,

Custer and the Seventh Cavalry, Generals Sheridan and Palmer, Lonesome
Charley Reynolds, Buffalo Bill Cody, and, last but not least, Spotted Tail and 600
of his best.[12]

Spotted Tail showed them how the Indians would cut out a small herd, cause
them to circle, making them mill into a small bunch, and then bring them down with
bows and arrows. Spotted Tail became incensed over the senseless slaughter of the
Indians' buffalo, just to please the Grand Duke and some back east politicians.

At one evening feast he was invited to say a few words. They got an earful.

He told them the unvarnished truth. He told them how poor his people were
and that the whites were displaying all their wealth and waste and having fun and
games slaughtering buffalo at the Indians expense. He told them that if they would
allow him two traders instead of one he could bargain for fairer prices and competition would bring prices down. By the way, he concluded, if the Russian prince
could hunt buffalo on the Republican why couldn't his tribe do the same?

After he spoke the Grand Duke gave the 600 Sicangu 100 fifty-cent pieces and
twenty blankets and called it square.[13]

Spotted Tail would square accounts with Buffalo Bill later. He held Buffalo Bill
in contempt.

A contemporary hunter, Old man Wiggins, had this to say about Spotted Tail
and Buffalo Bill: "Buffalo Bill? Oh yes I know him. "Friend of the red man, Huh! I
remember in the early seventies when old Spotted Tail wanted Bill's scalp and
Grand Duke Alexis and a lot of down east Senators and Congressmen."

Wiggins said that we'd have some buffalo left if old Spotted Tail had his way.
He claimed old Spot knew more than any whiteman, just the same as the beaver
knows more about cold weather than an Indian does.

He said the Grand Duke Alexis party hunted three months and that these forty
hunters shot an average of 37 buffalo a piece per day. They counted only those
that fell and not the wounded ones that staggered off to die.

The "sportsmen" fastened a blank sheet of paper to their lapel and every time
they felled a buffalo they punched a hole in the paper.

Wiggins said that Spotted Tail was mad enough to kill the hunters. The buffalo
were made for the Indians and he didn't want those royal bloods killing his meat
and leaving it for the coyotes to eat.[14]

Saving the Buffalo

South Dakota historians have credited Scotty Phillip with saving the buffalo.
He helped, but the Minniconjous gave him a great head start.

In 1881, 'Pete' Dupree, a breed Indian Rancher, captured five buffalo calves,
which had become exhausted in the chase of the last buffalo hunt. They were
loaded and taken to his ranch where they multiplied. While Scotty Phillip receives
all of the historical accolades for saving the northern buffalo herd, in fairness we
must relate the Indian spiritual story of their salvation.

Fred Dupree had come to the Cheyenne River area as an employee of the fur
trade in 1828 and died there in 1898. He married an Indian, raised an Indian family, turned to ranching and prospered.

Dupree had also been responsible for the return of white women hostages that had been taken during the Minnesota uprising.

The story of the saving of the northern buffalo herd is best told by Wilbur A. Riegert in his book, *Quest for the Pipe of the Sioux*, Published by Printing Inc., Copyright 1975 by Jean M Fritze, Keystone Route, Box 184, Rapid City S.D., 57701.

Riegert relates the following Indian history of the saving of the buffalo and the involvement of the Sacred Calf Pipe:

"After the mistreatment of the Pipe, the Sioux took action to protect the Pipe and keeper. Representatives of the districts of the reservation were chosen to visit the keeper and be present when and if the Pipe was to be used, as on very special occasions. One such event occurred . . . (when) . . . a blessing was given at the "kick off" for the first real buffalo hunt aimed at gathering buffalo to form a Sioux buffalo herd on the reservation. The attempt was made among the Minniconjous at Dupree, South Dakota."

"The Dupree family owned and leased much land in the Dupree area . . . So, on that occasion, the Sioux assembled on the grounds of the Dupris (Dupree) cattle ranch. The gathering was religiously interested and motivated. They had come to ask the Great Spirit to guide and protect the large group of men, women, and hardy youth preparing them to set out on the hunt. It would take them past Thunder Butte and to the northern Black Hills, where the buffalo were spotted by scouts. The report was that a good herd of bulls, cows and calves were seen. Such a hunt was never heard of before or attempted. So the religious convocation was large and included Miniconjou ministers and a Catholic priest. The meeting carried over into three days spent in prayer and feasting. To cap the whole celebration, the keeper of the Calf Pipe gave a special blessing, using the Pipe for the special occasion."

". . . Edward Dupris was the originator of the first buffalo herd in captivity. He was born in 1847 and died at 60 years of age . . . Aurelia Traversie Dupris was his wife and was born in 1864 and died in 1960 at the age of 96. All dates here pertaining to the Dupris family tree were given me by Andrew . . . Andrew had two brothers (Robert and Douglas) who were both killed by Russian-Germans in 1922 . . . .."

"All the Dupris family attended the convocation and received the blessing in the ceremonial with the Calf Pipe. The Pipe was lit and raised to the heavens, as the prayer man called upon the Great Spirit to witness and bless the convocation and the gathering of the buffalo. This was perhaps the most dramatic use of the Sacred Calf Pipe in its history . . . Then the Pipe was passed to Edward Dupris . He took one deep draw on it and passed it to his wife Aurelia . . . (who) was not allowed to draw upon the Pipe but was permitted to kiss the bowl, which she did. The Pipe was then passed back to the keeper who wrapped it and placed it back in safety. This was the story as told to me by Andrew Dupris himself."

"Preparations for the buffalo hunt were completed. Those to make the excursion were chosen, and shortly they were ready to start. The Dupris ranch and home were about one and a half miles northeast of Dupree. Three large and sturdy hay wagons of a sort were made ready, besides other wagons for transporting bulls and calves. The hunters were in their own glory. It was to be a buffalo hunt for a herd of their own, and with the special blessing they were in near ecstasy."

"One outstanding characteristic of the Sioux is their appreciation of the way to relate themselves to man, God, and His creation. To give thanks for blessings was almost second nature, as well as to be ready to look out for their fellow Lakota."

"The hunter's destination was a spot about 120 miles away towards the Slim Buttes in the northern part of the Black Hills. The terrain there is rough and virgin country, lined with cow trails and buffalo runs, dry creeks and washes. They crossed the Moreau and Belle Fourche rivers and Hay creek . . . .."

". . . They left the Dupris ranch early in September and returned in late October 1905 with four bulls and 42 calves . . . .."

Some of those who took part in this successful round-up were, Palmer Horsehoe, Alex Traversie, Straight Head, White Horse, Two Moons, Standing Straddle, Black Eagle, Iron Lightning, Joe Fox and Makes Room. The names and dates of the Indian and Dupree of round up buffalo varies. Perhaps there was more than one round up or memories of probable dates may have been confused.

In the *South Dakota Democrat* published at Chamberlain, South Dakota on July 31, 1890 the following report was filed:

"The big ranch belonging to Fred Dupree on the Cheyenne River is a point of considerable interest to persons visiting that portion of the ceded Sioux lands. He has a herd of tame buffaloes, caught wild years ago when young, but which now roam at will on his big ranch with his cattle. Dupree has lived with the Sioux for about thirty years, and it is claimed has been married to seven different squaws. The old man has accumulated quite a property since casting his fortune with the Indians and is very wealthy."

When Dupree died, Scotty Phillip conceived the idea that the buffalo must be saved. He bought the entire herd from the Dupree estate and established a buffalo pasture for them across the river west of Fort Pierre, South Dakota. One of the riders who handled the buffalo drive was "Buffalo George" who was one of those "notorious" outlaws in the early days of Oacoma.

"Bunk White", an early black cowboy, along with George Phillips and Buffalo George roped three gigantic buffalo bulls just to satisfy Scotty's curiosity as to whether cowboys, cow ponies and rope could handle these monsters.

In 1906 the Congress of the United State passed an act allowing an area of about thirty five hundred acres to be withdrawn from the public domain and rented to Scotty Phillip "exclusively for the pasturing of native buffalo and for no other purpose." The land was fenced and Uncle Sam charged an annual rental of fifty dollars.

From this herd nearly every buffalo presently in parks, Indian reservations and private ownership in the west was descended. When you travel through the great western plains and watch the buffalo on his native range, thank the Sacred Calf Pipe, Duprees, Scotty Phillip, and those "notorious" cowboys, like Buffalo George, Bunk White, and Dupree's Indian ranch hands.

Give us the Black Hills (or else!)

In June of 1873 the Government presented three proposals to Red Cloud and Spotted Tail at a council held at Red Cloud Agency in Nebraska. The Army wanted the Lakota to (1) give up hunting in Nebraska, (2) move their agency to the headwaters of the White River in South Dakota and (3) give up claims to the Black Hills.[15]

The Lakota objected to all three proposals except that Red Cloud returned on the second day and said they would move to the headwaters of the White River.

In Col. Smith's report of June 27th 1873 he stated:

". . . it is very evident that the Indians will not relinquish their rights to hunt or cede the territory outside of their reservation without a serious struggle." Col. Smith concluded:

"The commission also had a letter requesting them to use their influence with the Indians to give up the Black Hills within the limits of their reservation, the only portion worth anything to them, and nothing short of annihilation will get it from them."[16]

Except the removal of the agency, if accomplished, the mission may be considered a failure."[17] Spotted Tail, Whistler, Pawnee Killer, Two Strikes and No Flesh continued to hunt along the Republican River, in Nebraska. The white settlers would soon cause trouble. White settlers killed Whistler, who was minding his own business. The Commission and the Army were at odds. The Commission recognized the Indians' treaty rights to hunt. The army had other ideas. The Army argued that it would be better to shoot first and ask questions later.

The report of General Ord from the HQs of the Military Division of Missouri of May 20th, 1873 stated:

"The only suggestion which I have to make in this case is, that if it be entirely certain that these Indians intend to massacre the settlers, men, women, and children because Whistler was killed by some unknown persons, would it not be best to jump them first? Even civilized nations do this . . . .."[18]

Another ultimatum

To keep the Indians on the reservation the Office of Indian Affairs issued the following order to all its western agents on December 6th 1875:

"I am instructed . . . to direct you to notify Sitting Bull's band and other wild and lawless bands of Lakota Indians residing without the bounds of their reservation . . . that unless they shall remove within the bounds of their reservation (and remain there) before 31st of January next, they shall be deemed hostile, and treated accordingly by military force."[19]

The Wyoming Card

By 1874 the powers that be were again pestering Spotted Tail to move back to the dreaded Missouri River. He understood that "Brass Kettle" Howard, the agent from the Iowa and eastern Dakota contingent, knew that his agency was fat and they wanted the fat for themselves on the Missouri River. Spotted Tail had another ace up his sleeve. He played his Wyoming card.

The Sicangu chief traveled to Cheyenne to secure the interest of Wyoming trading entrepreneurs. He also wanted to get the best deal for his own people. By 1874 the beef appropriations under the "Treaty made under the Stars" had expired.

On January 28th, 1874, one day after the rations had expired, Spotted Tail and his entourage were in Cheyenne, Wyoming.

He came to address his grievances and especially to complain about the efforts of "Brass Kettle" Howard to remove his agency to the Missouri River.

Spotted Tail was taken into the home of a prominent citizen and attended the theatre at Cheyenne. The Daily Leader reported: "Spotted Tail and a few of his friends occupied one of the private boxes at McDaniels theatre last evening. He seemed to enjoy the performance as much as any one in the audience."[20]

On the 29th he met with acting Governor Brown and Spotted Tail insisted that his words be taken down verbatim as he said he wanted the Great Father to know exactly what he said.

The Cheyenne Daily Leader reported his exact words:

Spotted Tail:

"The last time I saw my Great Father he told me to let him know if I was in trouble anytime . . . . . I want to observe about the goods and provisions we have hauled from Cheyenne which is 200 miles instead of Fort Randall which is 300 miles . . . My Agent wants me to move again, but we desire to stay where we are. We have plenty of wood, water and good soil near our present agency."[21]

He related that the flour was bad. That instead of bacon they got salt pork, which they can't eat. It was yellow and smells badly. That their beef cattle were small, some smaller.

The chief explained that if the freight was hauled a short distance he could save money and have more supplies and that his own men could do the hauling, thus benefiting his own people.

The editor, tongue in cheek, couldn't believe that the government would force him to move against his will; stated that the Indians' rations were excellent; couldn't see the economic advantage of trade in Wyoming and thought that he should not have been recognized by anyone since he had come to Cheyenne without permission. Did the promise of Gold in the Hills blur his vision? Had the Stockgrowers Association influenced his decision?[22]

In fact the settlers of Dakota Territory were casting a jealous eye on the Indians' Black Hills. In January of 1874 the Dakota Territorial Council passed the following memorial to Congress:

A Memorial

"To the Honorable, the Senate and House of Representatives of the United States Congress Assembled.

Your memorialists the Legislative Assembly of the Territory of Dakota, most respectfully beg leave to petition your Honorable bodies to take immediate action in the matter of opening of the Black Hills of Dakota for settlement, because of its great mineral wealth and its being so well adapted for agricultural pursuits and respectfully call attention to the following reasons

1st. That General Custer has explored the Black Hills, and reports the finding of gold in every locality where the miners prospected,

2nd That no section of country in the west has more beautiful valleys than this hitherto unknown country, all being well watered and so favorably adapted to farming and stockraising.

3rd That gold, silver, platinum and inexhaustible pine forests were found.

4th That the most favorable reports published in the press throughout the country will scarcely convey an idea of the actual and enormous wealth of the region when developed by the diggers of our "Nation's specie".

5th That Prof. Hayden and Gen. Warren, in their several explorations and surveys of interior portions of the Black Hills, report 'officially' that they found gold, silver, iron, and forests of unknown limits within 130 miles of steam boat navigation on the Missouri River.

6th That the Sioux Indian treaty, still respected by the Government, but numberless times violated by the Sioux Indian, prevents whitemen from acquiring, Homesteads, Pre-emptions or mining rights within the great Sioux Reservation.

The Legislative Assembly of Dakota Territory most earnestly petitions Congress to abrogate the Treaty now in force, or if such action be deemed unjust to the Indians, in lieu thereof, Extinguish the Indian Title to that portion of the Reservation known as the Black Hills of Dakota. . . .."

Spotted Tail's education had come through the perfidy of the whites. When told by one agent that he would have to put up with some hardships, Spotted Tail replied that if the agent had lived through as many hardships as he had, the agent would have slit his throat long ago.

While the editor of the Cheyenne Daily Leader found the Indians' rations "excellent", Spotted Tail's characterization of the rations as "bad" was a classic understatement.

The Indians acknowledged good agents such as Lt. Jesse Lee and Dr. Irwin, who quit in disgust. They claimed the most notoriously corrupt agents were agents like Howard of the Iowa contingent, who were protected by Bishop Hare.

C.P. Jordan, who had been a trader at every location of the Sicangu agency, blew the whistle in 1890 and reported that the governments' own records showed that the Rosebud agency had been shorted for fiscal year 1890-1891 by 1,374,920 gross pounds live weight of beef.[23]

Fornication and Adultery

While Spotted Tail worried about the quality and amount of his rations and the movement of his people away from the Missouri River, the agents encountered what they considered to be the weightiest problem of all.

"Fornication and Adultery among the Indians, mixed bloods, and squawmen, are subjects demanding your immediate attention" wrote special agent Pollock from his office at Whetstone to the Commissioner of Indian Affairs on September 15,1878.[24]

No mention was made of the inadequate supplies or Spotted Tail's discontent with his location on the Missouri River. Pollock asked for specific advice on the following problem:

"The best educated and most influential half breed on the reservation having put away his wife . . . and took unto himself with great eclat, according to the Indian custom no less a personage than the "favorite daughter of Spotted Tail."

. . . Spotted Tail at first was deeply offended, but has since become reconciled and now asks that the offense be condoned, rather than that his daughter should be disgraced by being left a widow."[25]

With such posturing by the chief is it any wonder that he was considered a consummate diplomat?

The problem was of such import to the Commission on Indian Affairs that it demanded direction from the top. On June 17th 1878 Spotted Tail's agent, Lt. Lee, received the following orders:

". . . I answer that the enforcement of the rule is imperative and you will therefore notify Mr. Pratt that if, as it is alleged, he has an unmarried man employed as his book-keeper he must immediately upon receipt of such notice, dispense with his services."[26]

A Sunday at the Res

Yet another side of reservation life was reported. Compare the conditions described by Spotted Tail and Jordan, the fornication problems of agent Pollock with the following idyllic report of "A Sunday at the Spotted Tail Agency."

"Rafferty" of the Cheyenne Daily Leader reported in June of 1878 he enjoyed the most novel and interesting scenes at the agency.

"Rev. J.W. Cleveland of the Episcopal church assisted by sisters Pendelton and Lee called English services for the soldiers, teamsters, army officers, squawmen, and their wives.

The interior of the church was festooned with boughs of cedar and a wild canary strayed inside, flitting from bough to bough. At about 2:00 P.M. sixty mixed blood children attended services. Among them was a beautiful half breed daughter of General Sully, by his Lakota wife, who is now wedded to a half breed at Spotted Tail."[27]

Little did the reporter know that this beautiful half breed daughter, who was married to John Bordeaux would, after John's death in 1881, marry Reverend DeLoria and that union would produce Ella Cara Deloria, author of *Waterlily* and other important Native American books.

The glory of a General army officer in fathering a half breed child while still married to his white society wife was not considered by the paper or agent Pollock. Just who was doing all this fornication and adultery anyhow?

Let's Dance

Spotted Tail would continue his challenge to governmental authority at every turn. Not only did he organize a dreaded "barbarous" sun dance; he also organized a boycott of the government trader's store in Rosebud in an attempt to bring down "company store" prices.

Spotted Tail's "invitation to the dance" demonstrated his abilities to control the government agents and his shrewd intellect. In May of 1879 he had agent Cicero Newell send invitations by personal couriers to each reservation inviting all to attend a sun dance "at a place between Black Pipe and Gap Creek, next month in the full of the moon."[29]

Dances were set according to the full moon cycle so that bands could travel at night.[30]

At this time conditions were bad at Red Cloud's agency. On May 16th 1879 agent McGillicuddy wrote the following to Spotted Tail's agency:

"I am entirely out of bacon and coffee . . . I earnestly request you . . . (send) 12,000 lbs. of bacon and 5,000 lbs. of coffee . . ."[31]

Spotted Tail declined to send the supplies. He may have had good reason. On February 7th 1879, a report was telegraphed to Spotted Tail's agent Newell that 50 or 60 lodges of Spotted Tail's band were crossing into Canada to join Sitting Bull and the hostiles.[32] Spotted Tail knew that a well provisioned agency with traditional sun dances would cause more of his people to return to the reservation than threats and military action.

The government's response to the invitation to the dance was immediate and phony. They canceled the dance and sent Spotted Tail a copy of a letter "written" by Little No Heart, chief of the Minniconjou.

No Heart wrote:

"that his Indians had given up the greater portion of their old barbarous customs . . . that Spotted Tail has never advocated farming or stock raising and is living after the manner of his ancestors; yet he appears to be a favorite with our great father, and allows him to keep . . . all of their barbarous customs, and idle shiftless mode of life . . ." He also "wrote": "We don't want our young men encouraged to take hold of the 'sun dance pole', but to take hold of plow handles."[33]

The Commissioner excoriated Agent Cicero Newell. He wrote him on June 6th 1879:

". . . I am surprised that an agent who is expected, and has been instructed, to use his best efforts to promote the material and civilization of the Indians under his charge, should send a notice of this character on their behalf, to Indians of a neighboring reservation, and I can only attribute the act, to thoughtlessness or ignorance of the real nature and tendency of the heathenish ceremony referred to."

"This "sun dance" is directly antagonistic to all efforts made, and influences existing to promote the highest good of the Indians. It keeps alive their barbarous practices, incites hostilities to crimes and cruelties, and fosters a spirit of hatred and revenge especially in the young men of the tribe, and the agent is not only expected but required to employ all means and instrumentalitys, at his command, to break up this barbarous custom . . . you will advise Spotted Tail at once of the views of this office . . . and induce him and other leading members of the tribe. . . to prevent the Indians from engaging in such demoralizing practices."[34]

Like all young men everywhere they went to the dance. Spotted Tail defied the orders of the government and proceeded with his tribal ways of enforcement. He sent one of his bravest war leaders, White Thunder, who had killed the Omaha great chief Logan Fonetenelle, to "invite" the Lower Brules to the dance.[35]

After White Thunder delivered his message a large body of Lower Brule warriors rode through the Lower Brule Agency, chasing and "soldiering" every policeman they saw. They shot out the policemen's windows and killed their livestock. The next day all the Lower Brule policemen resigned. The Lower Brules spent three glorious weeks at Spotted Tails, dancing and eating the provisions that he had refused to send to McGillicuddy.[36]

Spotted Tail's Revolt

In September of 1879 some of Spotted Tail's children were sent to Carlisle. On his next trip east Spotted Tail visited his children. All hell broke loose.

He took his children out of school. The agents reported that:

"The conduct of Spotted Tail in the removal of his children from the training school at Carlisle brought down upon him the strongest condemnation of the other chiefs and the Indians not directly connected with him. (He) was made to feel that he merited not only the censure of the Hon. Secretary in his (Spotted Tail's) revolutionary course but the rebuke of the good and true Indians who had no desire to retrograde on the march to civilization . . . Signed John Cook . . ."[37]

Some historians have felt that this was a contributing cause to Spotted Tail's death. In fact the other chiefs were telling the Agent what he wanted to hear and the Agent in turn was telling the "Great Father" just what he wanted to hear. Such conduct, in twitching the Great Father's nose would have made him a hero, not a despised revolutionary chief.

Spotted Tail proved to be more enlightened than the government school system. In May of 1880 Spotted Tail counseled reform of the regulations adopted at Carlisle. He wanted the "guardhouse" at Carlisle stopped. He told Captain Pratt: "These Indian children had not been given up to be treated as ill-behaved soldiers and they were not to be treated as slaves."[38]

Spotted Tail proved he had a Lakota father's deep love for his many children. In addition to his concern about his boys at Carlisle he had a strong attachment to his girls as well. Much has been written about one of Spotted Tails daughter's infatuation with the military at Fort Laramie. Lt. Ware published a full account of her funeral at Fort Laramie.[39] He gave her the romanticized name of Ah-ho-ap' pa, Wheat flour.

Susan Bettelyon attended her military funeral and noted her name was Pehinziwin or Yellow Hair Woman.[40] The name and the military funeral lend credence to her rumored love of an army officer.

The Cheyenne Daily Leader on March 4th, 1887 reported the rumored love affair as follows:

"The tale which is by no means new runs thus"—"A favorite daughter of the old chief became enamored of an officer stationed at Camp Sheridan, near the agency. Her passion was not appreciated by the pale face . . . she . . . died of a broken heart . . . but called Spotted Tail to her side . . . (made) him promise not to fight the whiteman."[41]

The same issue of the paper reported:

"He has another daughter Shonkoo (Can-ku-Sa), which means Red Road who has recently been married to Lone Elk . . . Not long ago two Sisters of Charity visited their Agency, and were presented to Spotted Tail . . . He was well pleased to meet them and had a friendly "talk" with them at Colonel Mill's house. In the course of the conversation they asked him if he would like to give them Shonkoo to go and live with them in the convent. He said yes . . . he sent for Shonkoo . . . She (refused to answer his question about going with the Sisters) . . . .. That night she eloped with Lone Elk . . . She is considered quite pretty . . . understands English . . . and is proud enough to be a Princess . . . .."[42]

As with other great leaders, dealing with enemies was often easier than solving family affairs.

HURRAH FOR SPOTTED TAIL!

(Headline of Cheyenne Daily Leader when it was reported Spotted Tail had talked the northern hostiles into surrendering)

Back in 1876 General Crook appointed Spotted Tail as head chief of all the Lakota. In the same year Spotted Tail hand picked 250 men and set out to convince the northern hostile Indians to come to the agency.[44]

"Rafferty" reported that Spotted Tail was the originator of the plan.

Spotted Tail's hand is seen in the events leading up to his departure. Earlier Crook had sent a group of thirty Indians commanded by Few Tails on a peace mission. On the night of their first camp they were severely "soldiered" by Spotted Tail. Few Tails' band promptly returned to the agency. Spotted Tail was not going to let the army run the affair.[45]

After Spotted Tail left to seek the return of the hostiles, Lt. Clark approached Red Cloud. Clark told him "I don't want Spotted Tail to get ahead of you." He sent Red Cloud out with the promise that he would have Red Cloud replace Spotted Tail as the head chief of the Lakota. The government was now playing Mutt and Jeff.[46]

The Cheyenne Daily Leader reported "a band of Lakota had left the Red Cloud agency before the departure of Spotted Tail on his self imposed mission of peace,

and whose object was the same . . . were . . . bulldozed near Hat Creek by a large
war party and lost their ponies and arms."[47]

Unfortunately some historians, while recognizing the government's willingness
to foment petty jealousy, have themselves continued the process by comparing the
conduct of one chief against the other. It is not necessary to tarnish Red Cloud's
or Crazy Horse's reputation to brighten Spotted Tail's legacy. All were great chiefs
and each contributed to the glory of the Lakota in different ways.

The Cheyennes Surrender

In the early spring of 1877 Spotted Tail's efforts started to bear fruit. Rafferty
reported that on April 14th 1877, 1500 hostiles, mostly Northern Cheyenne,
arrived at Spotted Tail's agency in Nebraska. In early May the last of the hostiles
under Crazy Horse surrendered. Sitting Bull remained aloof and escaped to
Canada.[48]

Surely Crazy Horse saw his future before him on that day. As he was surrendering, the Northern Cheyenne, who had given up just one month earlier, were
placed under military escort, and sent to the Oklahoma Indian Territory. So much
for the promise of an agency on the Tongue River for the Northern Cheyenne and
Crazy Horse's band.

To demonstrate the tractability of these "hostiles" Crook sent a contingent of
only 15 men to escort them to the Indian Territory. The only trouble they had was
the activities of white settlers trying to "redeem" the Indians' horse herd.[49]

Sans Arc and Minniconjous Surrender

Also on April 14th the Sans Arc and Minniconjous under Roman Nose and
other chiefs surrendered. Their band contained approximately 1000 Indians. They
were given permission to lay down their arms according to their traditional cultural ways used when entering a friendly village.

At about 10:00 in the morning 300 warriors made a customary charge on the
agency from several directions, yelling war cries and trills and firing their guns in
the air. An hour later the main camp entered and established their camp. At this
time 30 chiefs and headmen rode in line to the fort, advancing slowly, and wheeled
to the left to greet General Crook, with Spotted Tail acting as master of cere-
monies. The son of Lone Horn rode first and laid down his arms. The other chiefs
followed suit.[50]

Crazy Horse arrives

Crazy Horse and his hostiles "surrendered" at the Red Cloud Agency on the
first Sunday in May, 1877. The formalities took place on 2:00 p.m. of that day with
1300 Indians and 2500 horses surrendered.

The chiefs who surrendered on that day were Crazy Horse, Little Hawk, He Dog
and Little Big Man. Many lodges were old and in rags. Most of the chiefs had never
been on a reservation. Little Hawk was wearing a silver Presidential medal presented to his father by President Monroe in 1817.

With this arrival the total number of northern hostiles who had surrendered at Red Cloud Agency since March was 3600 Indians.[51]

The Grand Review

On May 25th 1877, a grand review of the hostiles, pow wow and council was held at the Red Cloud Agency. 600 Indians who had enlisted in Lt. Clark's command performed close order cavalry drill before General Crook.

At noon on the 25th of May nearly 800 former hostiles who had enlisted in the Army passed in review in 18 platoons before General Crook and his staff.

Afterwards the chiefs formed in a line and rode within a few paces of General Crook, then dismounted and shook hands with him.

Crazy Horse, who met the General for the first time, knelt as he took the General's hand. His example was followed by most of the others. Little Big Man was conspicuous for his almost complete nudity.

The order of speakers was as follows: 1. Crazy Horse, 2. Young Man Afraid, 3. Red Cloud, 4. No Water, 5. Iron Hawk. They all requested to be moved to an agency in the north.

Crazy Horse told General Crook that he had been waiting ever since his arrival to see the General and now his heart had been made happy. He told Crook that in coming this way he "picked out a place where I wish to live hereafter. I put a stake in the ground to mark the spot. There is plenty of game in that country. All of my relatives here approve of my choice. I want them to go back with me and always live there together."

Spotted Tail was the last speaker. He had the knowledge that comes from bargaining with the U.S. since he gave himself up in 1856. Nearly twenty years of education and Spotted Tail was a very smart and quick learner indeed.

As if he could foretell the future he told the council that the U.S. had broken all its previous treaties; and complained that the present Commissioner of Indian Affairs was bald and it was his experience that all bald headed whites were liars. Spotted Tail wanted to go right to the top. He asked permission to go straight to Washington so that the Great Father could settle the Agency's location.[52]

The fate of Crazy Horse and all the Indians had already been determined by the Hayes administration. On June 7th, 1877 the Cheyenne Daily Leader reported that the Army was under orders to remove the Ponca to the Indian Territory to make room for the Lakota who would be moved to the Missouri River.[53]

Following the surrender of the northern hostiles, General Crook reported to the press that the Lakota were the most tractable Indians he had encountered and he expected no trouble.

Chapter Four End Notes

1. MS8 Ricker, Eli Seavey, Box 4, reel #3, #1655, Tablet #11, pp. 103-137.
2. Poole, D.C., *Among the Lakota of Dakota*, Minnesota Historical Society Press, 1988, p. 49.
3. MS8, Ricker Ms., Tablet #11, pp. 103-137.
4. Ibid.
5. Ibid.
6. Ibid.
7. Ibid.
8. *Cheyenne Daily Leader* March 4, 1877.
9. Kansas City Regional Archives, Letter from D.C., Poole to Gov. Burbank, May 4 1870.
10. Kansas City Regional Archives, Letter from D.C. Poole to Gov. Burbank April 28, 1870.
11. Kansas City Regional Archives, Letter from Ponca Agent, Hugo, to Gov., Burbank, September, 1870
12. Hyde, *Spotted Tail's Folk*, University of Oklahoma Press, Norman, 1961, p. 196.
13. State Journal, Lincoln Nebraska, December-January 1871- 72.
14. *Denver Field and Stream*, September, 1905.
15. National Archives Micro film MS #, Sinte Gleska University Library, Mission, S.D. Letter from Col. Smith to General Ord, June 27, 1873.
16. Ibid.
17. Ibid.
18. Ibid, endorsement of General Ord of May 20,1873
19. Kansas City Regional Archives, Letter from Acting Commissioner Smith, dated December 6, 1875
20. *Cheyenne Daily Leader*, January 28, 1874
21. Ibid.
22. Ibid.
23. Jordan files, South Dakota Heritage Center Archives
24. Jordan files, South Dakota Heritage Center Archives
25. Ibid.
26. Kansas City Regional Archives, Letter from Commissioner of Indian affairs to Spotted Tail's Agency, June 17, 1878
27. *Cheyenne Daily Leader*, June 1, 1878.
28. Susan Bettelyon Ms., South Dakota Heritage Center Archives.
29. Kansas City Regional Archives, Letter from Commissioner of Indian affairs to Cicero Newell, dated June 6, 1879.
30. Eugene F. Ware, *The Indian War of 1864*, p. 147.
31. Kansas City Regional Archives, Letter from V.T. McGillicuddy to Cicero Newell, May 16, 1879.
32. Kansas City Regional Archives, Telegram from Fort Keogh, Montana, February 7, 1879.
33. Kansas City Regional Archives, Letter written by No Heart.
34. Kansas City Regional Archives, Letter from Commissioner to Cicero Newell, June 6 1879.
35. Schusky, *The Forgotten Sioux*, Nelson-Hall, Chicago 1977, p.107.
36. Ibid.
37. Kansas City Regional Archives, hand written report of agent to Commissioner
38. Kingsbury, George. *History of Dakota Territory*, Vol. 2, page 1126. The Clarke Publishing Co., 1915
39. Ware, *Indian War of 1864*, infra p. 407.
40. Susan Bettlyon Ms., South Dakota Heritage Center. Translation by Rose Kills Enemy Kramer, SFIS 1993.
41. *Cheyenne Daily Leader*, March 4, 1887.
42. Ibid.
43. Kansas City Regional Archives, Letter from Cody and North to agent Pollock, November 7, 1878.
44. Susan Bettelyon Ms., South Dakota Heritage Center Archives.
45. *Cheyenne Daily Leader*, March 4, 1877.
46. *Cheyenne Daily Leader*, May 26, 1877.
47. *Cheyenne Daily Leader*, March 4, 1877.

48. *Cheyenne Daily Leader*, June, 7 1877.
49. Ibid.
50. Ibid.
51. *Cheyenne Daily Leader*, May 8, 1877.
52. *Cheyenne Daily Leader*, May 26, 1877.
53. *Cheyenne Daily Leader*, June 7, 1877.

CHAPTER FIVE
FOOL SOLDIER

In the winter of 1862 a group of Two Kettle and other Lakota rescued two white women and six children from a band of hostile Santee Sioux. The Sioux had taken them hostage following the Minnesota uprising at Lake Shetek in late August of 1862.

The Lake Shetek hostages were Mrs. John Wright, with an infant and a boy of two, Mrs. William J. Duly and two girls, Lillie Everett, a girl of eight years and two small daughters of Thomas Ireland. The hostages were captured by White Lodge's band of Santee Sioux and taken to West River, South Dakota.[1]

Perhaps no story reflects the differing viewpoints of white historians and Indian tradition more that the oral history related by the descendants of the Indians who rescued the white captives and the accounts of early white historians.

In 1902 Doane Robinson wrote: "these eleven boys, the eldest of whom was but twenty years of age, with that grave formality characteristic of the Indian in his native state, solemnly pledged themselves to withhold nothing in comfort, effort, life or property which might be necessary to sacrifice to serve white people."[2]

Robinson's article in *The Dakotan*, prompted Senator Gamble of South Dakota in February of 1906 to introduce legislation in the U.S. Congress appropriating $3,600.00 to pay the members of the "fool soldiers" or "young men's association." Martin Charger, Pretty Bear, Swift Bird, Charging Dog, One Rib, Red Dog and Walking Crane of the Cheyenne River Sioux Tribe and Fast Walker, Black Eagle, Don't Know How, Black War Club, Mdoka and Fool Dog of the Crow Creek Sioux Tribe and Mad Bear of the Standing Rock Sioux Tribe were identified in the bill for their services and sacrifices in returning the Shetek captives in November of 1862.[3]

Two very embarrassing facts, which were known both to Robinson and U.S. Government, were missing from the article in *The Dakotan* and Senator Gamble's report from the Committee on Indian Affairs.

No mention was made that in the August 27, 1863 Indian Commissioner Report, Samuel N. Latta wrote:

"Left St Louis with annuity goods on the Robert Campbell and reached Fort Pierre on the 20th of June. There were a large number of Sioux here in suffering condition and they received their goods with expressions of satisfaction. The Soldiers at Fort Randall had killed 7 friendly Two Kettles who had periled their lives in the release of some Minnesota prisoners from the Santees. I gave the relatives of the deceased a special present to reconcile them as far as possible."[4]

In one of his last speeches on United States Indian policy, Hon. Walter A. Burleigh, delegate to Congress and former Yankton Indian agent recounted the following terrible aftermath of the courageous rescue of the Minnesota uprising captives at Fort Randall, Dakota Territory.

"During the massacre in Minnesota in 1862 several white women and children were taken captives and carried to the Upper Missouri. Through the interposition of Colonel Galpin and a number of friendly Sioux, who exchanged their own horses for them, two women, and five little girls were ransomed and returned to their friends in Minnesota. The Indians who had performed this act of humanity traveled down to Yankton agency, a distance of 400 miles, where they were to be reimbursed for this act by the Government. Week after week passed away and neither clothing nor food came to the relief of these faithful friends. Despairing of early relief, one morning ten of their number came to me for a letter, stating who they were and gained permission to go out and hunt for the support of themselves and families. The third morning out, and when on Ponca Creek, about twenty miles back (west) of Fort Randall, which post was then garrisoned by the Sixth Iowa Cavalry, a Captain Moreland, in command of some twenty men overtook them. They presented him with the letter I had given them for their protection, whereupon the Captain requested them to leave their arms and go to the fort for food. The Indians obeyed, but had not proceeded eighty rods when the brutal captain ordered his men to fire upon the Indians, who were in advance, and murdered nine out of the ten in cold blood on the spot. The tenth member of the party escaped and bore the terrible tiding of this damnable tragedy to his kindred far up the Missouri, while the bones of his comrades still remain on that fatal spot to chronicle the foul deed and point unmistakably to the cause of the Sioux War which followed with fearful and just retaliation and cost the treasury of the nation more than thirty million dollars and the loss of hundreds of innocent lives."[5]

White historians and politicians other than Latta and Burleigh chose to let this massacre of friendly Sioux "rest in peace". The Indian descendants have remembered, but whites have not.

Failing to mention the tragic massacre of the rescuers, Doane Robinson in his article in *The Dakotan* summed up his feelings:

"When the circumstances surrounding this case are considered; when the Dakota country as it was in 1862 is taken into account; when the condition and environment of the young Tetons, unschooled, beyond the influence of the missionaries, unprompted to the heroic action which they performed, except by the instincts of humanity, unrewarded and without hope of reward, -are reckoned with, I submit the record of the world's history will be searched in vain for a parallel."

Martin Charger's Ancestry

At the time it was well known that Fool Soldier survivor Martin Charger may have been a descendant of Captain Meriwether Lewis.

Lewis and Clark spent the 26th, 27, and 28th of September 1804 camped with the Two Kettle Band.

The Two Kettle camp royally entertained the company. Captain Lewis spent time on shore before Captain Clark was carried to chief's lodge on an elegantly painted robe. He was not allowed to touch the ground until he was put down on a cushion of white dressed robes. Clark admits they were offered women but he steadfastly denies they accepted the offer. The Coues edition of the Journal of the Lewis and Clark Expedition states that the dances that evening were voluptuous and indecent. Other accounts relate that the Corps of Discovery did in fact have many sexual liaisons with the natives.[6]

On November 30, 1915 Doane Robinson received the following letter from Samuel Charger:

"I am interested in the history of SD as my father Martin Charger was a member of the crazy band who rescued some white captives and which is told in the history.

And in this history it says that Martin Charger was a grandson of Meriwether Lewis, Now I want to know where you got this information, because I asked my mother who is about 87 years of age and still living and this is what she told me.

That in about the year 1824 my Grand Father with some white men who was going down the river in a boat he went with them and visited with his fathers and got two horses from his father but did not like to stay with them so in the year 1825 he ran away from his father's home for he was raised amongst the Indians and so could not speak the English very good this was done when he was seventeen years of age. The reason he went south to look for his father was that he went to war and had a very poor horse and so could not be in the fight and made up his mind that someday he will go and look for his father and get some horses from him which he did. . . ..

Now I read in the papers a few years ago that congress appropriated some thing like $3,500 to give the Indians who rescued the white captives. Now I want to know to whom I can correspond with about this matter. . . .."

On December 6, 1915 Robinson responded:

". . . ..I met your father many times and greatly admired him. He told me himself through Mr. Barney Travesee, interpreter, that he understood he was descended from Captain Lewis, and Lewis La Plant told me that it was so generally understood when he came to this region in 1855.

Captain Lewis died in 1809. Consequently if your grandfather actually visited his father and secured horses from him, he must have been some other person than Lewis.

I expect to visit St. Louis in January next and I shall take particular pains to make inquiry pertaining to your father. . . .."

In notes to the "Biography of Martin Charger" Doane Robinson tries to unravel the mystery of the paternity of Martin Charger.

Robinson states that although early territorial historians such as Deland and others claim that Martin was a grandson of Meriwether Lewis he recollects that Louis La Plant told him that Charger was the son of the fur trader Reuben Lewis from St. Louis.

He states: " It may now be said with all confidence that Charger was in no wise related to Meriwether Lewis who met Charger's Indian friends at Fort Pierre in the early autumn of 1804. . . .. (The violent death of Meriwether Lewis in

September of 1806) utterly refutes any statement that Sioux relatives from Dakota ever found him in St. Louis. These facts seem to confirm the views of Louis La Plant that Charger was descended from Rueben Lewis, the fur trader."[7]

Earlier Robinson had noted that "Louis La Plant informs the writer that Charger's relationship to Captain Lewis was a matter of common notoriety among the Indians. . . . That it was well known that Charger's father who was then living was (Lewis's) Clark's son, and that he was very proud of it."[8]

Robinson surely should have known that Rueben Lewis was a full brother of Meriwether Lewis. Rueben was a partner in the St Louis Missouri Fur Company, which was formed on March 7, 1909. Meriwether had given him his Power of Attorney on April 30, 1801. Rueben was appointed by his brother who was then Governor as sub-agent for the Indian department of the upper country on October 12, 1809. Both were friends and neighbors of Thomas Jefferson.[9] In fact, Meriwether Lewis has a headstone marker at Monticello Cemetery.

The baptismal records of the Episcopal Diocese of South Dakota located in the archives of The Center for Western Studies at Augustana College in Sioux Falls, South Dakota show that: at White Swan in the Church of St Phillip, the Deacon on Tuesday June 18th 1872 the following persons were baptized By Rev. Joseph W. Cook:

Christian and surname: Joseph DeSonnet Lewis adult (age 68)
Place and DOB: Yankton Agency
Parents: Captain Meriwether Lewis & Winona
Walter S. Hall, witness
Andrew Jones, witness

Other family members baptized were: Winona or oldest girl, probably Santee. Annie Tamahace (Slim) or (Skinny); Francis Saswena aged 21, daughter of Joseph and Annie; (Saswena is a "made up" Indian word for Francis) Joseph Wanikya (Jesus) aged 19, son of Joseph and Annie; (translated as "he who gives life") John Paddock Matowakpana (Bear creek) "n" instead of "l" indicates Nakota dialect aged 8, son of Waanatan Lewis and Makipagiwin Lewis; Edwin Kemble Ehaheka (come last) aged 6, brother of John Paddock.

Notes found in the South Dakota Historical Society archives give the following biography of Martin Charger.

His father was Zomi, Long House later known as Desonett a half breed that was born about the year 1802 and is supposed to be the son of Merriwether Lewis.

The unsigned biography states that he went down the river in 1820 and found his father and two half sisters with whom he stayed from fall until spring and returned to live in Indian Country until he died at the age of 97 years in the year 1899 and is buried on the Lower Brule Reservation, opposite Crow Creek. The oldest boy was born in 1834, his Indian name is Waanatan. English translation being Charger. Martin married a Yankton Sioux woman named Walking Hail or Makipayiwin.

WHITE ACCOUNTS OF THE RESCUE

Galpin's account

Major Charles E Galpin, on his return from trading on the upper Missouri encountered the Santees under White Lodge near Standing Rock above Fort Pierre. His Lakota wife, mother of Charles Picotte, alerted him to the trickery of the Santees and after determining that they had white hostages, he and his boat made their escape.

When Galpin arrived in Yankton he took credit for the return of the white captives. He claimed that he sent a delegation to purchase the prisoners, who took with them twenty horses and a large supply of provisions to ransom the two women and six children.

On December 2 1862, Major Burleigh informed the Yankton agents that the captives had been released. They were sent to Fort Pierre where they were turned over to Colonel Pattee. This account states that the prisoners were then in the charge of Dupuis (Dupree) and Colin La Plant. After a fortnight at Fort Randall the captives were sent to Yankton.

No mention is made of the activities of Martin Charger and the "Fool Soldiers."[10]

Charles Barbier account

Charles P. Barbier was born June 12, 1833 in Abbevillers, France. He came to Dakota in May of 1859.

The following account was in the handwriting of Mr. Charles Barbier and was given to the South Dakota Historical Society by John P. Williamson, and published as written.

". . . .. They were ten from here and they named their chief which it was a name La Chappelle and I have seen him lots time, he look more like white man than Indian. Anyway he was resolute and say when they were ready, " If we don't be back in 10 or 11 days you cane see we are dead." along their road they find few tipi, so two or three Indians went with them, and when they got to those Santee they had to parley a great deal they wont gived up and they told them all right we go back, and send lots soldier up here, finely they give them up, they were in all 7 prisoner, 2 big women and a girl of 13 years and 4 boys of about 7 or 8 years, after ten day we saw them over the river, and what a pretty site it was we could not tell if they were white or Indian. . . .. what saved it was Galpine wife, she was a Sioux too, and that she ought to be rewarded and those 12 or 14 Indians that bring these 7 prisoner, we heard that Galpine got 5 thousand dollars from the government. . . .."

" . . . ..It seems to us after they stay about 2 week with us and when two men came with their team and wagon to take them down to White Swan for the stage they were more gay and we shook hands with them all and thanking Mrs. Wright for having been our cook, to make good bread, before that we did have very poore bread made of caleratus which we did not like very much and she laugh, Well I can thanke you all for your kindness and goodbye, The men took them peoples down were and Mrs. Wright talked a great deal of those 14 Indians, how good they were even give them their own shoes and horses because they had only one cart and the four boys and the girl was enough and she say so. I will write to Washington so they probably will be paid. . . .."[11]

Jay Arem, who was stationed at Fort Randall, wrote the editor of the Yankton Weekly Dakotian in June of 1863:

"Encamped at Fort Randall is the 1st Battalion of Iowa 6th Cavalry, under Lt. Col. Pollock. This officer is not encumbered with any superfluous amount of the "milk of human kindness" when treating with the treacherous red skins . . . The only copper faces about the garrison now, are our old standbys-the seven Santee prisoners-who have been in close confinement in the guardhouse for several months."[12]

Yankton Weekly Dakotian

"Hostilities have commenced. Seven Indians have been killed and one wounded, by the soldiers. . . .. Early on the morning of the 13th Capt. Moreland of the Iowa Sixth—with 30 men—20 from his company and 10, from Dakota Cavalry-went out with orders to pursue, overhaul and then take no prisoners, so the reports says. He went and succeeded in overtaking the party of Indians nine in number, near Laramie Crossing, on Ponca Creek 26 miles from the Fort. . . .. and before firing upon them (Captain Moreland) disarmed them . . . One of the number was provided with a paper, which he had received years ago, from General Harney, which bore testimony of the bearer's good character.

After disarming them . . . the Indians broke and ran. They were immediately fired upon and seven of the nine were killed and one badly wounded. The one bearing the paper was unhurt. None of the soldiers were injured. . . .. seven of Indians belonged to the Two Kettle band, and two to the Yanktons."

Yankton Weekly Dakotian, June 23, 1863.

It is interesting to note that the editor of the paper could correctly describe the dead Indians as "Two Kettle and Yankton Sioux " when the Army insisted they were Santee prisoners.

Somewhere near the old Laramie crossing in southern Gregory County is an unmarked testimonial to the generosity of these men and a shameful event in U.S. history that should be marked and remembered.

Lakota Oral Tradition

The American Indian Research Project (AIRP) at the Institute of American Indian Studies located at the University of South Dakota contains over 1,900 taped interviews, 70 percent of which were gathered in the field between 1967 and 1973. One of six original university oral history projects funded by the Doris Duke Foundation, each project's primary goal was to collect the history of American Indian people from their perspective.

The following are edited versions of the tape-recorded interviews of descendants of the "Fool Soldiers" that were made by the employees of the Institute.

It is difficult for a non-Indian to interpret and give effect to the meanings that were given in these interviews. However, I have taken the liberty to edit some of the interviews, taking pains to correctly state the relevant facts.

Esther Benoist

I tell you this in Lakota. You must have it translated. I want no mistakes. This is what my father Strikes Fire has said.

Every day some one would bring news of death in Minnesota. A group of Indians from Minnesota came to Crow Creek to seek an alliance. In 1862 or 1863 came to Ft Thompson area. They were in bad shape. The Two Kettles were split. Old ones wanted to fight whites and young did not. A Council was held. These Minnesota Indians had white captives including a woman and children.

Waneta and Strikes Fire with nine others wanted hostages released. Old people called them Fool Soldiers. They gathered supplies and went after the hostages. Strikes Fire wanted to quit. They bargained three days and traded nearly all their goods for the hostages. We took hostages to Charlie Premo's camp. He gave them supplies. We went to Ft Randall and Strikes Fire quit them.

I told you so! We never should have ransomed the white captives; we should have left things the way they were and gone back and then we wouldn't be fool soldiers."[13]

"Grandfather Strikes Fire wanted to leave the group when they found White Lodges camp and the captives. He was tired of being called a fool soldier, and he should have known better. Waneta changed his mind. He was part white you know in fact he was more white than Indian. He was Meriwether Lewis's grandson; everyone around here knows that. They traded all their goods for the captives, but Strikes Fire kept his horse, his blanket, and his gun. You tell the people back home that Strikes Fire my grandfather was not willing to buy you white people, he kept what he had and he's a true Indian."[15]

Frank Kills Enemy

"My Father's Name was Bear Rib, we were Two Kettle Sioux. Here is what he told me. Abraham Lincoln caused all that trouble in the first place. He broke all the treaties and hung all those Indians. Santees were different from us; they raided all over, and killed our buffalo. Gold miners came to our camp and told of Santees having white captives. Bear Rib and young Two Kettles wanted to punish Santees and rescue hostages.

He didn't know the names of the other Fool Soldiers. The white soldiers, you know, killed many, right after the captives' release.

Many young men left with them to seek the release of the captives, it was midwinter. Many storms. Found captives at mouth of Moreau River. They had trouble in camp. Many wanted to quit. Ten young braves left to return to Fort Thompson.

The remaining men secured the release of the hostages, but the Santees tricked them and kept some of the hostages.

They returned to the cabins on the river. There they found their ten friends who had voted to return all frozen to death in the snow. Made them think they were really foolish soldiers. Decided to wait out the storm."[14]

"My father told me that the commanding officer ordered all of the Indian rescuers placed in the stockade. They were given no food or water for a week and two died. Bear Rib, my father, and two friends were ordered out to dig a trench. The soldiers took six of the Indian rescuer friends of Bear Rib out to the trench and on Lincoln's orders shot them. They had to bury them. They were told to go home and tell our people what happened to these bad Indians.

Bear Rib went home. He was ridiculed and instead of being heroes was treated as fools. Members of the band painted Bear Rib's log house with white wash. Told him he was a whiteman so he should live in a white house. Bear Rib became very sick. The medicine man Blue Earth told him the best thing he could do was die.

He left the band and went to Pine Ridge. He changed his name to Kills Enemy and moved to Manderson SD. No one knew he was a member of the fool soldier band. He kept it secret

One of the captives was part Chippewa, but she looked white. Bear Rib was in love with her and would have married her and he wanted to run away with her and tried to talk her into running away with him."[18]

Phoebe LaPlant

"My Father was Joseph Swift Bird. He was a Fool Soldier. We left the Two Kettles and moved to Promise to escape ridicule. Other Fool Soldier families joined us.

Martin Charger and Strikes Fire wanted to rescue the captives. They were angry because the Santees would come in the summer and kill their buffalo. Martin Charger was the grandson of Meriwether Lewis."[16]

Susan Pine

"My father was Jonah One Rib. We moved here to escape being called Fool Soldiers. Jonah One Rib was leader. Martin Charger was important part of the Fool Soldiers. Charger was the grandson of Meriwether Lewis.

Lincoln caused it all. Father saw the hostages the way they were treated was not the Indian way. He was mad. The Santees also killed their buffalo.

Charlie Premo saved them from starvation and gave them supplies to reach Ft Randall.

At Fort Randall the soldiers put all the Indians in the guardhouse. Jonah One Rib and Martin Charger and a few others were allowed to return.

My father saw seven of his comrades shot by the soldiers at Fort Randall. He helped bury them. The soldiers made everybody watch. That's what will happen to you if you don't watch out, they told the witnesses. They took them one at a time and shot them one at a time.

On returning home he was ridiculed and called Jonah Fool Soldier.[17]

Albert Four Bear

"I am Martin Charger's grandson. You know my grandfather was part white. He was the grandson of Meriwether Lewis. He and other young men were angry with other tribes killing their buffalo.

There were 15 fool soldiers. Martin Charger and two or three others had their girl friends with them. You can fetch and carry and cook they told the women.

That French guy Charlie Primeau he saved all their lives They took the captives to Fort Randall. Then you know what happened? Then my grandfather and his friends were put in the stockade and told they were hostile savages, and the soldiers wanted to know where they had gotten the white women and they would not believe them. They decided to punish the Indians. Grandfather and two of his friends were made to dig a trench. Five of the Fool Soldiers were taken out and shot and grandfather and two friends had to bury them.

The soldiers said you go back and tell your people what will happen if they cause trouble.

They went back and built some nice log houses. The people came and whitewashed all of them and called them white lovers.

Most left the community. Many went to Manderson and some had gone north."[19]

Frank Flying By

"My father's name was Circle Hawk. He was Santee. He knew White Lodge in Minnesota. I want this very clear. He was not a fool soldier even though he traveled with them. He was a Santee. His father was like Little Crow not Martin Charger.

Half of the fool soldiers gave up and left to return to Ft Thompson. Circle Hawk was a friend of the Santees and did the bargaining.

On return trip found the ten frozen bodies of their departed comrades.

They took the captives to Fort Randall. The Fool Soldiers were thrown in the stockade. Circle Hawk and two other told to dig a trench. He ran away because he knew he would be killed.

Only four survivors of the original fool soldier band that came to Fort Randall."[20]

Francis Jackson

"Regina Spotted Horse my mother had been married to Martin Charger. He was a descendant of Meriwether Lewis.

Regina Spotted Horse went with Fool Soldiers. She went with them when they parlayed with Santees. Regina would not give up her horse for the trade. She told Martin Charger he was a fool and was whiter than a white man. I told you so, she said, as on their way back they found the frozen bodies of their departed friends.

On the way back Regina got really mad at Martin Charger. I am tired of cooking, washing and doing everything for you, she said. He lay around and she jerked the meat and dried the chokecherries, and besides he had given away all their supplies to ransom these white women and besides Martin Charger had his eyes on one of those white women and that made her madder yet. In fact he was sort of running around with her on the trip back.

I got even at Fort Randall she said. All the male Indians were put in jail. Jokes on him she said. She was not put in jail but only had to cook and wash for the white soldiers. Now she was really mad at him. He was in jail and she was doing menial work for the whites, all this for giving away all their possessions and rescuing those white women. The Indians had no food for week and after that the soldiers shot six fool soldiers and dumped them in the river."[21]

Mankato Record, Saturday October 25, 1862

"Some ten weeks have elapsed since the Indian massacre at Lake Shetek, when some fifteen or twenty persons were killed, and several horribly wounded left to perish. There has been no one sent there to relieve those who possibly might have survived for a few days or to bury the dead. Men women and children lie unburied where they fell, while their relatives and friends who escaped the horrible death, thus far have been unable to procure for their own loved ones even a Christian burial.

Every other place where Indian Barbarism left its prey, we believe has been visited and the unfortunate dead buried as well as possible; but for the survivors of Lake Shetek, reduced to penury and want, and weeping for lost relations there comes not even the consoling thought that those dear to them as life itself have had the customary rite of a decent burial."

And in this place in Gregory County, South Dakota, White Barbarism has left its prey over 130 years ago, the unfortunate dead thrown into a mass grave, their relatives reduced to penury and want, being ridiculed by their own for the "fool soldier" rescue of the white captives, their log cabins "white washed" and being forced to move and change identity there comes not even the consoling thought that those dear to the deceased as life itself have had the customary rite of a decent burial or a suitable marker to forever set the place where they were repaid for their kindness by being shot down in cold blood.

Chapter Five End Notes

1. *Mankato Record*, October 18 and 25, 1862.
2. *The Dakotan*, Vol. V No.4 August 1902.
3. Copy of Report of the Committee on Indian Affairs, South Dakota State Archives E99-D1-G6-45.
4. Vol 37 SDHC collections, *Digest of Indian Commissioner Reports*, p. 320.
5. *Dakota Territory*, George Kingsbury, (History of Dakota Territory) S.J. Clarke Publishing Company, Chicago, 1915, pp. 514-519.
6. Denig, Edwin Thompson, *Five Indian Tribes of the Upper Missouri*, pp. 28-29, University of Oklahoma Press, Norman, 1961. Moulton, Gary E. editor, The Journal of the Lewis and Clark Expedition Vol. 3, University of Nebraska Press, Lincoln and London, 1987, pp.113-120. Coues, Elliot. Editor, The History of the Lewis and Clark Expedition, Vol. 1 p. 136 Dover Publications Inc. N.Y. ISBN 0-486-21268-8. Ronda, James, P. Lewis and Clark among the Indians. Lincoln: University of Nebraska Press, 1984.
7. Vol. 22 SDHC *Biography of Martin Charger*, by Samuel Charger pp1-26.
8. VOL 27 SDHC pp. 85-85; Vol. 2 SDHC p 307.
9. Lewis Collection; Lisa Papers; Pierre Choteau Collection Thomas Jefferson papers Missouri Historical Society Library St. Louis, Missouri 63112-0040.
10. VOL 11 SDHC pp. 233.
11. Vol. X1 SDHC *Recollections of Ft LaFramboise in 1862 and the Rescue of the Lake Chetek Captives*, By Charles P. Barbier.
12. Jay Arem, of Fort Randall in a letter to *Yankton Weekly Dakotian* on June 9th, 1863.
13. Esther Benoist aged 89 years quoting her grandfather Strikes Fire.
14. Frank Kills Enemy, interview 1972 Thunder Hawk SD born at Pine Ridge in 1887.
15. Interview 6/4/72 Promise SD Esther Benoist aged 89 years quoting her grandfather Strikes Fire.
16. 6/5/72 Interview Phoebe LaPlant born 1882 Promise SD Descendant of Swift Bird a Fool Soldier.
17. 6/9/72 Interview Susan Pine born 1890 at Bull Head SD.
18. Frank Kills Enemy, interview 1972 Thunder Hawk SD born at Pine Ridge in 1887.
19. Interview 8/7/72 Albert Four Bear Sr. born 1889 at Gettysburg SD.
20. Interview 6/21/72 Frank Flying By born 1890 Ft. Thompson.
21. Interview 6/17/72 Francis Jackson born 1889 Cherry Creek SD.

Fool Soldiers

Martin Charger*	Strikes Fire*	Jonah One Rib*
Joseph Swift Bird*	Bear Rib*	Kills and Comes Back
Mad or Crazy Bear	Pretty Bear	Red Dog
Charging Dog	Circle Hawk* (Santee who traveled with Fool Soldiers)	

Survivors

Prisoners taken at Shetek Minnesota on 21 or 22nd of August, 1862

Mrs. Julia Wright, Wife of John A. Wright
Daughter, Aged Five Years
Mrs. Laura Duley
Daughter, Aged Nine Years
Son of J.M. Duley, Aged Five Years
Roseanna Ireland, Daughter of Thomas Ireland, Aged Nine Years
Ella Ireland, Daughter of Thomas Ireland, Aged Seven Years
Lilla Everett, Daughter of William Everett

CHAPTER SIX
NORTHERN CHEYENNE AND LAKOTA

The Northern Cheyenne were escorted to the Oklahoma Indian Territory in May of 1877. By September of 1878 they wanted to go home, to their friends in the north. Life in the Indian Territory had been disastrous. Scotty Phillip's favorite recollection of the Cheyenne was a comparison between 50 mounted, proud Cheyenne warriors as they rode into Ft. Robinson and surrendered and a month later when they had become a bunch of dispirited, ragged, wretched men.

In May of 1879 Dull Knife's and Little Wolf's band escaped from the Indian Territory. What a hullabaloo it caused. "Savages on the rampage again" shouted the newspapers. Two bands of wretched and homesick Northern Cheyennes who wanted to return to their sacred homeland.

They only fought when their route home was blocked. Their capture and treatment in December of 1878 and early 1879 would remind Spotted Tail and Red Cloud what could happen to their people if they did not wisely lead them. It would also provide a demonstration to the world that the Plains Indian does consider the holiness of the earth, respect for others and the value of "family" togetherness in hardship. The Oglalas would put their money where their mouth was for the Cheyennes.

When Dull Knife's and Little Wolf's band reached the Platte River in October of 1878 they decided to split. Little Wolf did not trust the "Great White Father" and decided to set off on his own to their home in Montana and Wyoming. Dull Knife, more the negotiator, decided to make camp with his friends and relatives the Oglalas at Camp Sheridan, not knowing that the Red Cloud camp had been moved.

On October 25th Dull Knife's band of Cheyennes was "captured" near the Platte River by Major C.H. Carlton of the 3d. Cavalry. Carlton directed them to be ready to move to Fort Robinson. The Cheyennes held a council and advised Carlton that they would die where they were in preference to returning to the Indian Territory. They knew that Fort Robinson was but the first leg on such a journey. Carlton then offered to take them to Camp Sheridan and again they declined believing they would all be killed if they left the river thicket where they were camped.

From the moment they heard that Carlton intended to take them to Fort Robinson the Cheyenne started digging pits and breastworks opposite each detachment of the troops. Death songs were sung.

Carlton would soon be reinforced by two companies of the 7th Cavalry. He was joined by a brass howitzer company under escort from Captain Monahan.

When the Army's reinforcements arrived, the Cheyenne announced they were now ready to move to Camp Sheridan. The Army, adhering once again to the white man's idea of unconditional surrender, announced that it was too late for that and told them they must go to Camp Robinson.

As an additional condition, since they had taken so long to make up their minds, they would have nothing to eat along the way.

Carlton reported that "It might have been considered that after the Indians had surrendered and had given up their arms the troops then murder them."[1]

Lone Bear and Two Lance, Sioux scouts, stayed with the Cheyennes during the night. Two Lance's daughter had married a Cheyenne and she and her children were in the Dull Knife band. Carlton promised that Two Lance could "rescue" his daughter and grandchildren from the Cheyenne.[2]

Carlton reported to his superiors that before Dull Knife's band would return to the Indian Territory it would be "necessary to tie and haul them." Red Cloud told the Army that the Cheyenne prisoners should be deprived of their knives. He said "they will kill themselves with knives to keep from going south"[3]

In November Carlton was sent after the elusive Little Wolf's band and the care of Dull Knife's band was given to Captain Wessels' 3rd Cavalry at Fort Robinson.[4] On December 30, 1878 confidential instructions were sent to General Crook to remove Dull Knife's band to Fort Leavenworth, Kansas. This was at the request of the Commissioner of Indian Affairs. The Commissioner wanted them held there so that those who had been engaged in the "horrible series of outrages in the state" could be brought to justice.[5]

The weather was arctic in severity. The Cheyenne were in rags. The Army requested clothing to be furnished for the trip. Bureaucratic buck passing set in. Finally Captain Wessels was ordered to supply clothing from the Army quartermaster at Fort Robinson. This was done, but Crook reported "It is easy to understand, however, that this action of mine could be productive of but little benefit, as there were 60 women and 40 children to be provided for and the Quartermaster Department is not supplied with clothing suitable for them . . . . .."[6]

Crook went forward with the plans for removal. He requested that the Indian Bureau superintend the removal and that the army merely act as guard. On January 7th, 1879 the Indian Bureau had telegraphed about clothing. Dull Knife's band informed Wessels on January 5th they were prepared to die before they would leave their sacred homeland. On January 9th the Cheyennes escaped from Fort Robinson.[7]

The Outbreak

Captain Wessels took charge of Dull Knife's band on December 4th 1878. Since they had been "prisoners of war" for over a month he assumed they had been disarmed. He reported:

"Still I knew that they had knives for I saw them daily and thought it possible there might be two or three pistols among them . . . .. Everything went nicely, the

Indians were good-natured, and said they were well treated, but told myself and other officers repeatedly that they would never go South. . . .."[8]

Wessels received orders to take the band to Sidney, Nebraska. He was to start as soon as possible. On the morning of January 3rd he called Hog, Crow, Dull Knife, Tangle Hair and Left Hand into his office and told them that the Great Father had decided they should be sent back to Indian Territory. He told them they would be placed on railroad cars in Sidney, Nebraska and sent by train to Fort Leavenworth.

Dull Knife spoke first. He said that this was the sacred home of the Northern Cheyenne, that their fathers were buried here and their children had been raised here. That they left Oklahoma to come here and here they would remain. He said that they did not get enough to eat in Oklahoma and that when they went south in the Spring of 1878 fifty eight people had died. Even the children would refuse to return. Hog repeated what Dull Knife said.

Wessels told them he was under orders and there was nothing he could do. He and Captain Vroom tried to persuade them that they would see that no harm would come to them between Fort Robinson and Sidney, Nebraska.[9]

Wessels determined that Hog was the leader of the Cheyennes. On the afternoon of the 4th of January he told Hog that the Cheyenne would be moved and that was all there was to it. There would be no more talk. He would act.[10] That night the Cheyenne were given their last supper. Wessels stopped all food and fuel. He would starve and freeze them out.

After 4 days of no food and fuel Wessels decided to trick Hog and chain him in irons. The following day on the 9th he had his men ready. He reported that Hog would not come but wanted him to go in their quarters where all might hear what I had to say. Wessels told him he might bring Crow and they came. In the meantime he sent for two men to the guard house for backup. When Hog and Crow entered he asked them if they would go south and continued talking while the room was filling with soldiers. . . Wessels gave the sign and the troop all jumped the two Indians at the same time."[11]

Crow gave up at once. Hog put up a struggle and wounded Private Ferguson of Co. E, 3d Cavalry. Hog had three knives on his person and was handcuffed and placed in irons. He told Wessels that if he would let him loose he would convince his people to go south. Wessels then allowed relatives of the men to come with them. However when Hog's wife went back to get some things the band refused to let her return.[12]

During the afternoon the Cheyennes tried to break down the doors to their barracks. That evening Hog was allowed to talk to the main body of Cheyennes. At that time he was allowed to take his and Crow's relatives with him.[13]

Lieutenant Simpson, officer of the day, reported that at about 10:00 o'clock the Indians shot and killed the sentry and wounded two others. The Cheyennes broke out of the barracks and the pursuit began.[14]

The escapees consisted of 49 men, 51 women and 48 children. The army killed 64, 18 surrendered and 35 were recaptured, many were unaccounted for and of the Cheyennes who were pursued only 9 were taken alive. Five soldiers were killed.

The Fight

General Crook's investigation stated:

"The squaws say that the men feared hanging if they returned south, and that in this affair all expected to die. From the time they knew their removal was decided upon they were in such a state of mind that were the movement to be attempted in any way, it would simply be a question as to who should be killed white man or Indian. . . .."[15]

Newspaper clipping January 18, 1879

"Fort Robinson, Nebraska. A conference was held here this morning between Chief Red Cloud and Lieutenant Schuyler of General Crook's staff regarding the propriety of enlisting some Sioux warriors to be employed as scouts against the brave little band of Cheyennes now corralled at Crow Ridge thirty miles distant. . . ... The old chief, in a very grave voice and without lifting his eyes from the ground said: "My people are sad at heart since their brethren were killed here some moons ago. I am very angry with the whites and I certainly will not assist them. . . .."

Woman's Dress, the scout whose lies led to the murder of Crazy Horse, was also an actor in this tragic affair. Woman's Dress became a scout for the Army and he was with Wessel's command that fought the brave little band at Crow Ridge. His sister was married to a Cheyenne and as a reward for his services he requested that his relatives be released to him.[16]

On January 24th the final battle took place at about 2:30 in the afternoon. Crook reported that the battle occurred at a point ten miles east of the telegraph line from Robinson to Hat Creek and five miles north of the stage road. The Cheyennes fought with courage and fierceness and refused all terms but death.

The Army's body count was: "killed seventeen warriors, four women and two children. Nine captured, only three of whom were not wounded. One fatally wounded."[17]

Widows and Orphans

The army's slaughter of the Cheyennes left many widows and orphans. The generosity of the Oglala toward the Cheyenne was demonstrated by Red Cloud's concern for widows and orphans.

Red Cloud made a formal request through the offices of C. Shurz, Secretary of Interior, that the widows and orphans of the Cheyennes at Fort Robinson might be given over to the care of the Oglala Sioux. On January 30 the army issued the order assigning them to Red Cloud.[18]

Nearly 58 Cheyennes were assigned to Pine Ridge and about 20 were sent to the Indian Territory. Their struggle to return to their homeland was not over.

The Second Journey North

The remnants of Dull Knife's band that had been shipped south were assigned to the Southern Cheyenne reservation at Fort Reno, Indian Territory. They constantly lobbied for a return to their homeland. Despite requests from General Pope and Sheridan that they be allowed to return, General Sherman was adamant. He stated: "in view of the remarks and recommendations of the Generals of the Army, the Department is constrained to decline the permission requested."[19]

Finally, on August 25th, 1881 the Department of Interior with bureaucratic rigidity allowed Little Chief and his band of "two hundred and twenty one men women and children" who had been counted as going to the Indian Territory some time previous, could return, but none other than that number could return.[20] The Secretary would not let any other members of his band go north.

Little Chief requested that 30 of Red Cloud's relatives who had married Cheyennes be allowed to go home to their reservation with the Cheyennes.[21] This request was also denied.

On January 5th, 1882, three years after the Fort Robinson outbreak, Little Chief was escorted into McGillycuddy's Pine Ridge agency with three hundred and seventeen Indians. Exactly eighty two more than Agent Miles at the Southern Cheyenne and Arapaho agency had turned over to Capt. Thompson for transfer to Pine Ridge.

McGillycuddy was directed to find how this happened.[22] Here is Little Chief's reply:

"Little Chief gives as a reason that there was an error in the count as made before starting and there were a large number of children born in transit."[23]

Hog and six others were indicted for murder in Kansas. Their cases were dismissed and they were returned to the Indian Country.[24] They returned to the Pine Ridge where they entertained Harry Oelrich and his back east friends at 4th of July celebrations.

Cigar Store Indians

In the late 1880s Harry Oelrich formed the Anglo-American Cattle Company. Much of its venture capital was British. Harry was elected general manager and was sent west, "to learn the business".

In 1882 he bought the T 0 T Ranch which was located near Edgemont, South Dakota. Included in the deal was 7000 head of cattle. Later in the same year, he bought the Bar T Ranch from E. W. Whitcomb, whose fortunes had improved since he had camped out in tents with his Indian family immediately after the Civil War and had hired Jacob Harmon and Jack Sully. He sold Oelrich 20000 cattle and 200 horses along with the ranch holdings that were located along Hat Creek in southwestern South Dakota.

Oelrich also purchased the T A N ranch with 7000 head of cattle. Harry "started out" with 34,000 head of cattle on the books, a law degree from Columbia, an education broadened by travel abroad and a thorough knowledge of polo ponies.

Harry started his dream by building large feed lots to fatten cattle for slaughter. A town was laid out and was booming. It is now known as Oelrichs, South

Dakota. Harry had a problem. His town was so far from the market for fattened beef that loss of weight between Oelrichs and Chicago made the feeding venture unprofitable.

While Harry was at Oelrichs he invited and received all the dignitaries of the time. They would come by private railcar and stay to watch the great spectacles of the west that Harry would display for their pleasure, especially on the fourth of July. He would invite the Lakota, Cheyenne and the cowboys to stage mock battles. The Lakota would fight the Cheyenne as Calamity Jane, Wild Bill and numerous Indian chiefs including Hog and Little Chief added pageantry to the event. All displayed for the edification of his lacy sleeved friends.

Summer offered geologic trips to the Badlands for gathering of fossil bones and sightseeing. Interesting as all these sights would have been to the eastern eyes the greatest attraction was always the mock Indian battle on the fourth of July.

The best 'battle' was July fourth, 1887, three and one half years prior to the battle of Wounded Knee, which occurred around 50 miles to the east of Oelrichs.

On this day the siding was filled with private railroad cars of the many easterners who had been invited to witness the event.

Harry had spared no expense. He worked out a program that required courage, patience and action of such a violent nature, that the Lakota and Cheyenne could at any minute turn the whole affair into the real thing. Harry was taking a chance, as usual.

A thousand Sioux and Cheyennes were invited to the open air stage to fight in a sham reenactment of the battle when the Lakota had driven the Cheyennes from the sacred Black Hills.

By the first of July, the Indians began to arrive. Soon the town was surrounded by teepees. Harry had to distribute food to the Indians and feed them throughout their entire stay. Before the day was over the whites started to look just a little bit whiter. In the morning, prior to the afternoon battle, the Indians painted themselves with war paint and started to mingle with the white spectators. Before the "battle" began, Harry and friends gave many speeches.

Not to be out done, Chief Short Bull, who had made a pilgrimage to Wovoka and would return be a leader of a Rosebud faction of ghost shirt dancers, began to speak. He praised Harry. He thanked them for the food. He thanked him for the railroad and was pleased that all of the white people of the area were enjoying such great fortune with the coming of the railroad.

Then he tuned her up, so they say. He started talking about the deplorable conditions of his Dakota people. He started telling them how the white people had broken all their treaties with the Sioux. The Indians, painted in their warpaint, began to 'hou' his statements and things were really getting heated up. These low 'hous' of encouragement inspired Short Bull and he really laid it on. Harry started to get worried, so in the middle of Short Bull's recitation of the duplicity of the white man Harry ordered the band to strike up a lively tune, drowning out the further remarks of Chief Short Bull.

Shortly before the battle, the Indian women gathered, and started to dance and sing encouragement to their men folk who would be fighting in the battle. The warriors really got worked up and excited, which led many of the onlookers to start to quake in their laced up boots.

The show started with the Cheyennes in camp and the Sioux charging them on the plain in front of the "witnesses". The Sioux warriors dashed about the field, shooting, shouting and routing the Cheyennes until they left the scene of battle.[25]

After the celebration the Lakota and the Cheyenne returned to the reservation. They would watch their heritage and culture disappear, adopt the coffee cooler life and await the coming of the Messiah and the Seventh Cavalry.

Chapter Six End Notes

1. National Archives Micro film MS. #666 #449 (71) NA Letter from Carlton to Crook dated October 29, 1878, Sinte Gleska University Library, Mission, S.D.
2. Ibid. Crook report of outbreak.
3. Ibid.
4. Ibid.
5. Ibid.
6. Ibid.
7. Ibid.
8. Ibid. Wessels report to Department of Army.
9. Ibid.
10. Ibid.
11. Ibid.
12. Ibid.
13. Ibid.
14. Ibid.
15. Ibid. Crook's investigation.
16. Ibid. Captain Vroom letter to Crook dated January 16.
17. Ibid. Crook report.
18. Ibid. Telegram from Bureau to Sheridan dated January 30, 1879.
19. Ibid. Letter Department of Army.
20. Ibid. Department of Interior signed by Carl Schurz, dated August 25, 1881.
21. Ibid. Department of Interior letter dated August 29, 1881.
22. Ibid. Department of Interior report dated January 10, 1882.
23. Ibid. McGillycuddy report December 31, 1882.
24. South Dakota Historical Collections, Digest of Indian Commissioner Reports 1879 report of Commissioner Hayt at page 385.
25. A.H. Schatz, *Opening a Cow Country*, Edwards Bros Inc., 1939 Ann Arbor Mi.

CHAPTER SEVEN
FIRST LET'S GET RID OF THE LEADERS

Coffee cooler life

The white man's "good life" caused problems for Crazy Horse. A telegram dated May 15th 1877 reported:

"Crazy Horse has been very sick since his arrival here; for several days he was not expected to live; since Sunday, however he has been improving. His illness was caused by over-eating and the sudden change from buffalo straight, and but little of that, to wheat bread, coffee, sugar and strawberries and cream, which are furnished at this place of plenty and it nearly killed him."

Crazy Horse got sick from something he ate all right, but you can bet it wasn't from "strawberries and cream" out at the Red Cloud agency, unless "cloak and dagger" Clark had a hand in the preparation.[1]

Lt. W.P. Clark had enlisted Crazy Horse and fifteen of his headmen in the Army in May of 1877. They were sworn into the Army and lifted their arms to true and faithful service to Uncle Sam. The sullen look of the hostiles was fast disappearing and Spotted Tail, Red Cloud and Crazy Horse were advanced to the rank of sergeants.

The Cheyenne Daily Leader quoted Crazy Horse in May of 1877 as saying that he wanted "to get along straight and well" at the agency, and "that he would like a hundred of his best men enlisted" and "that he wanted his agency in the north."[2]

The conspiracy to kill Crazy Horse

In late August of 1877, Lt. Clark called a meeting of the prominent Oglala chiefs, including Red Cloud, Young Man Afraid, Little Wound, Red Dog, No Flesh, Yellow Bear, High Wolf, Slow Bull, Black Bear, American Horse, Three Bears, Blue Horse and No Water. The chiefs did the white man's bidding and determined that Crazy Horse must be "put out of the way." In fact No Water rode two horses to death trying to catch Crazy Horse. Crazy Horse had earlier stolen No Water's woman and now he could "justifiably" seek his revenge.[3] Crazy Horse escaped from No Water by galloping his horse downhill and walking it uphill.

When asked if there was a conspiracy to kill Crazy Horse, Spotted Tail at first denied there was any such cabal. When pressed he said: "Yes there is a conspiracy, but we will be the winner."[4]

Crazy Horse learned of the plot and escaped to Spotted Tail's agency. Spotted Tail advised him that he would have to abide by his rules, but he was welcome.

Since Crazy Horse sought Spotted Tail's camp for refuge, Spotted Tail was probably not a participant in the plot to kill him. Always the politician, Spotted Tail praised Crazy Horse's people. After the killing of Crazy Horse, they sought refuge with Spotted Tail and shunned their own band.

Surrender

Crazy Horse had manifested an intense reluctance to return to the fort. He said he had no friends, white or Indian, at Fort Robinson. He sensed that he would be in physical danger. He agreed to go with the understanding that he would be allowed to explain himself and that his people could be transferred to Spotted Tail's agency where he could live in peace.[6]

Crazy Horse left with Louis Bordeau, Lt. Lee and Spotted Tail's guards. They were going to report to Fort Robinson. Lt. Lee, sensing something was afoot, and not being party to the conspiracy, sent a runner requesting that Crazy Horse be taken to the agent and not the military authorities. The officers in charge ordered that he must bring Crazy Horse to the officer of the day at Fort Robinson.[7]

The conspiracy to get him "out of the way" continued at the fort. Crazy Horse was killed and some historians have accepted the "plausible denial" of the Army that Crazy Horse stabbed himself in the struggle.

Cloak and dagger man

Lt. Clark wrote in his report of September 10, 1877:

"He (Crazy Horse) seemed to think it was done by one of the soldiers' bayonets, but it is impossible to ascertain about the matter as the doctors from the appearance of the wound thought it must have been done with his own knife . . . .."

The men who were present knew exactly which soldier had done the killing. In Clark's book, *The Indian sign language*, published in 1884, seven years after the event, he wrote the following account:

"In 1877 it became necessary for the military authorities to know something of the movements and plans of the great war chief, Crazy Horse, and to discover these one of the enlisted scouts (Womans Dress) became smitten with the charms of a dusky maiden who lived in the tepee adjoining that of the chief, and as she reciprocated the tender feeling, the scout would stand just outside Crazy Horse's lodge, holding the girl in a fond embrace, while his quick ears discovered a conspiracy, which, if it had not been for his cunning and shrewdness and prompt and loyal action to the whites, would in all probability have terminated in the murder of a general officer, but which eventually led to the necessary killing of the chief himself."[8]

When was Clark telling the truth? When he stated that he probably died from his own stab wounds or when he later wrote that it became necessary to kill Crazy Horse?

A soldier's account

The Cheyenne Daily Leader reported on October 6, 1877 that Edwin Wood, a soldier stationed at Fort Robinson, wrote the following letter to his parents:

"We started out on the 4th of September, with eight companies of the third cavalry, to bring Crazy Horse and his band into the agency, but did not succeed in capturing him. The next day he was brought in by a lot of friendly Indians . . . when the carriage drove to the guard house, Crazy Horse got out and walked a short distance; then refused to go in . . . there are all sorts of rumors about the way he was killed by another Indian called Big Little Man; but I know that he was killed by one of the guards myself, and was there when he was stabbed, and (I) know the man who did it."[9]

Encouraging chiefs to get troublemakers "out of the way" was not an uncommon occurrence. "Sioux Jim" and his sons were notorious robbers and killers in the Loafer Band. The army set a trap to catch him, but he escaped.

As the soldiers were riding away, taking one of Jim's captured sons to Fort Robinson, Chief American Horse came riding up shouting, "Hold on! come back! I've got Sioux Jim! I've killed him!" American Horse had indeed killed "Sioux Jim". John Bear had ensured his departure by placing an additional bullet right between his eyes.[10]

The Cheyenne Daily Leader of May 22nd 1877 reported that although Crazy Horse was honored as a warrior, he had not come to the agencies before his surrender. The agency chiefs were jealous of him. The paper reported that he was a small man and showed many scars of his combat which gave him an ugly appearance.[11] The paper concluded that he was an extremely brave chief but not "long headed."[12]

Exodus

A Fond Farewell The President closes his council with the Red Beggars and bids them homeward, pack their baggage and remove to the banks of the Big Muddy, where Sugar and Coffee, Beef and Blankets, Bread and Beans, Soap and Sow Belly await them.

—Headline in Cheyenne Daily Leader October 1877

Hurrah for Spotted Tail indeed!

After Crazy Horse's death and a perfunctory trip to see President Hayes as his reward in bringing in the hostiles, the government ordered Spotted Tail to move his agency to the dreaded Missouri River.

The order and plans for removal were made in April of 1877. When the move was made in November of 1878 the Government, as usual, was not properly prepared.

The two bands, Oglalas and Sicangus, did have two things to their advantage. The Oglalas were headed by Dr. Irwin and the Sicangus by Lt. Lee, both considerate and just Superintendents. Col. C.P. Jordan, who was a clerk at the Red Cloud Agency wrote the following account of the exodus:

"The two bands were accordingly removed in November of 1878. As I was chief clerk with the Ogalallas I will deal only with their movements. We started the exodus from the old Red Cloud's agency near Fort Robinson. We had some 10,000 people, a pioneer party of soldiers, two companies of cavalry under Captain Lawton, Indian traders and camp followers, 2000 head of cattle, a government mule train, with military supplies and a large bull train loaded with Indian rations.

We were enroute 31 days making a distance of 235 miles, locating our Indians at the forks of the White river (north and west of White River Town where the White River and the Little White River meet) . . . (The) military and agent and staff proceeded to the Missouri river some 65 miles further, where headquarters were established. The soldiers located at a new post on the Missouri river about a mile from the agency and were in command of Captain P.D. Vroom, 3rd US cavalry . . . (The Oglalas became restless) and stampeded back to their old agency at Red Cloud. The Sicangus were not far behind. Spotted Tail told the government if they didn't let his people return he would burn all the government buildings on the reservation."[13]

Spotted Tail's murder

Most of the history of Spotted Tail's death has concerned itself with the legal jurisdiction problem. In the process, the facts concerning the killing were not reported. The Government and Spotted Tail's tiospaye squelched most of the testimony of witnesses.

The first accounts reported that his death was caused by a conspiracy between Crow Dog, Black Crow and others and that Spotted Tail was armed when he was shot by Crow Dog. In fact, Black Crow openly boasted of the conspiracy.[14]

The motives for Spotted Tail's death were complex. He had opposition from Black Crow and his band. Crow Dog had historical reasons to seek revenge. Spotted Tail could be tyrannical and "soldiered" dissent. He was also a rumored "wife stealer." He Dog was suspicious of Spotted Tail's dealings with Nebraska ranchers. Now the government wanted him "out of the way."[15]

Spotted Tail was aware that there was a conspiracy and on the fateful day he was armed, unafraid and ready. Both Louis Bourdeaux and Alex Shaw, confidantes of Spotted Tail, mentioned that there was a family feud between Crow Dog and Spotted Tail's families.

Crow Dog told Alex Shaw in 1907 that he killed Spotted Tail because with him "out of the way," there would be room for others. Crow Dog also reminded him that Spotted Tail's grandfather had killed a member of Crow Dog's ancestors in the distant past. Just before his death, Shaw personally warned Spotted Tail of the conspiracy to kill him. Here's how Shaw put it:

"Spotted Tail replied with his soft and assuring smile: 'I am not afraid; he is not brave; he has never killed anyone; he will not kill anybody now."[16]

Sequestered testimony

The witnesses who knew of Spotted Tail's actions on that day were not called to testify or suffered "memory loss." The trial court ruled that Pretty Camp, Crow Dog's wife, could not testify. She would have testified that she was with Crow Dog and that Spotted Tail rode up, dismounted, and pulled his pistol before he was shot.[17]

No Flesh, a prominent Oglala Lakota chief, signed the most interesting affidavit of all. He said:

"(Following the trial) Bears Head . . . came to my house in the presence of Red Dog, White Face and Yellow Eyes (Oglalas)...Bear Head told him . . . Spotted Tail had a pistol and none dare tell it . . . on that day there was a council . . . and after the council looking off to one side I saw a wagon with horses attached standing in the road and Spotted Tail standing by the side of his horse with a pistol in his right hand at one side of the wagon . . . I then started toward the wagon . . . I saw Spotted Tail moving towards the head of the team and after taking a few steps, I saw him stop and instantly move backward in a crouching position. In an instant afterwards I heard the report of a gun, and saw Spotted Tail reel and fall to the ground. . . .."[18]

V.T. McGillycuddy, agent at Pine Ridge, who just months before had wished both Red Cloud and Spotted Tail dead, signed the following affidavit:

"1. That bribery and intimidation was used with said witnesses as against Crow Dog's interest at the trial.

2. That I have no doubt Spotted Tail was fully armed at the time of his death and by threats made by both parties at various times prior to the killing-it was merely a question of chance as to which should be killed first.

3. In my opinion, the well known reputation which Spotted Tail had acquired by having killed several Indians in the same manner in which he himself was killed fully warranted Crow Dog killing Spotted Tail as a matter of self defense".[19]

The Reporter's story

William Henry Wright, reporter for the Black Hills Daily Times, camped on the Rosebud gathering facts about the killing. He believed that Spotted Tail was armed at the time of his murder and that his relatives and friends had tried to cover up that fact. It is argued that is was inconceivable considering the facts and circumstances that Spotted Tail would have gone anywhere unarmed.

Wright interviewed Saffron Iott (Aiotte aka Iotte or Iyotte), one of Spotted Tail's trusted interpreters, who was with him when he made his journey to talk to the Governor of Wyoming in 1874. Iott saw Spotted Tail on the day he was killed and Spotted Tail had a "stolen" woman with him. Iott told him the Indians would not put up with it longer and that they would kill him.

Spotted Tail pulled out his revolver and said: "This never slips."

The reporter also stated that Spotted Tail Jr. had given gifts to those that testified at Deadwood who refused to say that Spotted Tail was armed.[20]

Last Hurrah

Thus did the great leader of the Sicangu Lakota meet his death. He was a powerful and intelligent leader who bargained as effectively as any man could with a perfidious and duplicitous government. He left his own epitaph. It was his last speech to the Great Father on October 1, 1877. He said:

"We don't want to move just now; we want some time to sell what property we have at our present home; we will move in the spring; or at anytime after that; we want our provisions removed to the agency I named (he wanted his agency on Wounded Knee Creek.)"

"You tell us that you increase. We want to increase too, in property and in numbers. You said you wished us to live like whitemen, and so we are here today dressed in whitemen's clothes. I want the kind of cattle the white men have-Short Horns. I want everything in writing before I go home so there will be no mistake. We want teachers of English and we want Catholic priests to teach us. We should like a saw and grist mill and agricultural implements and seeds; we want five or six stores; then we could buy cheaper at one than the other . . . .."

"Where we are right now we are prepared for the winter. Whitemen never throw away their labor. What whitemen have they love and it is the same with us, we don't want to throw our labor away.[21]

The President, despite Spotted Tail's plea, ordered the Sicangu to the dreaded Missouri River. Thus the long, slow, painful mid winter exodus began. It would be the last removal to the Missouri and it would be Spotted Tail's last endeavor to "get it in writing."

Secretary of the Interior Carl Schurz gave Spotted Tail his government's reply. "All we desire you to do now is to aid him (the Great Father) in making it possible for him to help you."[22] Sound familiar?

Government policy to kill the leaders

Had the government reached a point in its dealings with these shrewd chiefs that it would be necessary to "put them out of the way"?

The ubiquitous V.T. McGillicuddy, Schurz's agent at Pine Ridge, and the physician who had examined Crazy Horse and stated that it was entirely possible he had died of self inflicted wounds, were anxious to depose Red Cloud, Spotted Tail and any other "old fraud" who stood in the way of the melting pot theory.

The agents were doing all in their power to undermine the chief's desire to keep the Lakota's tribal culture and government. Unfortunately some present day tribal members are unaware that Spotted Tail, while giving up war, fought in the most effective way available to keep native culture and spirituality. He was no traitor to their cause.

McGillicuddy, Schurz and the eastern lacy sleeved set were pleased that the tribal jealousies they had fomented led to death of Spotted Tail. For them, it was a fortuitous circumstance.

McGillicuddy, in boldly racial tones, would write in his 1880 report to Commissioner of Indian Affairs:

"I have ... opposition ... from Red Cloud ... (and) ... Spotted Tail (who) form as egregious a pair of old frauds in the way of aids to their people in civilization as it has ever been my fortune or misfortune to encounter. When these two old men shall have been finally gathered to their fathers, we can truly speak of them as good Indians and only regret that Providence, in its inscrutable way, had so long delayed their departure."[23]

So sayeth the lord.

The government's policy had now become sinister and sanguine. The Lakota understood that this policy meant that Spotted Tail, Red Cloud and Sitting Bull must be "put out of the way." If the Indians could be fomented into permanently ridding them of these "old frauds," who would care?

Bishop William H. Hare, missionaries William J. Cleveland, Joseph M. Cook, John P. Williamson, Alfred L Riggs and Indian agent Jas. G. Wright petitioned the President that ... "Crow Dog ... is about to suffer hanging for an offense for which he has already been fully punished and for which he has already adequately atoned under the customs of the tribe ... to which he was amenable."[24]

Thus Spotted Tail would be put away and his killer set free by a self righteous governments' use of the very cultural system he would gladly die to preserve and they had vowed to destroy.

Chapter Seven End Notes

1. *Cheyenne Daily Leader*, May 16, 1877.
2. Ibid.
3. Friswold-Clark, *The Killing of Crazy Horse*, University of Nebraska Press, Lincoln-London, 1988, p. 79.
4. MS8 Ricker, Eli Seavey, Box 4, reel #3, #1655, Tablet #11, pp. 103-137.
5. William Bordeau Ms., SFIS Library, St. Francis, S.D.
6. MS8 Ricker, Eli Seavey, Box 4, reel #3, #1655, Tablet #11, pp. 103-137.
7. William Bordeau Ms., SFIS Library, St. Francis, S.D.
8. W.P. Clark, *The Indian Sign Language*, University of Nebraska Press, Lincoln-London, 1982, p 130.
9. *Cheyenne Daily Leader*, October 6, 1877.
10. MS8 Ricker, Eli Seavey, Box 4, reel #3, #1655, Tablet #11, pp. 103-137.
11. *Cheyenne Daily Leader*, May 22, 1877.
12. Ibid.
13. Jordan files, South Dakota Heritage Center Archives.
14. *Denver Republican*, August 16, 1881.
15. He Dog Community oral tradition. Interview Mary Waln, 1993. Susan Bettelyon Ms.
16. MS8 Ricker, Eli Seavey, Box 4, Reel #3, #1655, Tablet # 11, pp. 103-137.
17. Crow Dog File, South Dakota Heritage Center Archives.
18. Ibid, No Flesh affidavit.
19. Ibid, McGillicuddy affidavit.
20. Ibid, William Henry Wright affidavit, dated September 25, 1883.
21. *Cheyenne Daily Leader*, October 6, 1877.
22. Ibid.
23. McGillicuddy report to Commissioner, 1881.
24. Crow Dog Files SDHC, Pierre SD.

CHAPTER EIGHT
EARLY TRESPASSERS

The Pine Ridge Reservation grazing area was cherished by the Lakota and coveted by the whites. If the eastern and foreign lacy sleeved ranching set could not own the reservation outright they would use it anyway. Trespassing at will, they used the Indians' homeland to fatten their cattle and their purses. H.A. Dawson, who came west as an Indian Bureau clerk, "ranched" on Indian land and became one of the largest cattle owners in the state. Mostly at the Indians' expense. The Lakota had to fight not only the direct expropriation of their homeland but trespassers and influence peddlers as well.

In 1857, Lt.Warren reported that the Lakota used this land as a holding area for large herds of buffalo.[1] G.E. Lemmon a prominent rancher, known as the Boss Cowman, called it the best breeding ground to be found. He said that cattle could be raised cheaper there than any place he knew.[2]

In the early 1880s and 1890s it was illegal to pasture cattle on the Pine Ridge Reservation. The stockgrowers, however, trampled on the Indians' rights, pushed their cattle on the reservation and hired the toughest cowboys to patrol their trespassing stock.[3]

Lemmon admitted that in the 80s he ranged 10,000 trespassing cattle on the reservation, paying a "trespass fee" of a few lump jawed old mossy horned steers to the Indians.[4]

Things were so rotten that in 1884 the Custer County assessor raised the valuation on the Sheidley Cattle Company to $124,000. The Company went to court and argued that the cattle trespassing on the reservation could not be assessed. The judge agreed and lowered their assessment to $25,275.00.[5]

In 1897, Agent V.T. McGillicuddy registered the Indian brand of FOF. The cowboys called this brand the "Flying Asshole".[6] In the same year the Hunter and Co. cattle outfit branded T0T. Is it any wonder that Ed McGaa would state that many FOF cattle were rounded up and resold to the government.[7] A friendly brand inspector could read a FOF brand for a TOT just about any time he wanted.

By 1897 the vast range north of the White River was overgrazed. The "smart" operators of the Western South Dakota Stockgrowers (WSDSG), like Keliher and H.A. Dawson, often in complicity with the Agency, wintered their stock on the Pine Ridge reservation. Red Cloud with the help of an acting military agent, Captain Clapp of the 16th Infantry USA, would soon give them a wake up call.

The Western South Dakota Stockgrowers had a cozy arrangement on most of the reservations. F. M. Stewart, the Association's Secretary, was traveling under an assumed name. His alias "Stewart" was adopted to keep his real brother, an agent at Pine Ridge, from being questioned if "Stewart" and his buddies got preferential treatment.[8]

The Stockgrowers had treated the Pine Ridge as their own private domain even prior to Red Cloud's arrival. When Red Cloud and his band moved back to the Pine Ridge, the Stockgrower's cattle had already established squatters rights. Was this early trespassing presence of the Western South Dakota and Wyoming Stockgrowers Association's cattle on the northern, western and southwestern boundary of the Pine Ridge reservation one of the reasons the government was so adamant in its efforts to locate Red Cloud and Spotted Tail to the dreaded Missouri River agencies?

Baron E. Mandat-Grancey, a Frenchmen who ranched at Buffalo Gap in 1887, called a spade a spade. "The (Association) has the right to take (cattle or horses) in any manner it sees fit. The agents of the Association are generally men who have excellent revolvers and make use of them with great facility . . . . . Colonel Log has created a black list of those cowboys who cannot become members of the Association. In the two territories where the Association operates, Wyoming and Dakota, there are eight or ten great newspapers which are inspired by it. So, from a political point of view, it is all powerful. The railroad companies alone dare sometimes to fight it."[9]

A new acting agent was appointed at Pine Ridge on January 1, 1896. He was Captain William H. Clapp 16th Infantry, USA. On May 17th 1897 Clapp addressed the following order to all interested Indian operators on the reservation:

Pine Ridge Agency, May 17, 1897

"To R.C. Stirk, W.D. McGaa, Charles Jones, Billy Palmer, Taylor Palmer, Mart Gibbons, Charley Gifford, John Gifford, George Gifford, Ben Roland, Alex Adams, John Steele, John Pourier, Charley Cooney, Billy Twiss, George Harvey and Joseph Brown, together with any others living in Wounded Knee, Porcupine and Medicine Root Districts, this reservation, who are interested in preserving the grazing from being destroyed by trespassing stock;

"You are authorized and requested to round-up and bring to this agency all stray stock found grazing on your localities on the reservation, not the property of Indians, and drive the same to the agency corral, where it will be taken in charge by the proper officers of the court."

"It is understood that no pay will be given to you, or any of you, for this work, but that it is done free of charge in order to protect your own interests on the range."[10]

The Western South Dakota Stockgrower Association's round-ups for the spring of 1897 had been previously scheduled and the Association had set the Pine Ridge roundup to "start from the north side of the White River on June 1st and all concentrate to Wakpamini Lake where the round-up will end on June 25th, 1897."[11]

By scheduling the "Indian" round up" up weeks before the Association's annual spring round up Captain Clapp was stealing a march on a very powerful organization indeed.[12]

Clapp posted the following notice:

NOTICE

Section 2117, Revised Statutes U.S., provides: "Every person who drives or otherwise conveys any stock of horses, mules or cattle to range and feed on any land belonging to any Indian or Indian tribe without the consent of such tribe is liable to a penalty of one dollar for each animal of such stock."

Regarding which section the Hon. Attorney General of the U.S. has prepared the following opinion:

"It appears that when any stock of horses, mules or cattle are driven or conveyed so near to Indian lands, that from the nature and habit of the animals they will probably go upon such lands, especially when the circumstances show an intention on the part of the person so driving or conveying to have them go there, if the cattle should be found upon the lands without the consent of the tribe, such person would be liable to the penalty imposed by Section 2117 Revised Statutes. To incur that penalty, it is not necessary that the stock be actually driven upon the Indian lands; it is sufficient if they are so driven as to range and feed thereon."

Owners of stock held near the lines of this reservation are warned that in future stock trespassing on the Indian lands of this reservation in violation of Section 2117 Revised Statute are construed by the Hon. Attorney General, will be proceeded against as the law allows.

—W.H. CLAPP,
Captain 16th Infantry, Acting Indian Agent
Pine Ridge Agency, May 22, 1897.

He would soon reap the whirlwind of an irate, lacy sleeved ranching set who considered the property of others, especially Indians, as their own private domain. The Indian operators rounded up livestock belonging to over 48 different owners. Anderson and Rounds, Corb Morse, Keliher, John Hart, H.A. Dawson, the Johnson Bros, and Grant and Gandy were the biggest offenders.[13]

The possibility that the Stockgrowers could lose their free Indian range brought out their biggest guns. G.E. Lemmon, the great "boss cowman"; W.W. Anderson, a high powered Washington attorney, and Wood and Buell, attorneys at law from Rapid City, the best local talent money could buy, appeared on behalf of the Association in the investigation that would follow.[14]

When the Association asked for an investigation, things happened. The Indian Department sent that famous "friend of the Indian" James McLaughlin to investigate the problem caused by agent Clapp.

Hearings were held on July 15th, 1897 just 60 days after Clapp ordered trespassing cattle impounded. Who but the powerful could demand and get such service from the Department that was established to protect the Indians' interests? After July in Pine Ridge, McLaughlin would journey to Rosebud to try to get Stockgrower related concessions from the Sicangu.[15]

Agent Clapp had no representation. He was left to defend his actions on his own. Neither the Government itself nor any of the darlings of the eastern establishment came to his defense. Very powerful people were arrayed against him. He was playing with a "cold" deck.

Red Cloud, now old and having made his last journey to the Great Father offered insight and a history of the activities of the Association and G.E. Lemmon that deserves a direct quote.

Red Cloud testified:

"I will tell about these cattle. I lived down here on the Missouri River, I moved back here. In this country when I moved back here there was cattle back here. I saw them with my own eyes. Me and McGillycuddy was here and we had a hard time. There was another agent here, Col. Galligher, and we had a hard time. And there was another agent here, Capt. Brown and we had a hard time every winter. These cattle got around here, and came right to my house and the agents didn't help drive them off and we had to do it."[16]

Transcript of the proceedings

"(W.W. Anderson, Stockgrowers attorney) Q. Was this Indian stock or was it all whitemen's cattle?

A. (Red Cloud) It was outside cattle, the reservation was filled with it and the agent was here and knows all about it.

Now my friend here Crooked Ass (G.E.Lemmon) had cattle here for some time; the reservation was full of it. Now my friends you all sleep, and what we do is just to wake you up[17]"

Hunts His Horses, who lived along Medicine Root and Bear-in-the-Lodge Creek, testified that the area had been "chock full" of trespassing cattle for the last ten years.[18]

Red Shirt testified "I have been along the Cheyenne River three years and the country has always been plumb full of outside cattle and horses. Last winter just as soon as it snowed there was no grass anywhere. My friends take pity on us, you ought not to fight this case; give us a little show."[19]

Red Shirt, No Water and He Dog testified that the outside cattle ate all the winter range and that Indian cattle would die up in the winter because of such trespassing.[20]

The Medicine Root and Bear-in-the-Lodge Creeks of the Pine Ridge are one of the most picturesque and prime grazing areas in the west. It is filled not only with scenic beauty but also vast grazing meadows and an abundance of ever flowing springs and wooded valleys which offer winter and summer protection for livestock.

The Association's defense was: (1) The Indians who had complained were not full bloods but were "squawmen"; (2) unusual winter storms had driven the cattle onto the reservation in 1897 (the "Act of God" defense); and (3) it was necessary to the booming cattle industry of the State of South Dakota that such trespassing be allowed.[21]

The "squawmen" testified that as many as 2000 head of livestock would trespass at a time in their area thus leaving the winter pasture in such a condition that the Indians' cattle would die for lack of winter forage.[22]

Captain Clapp called over 25 witnesses. The Association brought out its big gun, Boss Cowman to the whites but known to Red Cloud as "Crooked Ass".

"Crooked Ass" Lemmon testified that he handled 20,000 head of cattle a year and that he shipped an average of seven to nine thousand steers to market each year. He also denied that Association members had grazed reservation grass and that they had sufficient range without trespassing on the reservations.[23]

Clapp, sensing the power that was arrayed against him and the Indians, cross examined Lemmon as follows:

Q. You are a member of the Western South Dakota Stock Growers' Association are you not?

A. Yes sir.

Q. Are there others than yourself who are members of that Association here present?

A. Yes sir.

Q. Name them. I should like to have it appear that there are a good many against me here."[24]

Lemmon named a plethora of members who were present, including Judge Gardner, W.W. Anderson, Keliher, John Hart, Eugene Holcomb, T.B. Irwin, Reed, Gannow, Hasser, Wood, Massingale, Dawson, John Stevens and F. M. "Stewart" the Association's secretary.[25]

Captain Clapp presented a powerful closing argument. He argued:

"I have been Acting Agent here since January 1, 1896, and from the first have recognized the pressing necessity for encouraging the Indians to engage each year more and more in the stock industry, that being the sole and only way they can become self supporting. The treaty under which they are now being fed and clothed covered when made 30 years, 27 of which have already elapsed, and very soon such aid as they receive will be in the nature of a gratuity rather than a right, and may be much less in amount than they are now receiving. There is therefore no time to lose, and these Indians must be pushed as fast as possible."

"I found everything going well but for one drawback. It has always been the case where Indians owned property white men covet, that the equities have been little observed, and in one way or another the Indian has been robbed and whee-dled out of his possessions, or have been taken away from him by force and small compensation afterward awarded. These Indians, once the owners of vast territory, were finally placed on their present reservation and their occupancy of it solemnly guaranteed by treaty; but the cattle ranges becoming overcrowded, the borders of the reservation on the north and west were fringed with ranches and stocked with cattle and horses to an extent rendering it certain that the owners expected their stock to range on the reservation. Not less than 10,000 head of stock are held along the northern border, where but for the reservation, not more than one tenth of that number could be subsisted. . . .. (That) the native grasses have been killed and the ground taken possession of by cacti and weeds. . .(and) it will take several years to restore . . . .."

"It is idle to claim that this state of things was unknown to the ranchmen; they have at all time known where their stock ranged and to what extent."[26]

The Association argued that unless the livestock were intentionally driven on the reservation that the provisions of the law did not apply. They quoted an opinion of the Attorney General that "where stock of horses, mules or cattle are found ranging or feeding upon the unenclosed lands belonging to any Indian or Indian tribe, without the consent of such Indians or Indian Tribe, but not driven or otherwise conveyed thereon by any person, Section 2117 Rev. Stats. does not, in my opinion, provide a remedy for the case."[27]

The Association blamed the "squawmen". Attorney Anderson argued that these men, and especially those recently married to Indians are living on the reservation holding large herds of cattle, purchased with secret money from the outside and are occupying the choicest grazing areas. He maintained that they enjoy all the privileges of both white and Indians and shield themselves from their own wrong doing behind their Indian wives.[28]

Anderson, like the politician who chops down the tree in order to have a stump to stand on in order to rail against the destruction of the forest, stated: "To allow these men (the "squawmen") to remain upon (the reservation) without putting some restrictions upon them, seems like putting a premium on rascality on the part of the government." To allow this to continue, he said: "(would give) these squaw men and half breeds a monopoly of the best grazing lands on the Indian reserve . . . .."[29]

Anderson also argued that the Clapp should be reported to the Society for the Prevention of Cruelty to Animals. He stated: "That part of the evidence showing a number of cattle rounded up in the dead of winter and forced through the ice on the river by whip and dog, is certainly . . . wanton cruelty."[30]

In his ruling, Inspector McLaughlin, true to the Indian Department and Bureau form, chastised Captain Clapp and effectively washed his hands of the matter.

He regarded Captain Clapp's order to round up the Association's cattle as "premature, and more susceptible to criticism than any of his administrative acts."[31]

The order, he ruled, caught the Association unawares and at a disadvantage and was done when Clapp knew that the Association was about to undertake its annual spring reservation round up. The great "friend of the Indian" ruled that "under the circumstances, with foreign cattle having been thus ranging for several years past, it would have been proper to have notified the stock association that all foreign stock found on the Reservation after a certain date would be rounded up and impounded, else have deferred the matter until after June 1st, the day set for the general round-up to begin, and which would have been only fourteen days to elapse after the issue of his impounding permit of May 17th."[32]

Thus did Agent Clapp catch hell for locking the barn door before the horses escaped.

The Inspector noted in passing that the Indians had vested rights, but "Public policy demands that every honorable industry be fostered rather than retarded and believing that the stock industry of South Dakota, which represents approximately $20,000,000.00 might be seriously affected should section 2117 of the Revised Statute be strictly enforced in such instances . . .(he) hope(d) for a just and early settlement of the matter."[33]

McLaughlin ruled that the Indians must build a 60 mile fence on the northern boundary and that the matter of the impounding of cattle be settled in the Federal Courts.[34]

On the date of the Inspector's report, attorney Anderson requested a private audience with the Secretary of Interior. Captain Clapp was not notified. Of course the Association would use every political means at its command to overcome the activities of Captain Clapp.[35]

Justice moved swiftly for the Association. On September 22, 1897 the Secretary of the Interior received a communication from the Attorney General, dated September 15th, in which he stated that he had instructed the U.S. Attorney for South Dakota to nolle prosequi (dismiss) the cases.[36]

The Association members retrieved their stock without penalty and with the ruling that they would not be prosecuted now trespassed on the Rosebud reservation, where squawmen like Jack Sully would take the trespassing cattle into their own hands.

The Inspector traveled to Rosebud where he tried to get the Sicangu to open a cattle trail across their reservation from the White River to Valentine. One may be sure that this hearing was also held at the behest of the Stockgrowers, as they wanted to ship their cattle directly on the rail head at Valentine and not take the more expensive Rapid City run.

The Sicangu knew they could not trust the Association, the Inspector or the Great White Father. They responded in the same direct manner as Red Cloud had when he gave his wake up call.

Two Strike, Hollow Horn Bear, He Dog, Quick Bear, Good Voice, Sky Bull, Bull Dog, Spotted Elk and White Horse all told McLauglin: "We tell you plainly that we have no roads to lend or sell. Tell the Great Father this and don't worry asking us for more roads."[37]

Dawson and other members of the association would soon move their cattle to the Rosebud and Stockgrower hired guns, vigilantes, ambush and death would follow in their wake.

A Different Missionary

From 1865 to 1890 The Indian Rights Association composed of eastern gentility gathered to decide the fate of the Indian in the west. They still do. But now those who wish to manage the Indian "ghost write" and solicit in their name.

The enlightened few met at the Lake Mohonk resort on the Hudson River in upstate New York. Imagine if you will, these gentle folks meeting in a Grand Hotel where cursing, card playing, dancing, Sabbath breaking and strong drink was banned, sitting down to tea and deciding the fate of the west and the western Indians.

This was well bred establishmentarianism at its best. No cowboys or real Indians were allowed. The Indian Rights Association met here each fall, and plotted the fate of poor Lo according to their culture and without regard to the Indian, the people of the west or any other part of American society. They were a very powerful lobby indeed.

Along with their obvious humanitarian motives they wished that the Indian be brought into the mainstream of American society. This left no room for the Indians' own culture or for choosing any religion the Indians wanted, including their own. Anything else would be "unamerican".

The Indian Rights Association, despite protests from leaders like Spotted Tail to "Leave us alone" and "Let us be Indian", continued to micro-manage the life, culture and spirituality of the Sioux in their own image. Thus "distance did lend enchantment to the view."

It was this group that decided to destroy the Indian tribal and cultural system. They wanted to put each individual Indian into the mainstream and they recommended the abolition of the reservation system using the Dawes Severalty Act of 1887. This misguided group should have known that the white man's greed would make their dissolution policy into the death of the culture of the Plains Indian. They also desired that the reservations be turned over to various religious groups and that each reservation would be in the charge of a single religious group and other denominations would not be tolerated.

Red Cloud printed his objections to the Dawes Act in a letter to the Boston Pilot. The Pilot was edited by John Boyle O'Reilly who shared ownership with the Catholic Archdiocese. O'Reilly, an Irish patriot who had escaped from Australia, wrote an editorial which supported Red Could's objections. Notwithstanding the objections of Red Cloud and O'Reilly the Dawes Act became law.

Surely, O'Reilly must have had the Indian Rights Association in mind when he wrote in 1885:

"The vulgar show of the pompous feast
Where the heaviest purse is the highest priest;
The organised charity, scrimped and iced,
In the name of a cautious, statistical Christ..."

Earlier, after the "'Custer massacre', O'Reilly had described the policy of the Indian Bureau as "methodistic cant, it protection high handed coercion, its object plunder. And its results disgrace and death of the Indians."

The Dawes Severalty Act forced uneducated Indians to accept allotments of land. Indians had traditionally held all of their land as part of the whole tribe. This Act still clouds the title to lands that were forced upon Indians, then plundered. The policy became a complete disaster not only because it forced land into private ownership contrary to Indian tradition but also because of the greed of many white land agents in the west who cheated every Indian they could out of their allotments.

A favorite method of early white entrepreneurs was to find some old shack in "Indian town", on the other side of the tracks, in a town like Winner, S.D. and trade it to an Indian family for their 160 acre rural allotment. Not to be so generous, they usually took back a mortgage on the shack, which would soon be foreclosed on by the entrepreneurs and recycled into a new exchange. Thus did the Dawes Severalty Act educate the Indian of the white man's world.

When Spotted Tail rescued his children from the clutches of Captain Pratt at Carlisle, the Indian Rights Organization, "the organised charity," started a campaign to undermine Spotted Tail's stature as a leader of his people.

At the same time, under the "Peace Policy" of President Grant, the Quakers controlled the Indian agents and each reservation was parceled out to the various religions. Under the former policy of allowing the churches to freely work among the Indians, the Catholic Church had made the most progress. The Catholic church felt that they were being discriminated against by the government and, in fact, many of the Indian chiefs petitioned the government to send them "black robes" to educate their children.

Government action across the ocean would also affect the plight of the Lakota. In Germany the "kultur kampf" policy of Bismarck, which seemed to follow the American thinking that Catholics could not be good citizens led to the expulsion of many German Catholics from Germany. As with other expulsions from this land, Germany's loss would often be the Lakota's gain.

The conduct of the American Protestant elite at Lake Mohonk and Bismarck's "kultur kampf" coupled with the generosity of the Drexel family of Philadelphia would leave profound and long lived marks on the Indians of western South Dakota.

The "Peace policy" assigned the Standing Rock and Devil's Lake Reservations to the Catholic Church; all others were assigned to Protestant denominations.

Bishop Martin Marty, who had been born in Switzerland, became one of the first missionaries assigned under the "Peace Policy". He established missions on those reservations and attempted to establish a school at Wheeler, Gregory County, South Dakota.

In 1883, a priest of Indian descent, Father Francis M. Craft was sent to the Rosebud Reservation. He was the son of a prominent New York surgeon and was outspoken in his defense of the Indians. He and Father Bushman erected a school at St Francis Mission on the Rosebud Reservation. Craft, who was always a militant advocate for the Indians, was distrusted by the government who asked for his removal from the Rosebud Reservation. Father Craft, the ever active missionary, remained in the government's hair and went to Wounded Knee to minister to Big Foot's band before the massacre had begun, as many of his band were Catholics.

Craft founded a Native American order of nuns who volunteered as nurses during the Spanish-American war.

The first buildings at St. Francis Mission were built with generous donations from Katherine Drexel of Philadelphia.

In 1885 Bishop Marty appealed to the Jesuits for aid in the care of the Indians of western South Dakota. Father Jutz was sent to St Francis. On September 7th, 1885, the United States government gave the Catholics permission to establish a school at Pine Ridge. This Mission, called Holy Rosary, was in the hands of the Jesuit fathers of the German province who had left Germany as a result of Bismarck's policy.

Jesuits under the leadership of Brother Andrew Hartman and local Indians made their own brick and built the Mission, which was completed in 1888. Katherine Drexel also donated to this building project.

Katherine Drexel, who was to become the founder of the Sisters of the Blessed Sacrament, donated to missions or schools at Bad River, St Francis, Crow Creek, Pine Ridge, and Rosebud in South Dakota. She also contributed large sums to black parishes including a contribution to a black parish at Cascade, near present day Hot Springs, South Dakota.

Father Jutz, at Holy Rosary, saved hundreds of Indians when he persuaded Short Bull and his followers to return to the Pine Ridge Agency during the Wounded Knee massacre of 1890.

However, Germany's greatest gift to the west and the Lakota was Father Eugene Buechel, S.J. The excesses of the early missionaries has been described by others. In the process, remarkable men have been slighted by history. Buechel is one.

Buechel kept a daily diary of everything he did on the Pine Ridge and Rosebud reservation during fifty years of his ministry. He preserved more of the Indians' culture for future generations than any other white man in the Lakotas' history.

Father Buechel began as a scholastic at St. Francis, was transferred to Holy Rosary, and then returned to St Francis in 1916 after a disastrous fire had destroyed all the buildings except the boys' dormitory.

The buildings were re-built under the direction of Brother Andrew Hartman, another German refugee. The foundation of the huge building was laid in March and the school was ready for occupancy by Thanksgiving. Funds for the building were again furnished by Katherine Drexel. The building was constructed with all local and volunteer Indian help. The building contained more square footage than the recently completed seven and one half million dollar government financed school at St. Francis. (dedicated in 1991)

Eugene Buechel kept a record of over 2,500 photographs of Indian people taken by him from 1900 until his death. The recording of these photos demonstrated Beuchel's unique talent for preserving Lakota tradition and culture. Each photo was meticulously numbered. In his diary Beuchel, when visiting an Indian family or event where the photo was taken, placed that number in the margin of his diary of the event. Thus substance was given to form.

He also transcribed the Lakota language into written form, collecting and publishing a dictionary of over 30,000 Lakota words and compiling a Lakota grammar; collected and cataloged native Lakota flora and fauna; collected histories of Indian families, Indian tales and lore, Indian star study, and priceless Indian art and artifacts, all of which has been preserved for the benefit of the Lakota.

Throughout the west many Institutions and Universities have treated the Reservations and Badlands areas as a gathering place for collections which are hoarded back east and never displayed where they belong. For saving these artifacts of Indian culture, Buechel deserves a place in Lakota and American history.

Buechel demonstrated all the traits of genius. He was truly deserving of his Indian name Wanbli Sapa (Black Eagle).

All of this however, does not do justice to him. In addition to the dictionary, grammar, astronomy charts, family and folklore tales, photographs, museum collection and flora and fauna collection, he was a true missionary to every Indian on the reservation.

He, more than any other, understood and expressed the plight of the Indian in his dealing with the often greedy white man. Wanbli Sapa compared the Lakota to the biblical traveler who had fallen among thieves, was robbed, stripped and left for dead. Buechel told the Lakota that in spite of all the white man's injustice, God loved them. His life was a sign of that love.

Father Eugene Buechel was born in Schlieda, Thuringia, Germany, on October 20, 1874. He attended Volkschule and Gymnasium in Fulda, Germany, from 1881 to 1896. In 1896-7 he studied in a seminary in Fulda, Germany. In October, 1897 he entered the Jesuit Order in Blyenback, Holland. In 1900 he came to the United States and was ordained in 1906. He died on October 27th, 1954. He is buried at St. Charles church cemetery at St. Francis, South Dakota with his Indian friends. During his last illness, Buechel refused to converse or pray in his native German, or English, but said his final prayers and farewell in Lakota.[38]

Chapter Eight End Notes

1. Lt. G.K. Warren, Preliminary report of exploration in Nebraska in 1855-56-57; SDHC, 1992 Vol XI, pp. 1-50.
2. A.H. Schatz, *Opening a Cow Country*, Edwards Bros Inc., 1939 Ann Arbor Mi., pp.5-6.
3. Ibid p. 12.
4. Lemmon-Yost, *Boss Cowman*, University of Nebraska Press 1969, p. 256.
5. Bob Lee and Dick Williams, *Last Grass Frontier*, Black Hills Publ., Inc., 1964 p. 197.
6. Ibid p. 75.
7. Gilbert, Hila; *Big Bat Pourier*, The Wells Co., Sheridan Wyo., 1968, p. 73.
8. Phillip S. Hall, *To Have This Land*, USD Press, 1991, p.15110.
9. Transcript of testimony -In the Matter of the Investigation of the Impounding and Holding of certain cattle by the Agent at Pine Ridge Agency, National Archives Micro film M # 1070-roll 37 attached to transcript.
12. Ibid WSDSG Round up orders attached to transcript.
13. Ibid pp. 276-277.
14. Ibid p. 1.
15. Ibid p. 1.
16. Ibid
17. Transcript hearing, p. 1.
18. Ibid p. 7.
19. Ibid p. 5.
20. Ibid p. 12.
21. Ibid pp. 9, 10, 14.
22. Ibid pp. 1-118.
23. Ibid pp. 145-148.
24. Ibid.
25. Ibid.
26. Ibid.
27. Letter to James McLaughlin July 28, 1897.
28. Brief of W.W. Anderson dated July 30, 1897.
29. Ibid.
30. Ibid.
31. Ibid.
32. Decision of Inspector McLaughlin dated August 19,1897.
33. Ibid.
34. Ibid.
35. Ibid.
36. Note in Transcript hearing file.
37. *Chamberlain Democrat*, Sept 2, 1897.
38. Buechel material was taken from conversations with Glendon Welshons, S.J. at St Francis Mission, 1990-1991.)

CHAPTER NINE
REMEMBRANCES

Agent D.C. Poole, who knew Spotted Tail intimately in 1869-70, described the good nature and hospitality of Spotted Tail toward his Lakota relatives.

"Hospitality was certainly one of the cardinal virtues of these people, and often led to a scarcity of supply at some lodge . . . ..

There were many arrivals at Spotted Tail's camp. . .from Red Cloud's camp. . . (and) other agencies, besides constant going to a fro of Indians from the hostile camps"[1]

Thus did Spotted Tail's old friend Red Leaf, who had turned himself in with Spotted Tail, Whistler, who had been hunting along the Republican, Roman Nose and Pawnee Killer and their bands visit Spotted Tail in 1869-70. Many of these bands would agree to come to the reservation with Spotted Tail when he went on his mission of peace, some 7 years later.

Comparisons of the strength and vitality of the "hostiles", as opposed to the Agency Indians has often been noted. Poole said it best.

"Red Leaf's followers, men, women and children, had a much wilder appearance than their friends at the agency. In place of woolen blankets and calico dresses . . . they wore gaily painted and ornamented robes, buckskin leggins, and garments made of dressed deer and antelope skins, decorated with beads and bright-colored porcupine quills. . . ..

"Their presence carried with it the impress of their wild, native independence. Their manner had more of ease and confidence, their step was more elastic and firm, and their eyes more keen in the quick glance of observation, than the agency Indians. Beside them the latter appeared to be in a stage of semi-somnambulism . . . .."

"If they were thus attractive to me, it was not strange that their own kith and kin should be still more interested in them, still true representatives of their race, every mark of admiration and esteem."[2]

Thus did the majesty of Spotted Tail and the wild bands pass from history.

This great leader was never boastful or disagreeable. He never mentioned himself when it could be avoided, and would never relate his adventures and bloody conflicts, which, his friends say, were many.[3]

The leadership, intelligence, bravery, modesty, hospitality and relentless dedication to the welfare of his people in a time of unprecedented historical and cultural change places Spotted Tail at the head of his class.

Jordan's Epitaph

Col. Jordan described Spotted Tail as follows:

"He was a remarkable red man who was possessed of many qualities of a high order. As an orator, diplomat and acute logical reasoner few Indians have excelled him. He was said to have been dignified and commanding and, for one of his race, was possessed of mature judgment and great kindness of heart . . . He ranks amongst the highest of the epoch in which he lived . . . Spotted Tail's career is more conspicuous for conscientious and intelligent loyalty and devotion to . . . the interests of his people . . . .. Spotted Tail was an exceptionally magnetic and able orator, and I doubt if ever a commissioner or government official has had to contend with a more shrewd Indian. He had a habit of programming questions and advancing arguments that often puzzled them to answer either to his or their satisfaction".[4]

Aftermath

Ironically, Crow Dog, now much admired because he was a "traditional Lakota", was the leading orator and proponent of the cession of nine million acres to the U.S. in 1889.

The Associated Press reported that Crow Dog's speech in favor of this great land cession by the Lakota to the U.S. was "the most powerful argument ever delivered by any Indian on the reservation."[5]

Even more ironic is that when the negotiations were moved to Pine Ridge, the Chief who supported the cession was none other than No Flesh. The same chief who had rode two horses to death trying to capture Crazy Horse and who was an accomplice to his murder.[6]

When the Rosebud Reservation was opened for settlement it was provided that sections 16 and 36 throughout the entire tract be ceded to the State of South Dakota. The State paid nothing for all of such land. Not only that, they had first choice.[7] On June 22, 1896 the State was given 18,935.94 acres of the old Winnebago reservation north of Chamberlain.[8]

The governmental elimination of the "old frauds" Spotted Tail, Red Cloud, Crazy Horse and Sitting Bull had paved the way for anybody and everybody defrauding the leaderless Lakota of what remained of their homeland, including the State of South Dakota. With the "old frauds" killed or deposed, the Federal Government could also work its will on the Lakota.

In a 28 page letter to General Nelson A. Miles in 1891, C.P. Jordan set forth the Indian's complaints about the treatment of the Rosebud Agency Indians by the Indian Department and added:

"It is perhaps needless for me to add in conclusion that if it were even suspicioned that I stated the facts and expressed the opinions herein contained I would be made to suffer for it-and particularly while the present system of Indian management continues."

"Should you have occasion to write to me please send the letter sealed to C.W. Cornell, Valentine Neb.–to be by him enclosed and forwarded to me–in order that the authorities here may not learn I am in correspondence with you."

Jordan's letter indicates that the starvation of the Indians by the government cut in beef allotments was worse than reported.

Jordan had kept strict accounts. He listed the account shortages from July 1st 1890 to June 30th, 1891.

He states that the Indian census was reduced from 7,000 to 5354 and that the reduction took place effective July 1st, 1890. This amounted to a reduction of 25% of the Indians' rations to which they had been accustomed. Each of the 5354 persons were entitled to 3 lbs gross beef per diem.

C.P. Jordan states that from July 1, 1890 to September 1, 1890 the Agency should have received 1,477,704 lbs gross weight of beef. The government issued only 987,900 gross lbs and had shorted the agency 489,804 gross lbs. At an average live weight of 800 lbs per head this would have been a shortage of 612 head for the two month period.

From October 1, 1890 to June 30, 1891 the Indians were shorted 885,116 lbs gross. At 800 lbs per head this would have been an additional shortage of 1,106 head for 273 days.[9]

Is it any wonder that the Lakota looked elsewhere for food to survive? With cuts in rations and shortages as stated by C.P. Jordan in his "secret letter" to Miles it is not surprising that hundreds of Lakota stampeded to Pine Ridge to follow the Ghost Dance spiritualism. The spirit of the Lakota would not die. They would first save the buffalo and then start to save themselves.

Chapter Nine End Notes

1. Poole, D.C., *Among the Lakota of Dakota*, Minnesota Historical Society Press, 1988, pp. 101-107.
2. Ibid.
3. Ibid. p. 92.
4. Jordan Files, South Dakota Heritage Center.
5. Kingsbury, George, *History of Dakota Territory, Vol. 2* page 1269, The Clarke Co., 1915.
6. Ibid. p. 1271.
7. Smith, George Martin, *History of Dakota Territory Vol. III* page 96-97.
8. Report of the School and Public Lands June 30, 1896 p. ix.
9. Jordan file, South Dakota Heritage Center, Pierre, SD.

MIDDLE WORD

Soon the missionaries, settlers, squawmen, rustlers, stockgrowers, murderers, foreigners, dreamers, honyockers, homesteaders, hired guns, hit men, frauds, liars and cheats would replace the army and the government in the envious assault on whatever the Plains Indians had managed to keep.

The initial grating between and among these two cultures has been left untold. It lasted just a few short years. It did foretell what was to come. The life and death of those who struggled to survive that great cultural clash would continue on the plains.

The continued struggles between the native and the white cultures; the fights between the bands themselves and then between full bloods and half bloods and the quarrels between the divergent white religions and economic interests would continue. They would eventually define a time and place. They would become West River.

PHOTOGRAPHS

Spotted Tail with his sons at Carlisle.
Photo courtesy of South Dakota Historical Society, Pierre, S.D.

Knew Denver as Village

J. C. HARMON, who came back to Denver after an absence of nearly three score years to find a metropolis where there had been a village.

J.C. Harmon photo printed in Denver Post, September 20, 1925.

Photo taken at one of Harry Oelrich's 4th of July spectaculars.
Left to Right: Interpreter, Harry Oelrich, Little Wolf, Running or
Wild Hog, and Standing Elk, all Cheyenne warriors.

Mrs. Wright, Mrs. Duly and children rescued by the Fool Soldiers.
Photo courtesy of South Dakota Historical Society, Pierre, S.D.

Members of the Fool Soldiers.
Strike Fire, Mad Bear, Walter Swift Bird, Martin Charger, and Four Bear.
Photo courtesy of South Dakota Historical Society, Pierre, S.D.

Fast Walker,
Crow Creek Indian,
helped rescue hostages.

Don't Know How (On Spe Sni) Yankton,
helped rescue hostages.

Chief Brave Wolf and Foolish Bear
at Ft. Berthold pictured with
Sacred Medicine Bundle.
Foolish Bear helped rescue Lake
Shetek hostages.

Four Bears, Two Kettle Sioux, one
of the Fool Soldiers.

Bear's Rib,
member of Fool Soldier Band.

Martin Charger
Photo courtesy of South Dakota
Historical Society, Pierre, S.D.

Marshall Petrie with
Walking Shield, convicted of
murder and hung in 1902.
*Photo courtesy of South Dakota
Historical Society, Pierre, S.D.*

George Bear, convicted
and hung for murder in 1902.
Pictured with Deputy Taylor. Buried
near Milk's camp, Gregory County, S.D.

Rev. Florentine Digmann, S.J.
Photo courtesy of Buechel
Memorial Museum, St. Francis, S.D.

Two Sticks
(taken while held in Deadwood)
Photo courtesy of Adams Memorial
Museum Deadwood, S.D.

Gathering at Sully Funeral at homesite.
Photo courtesy of South Dakota Historical Society, Pierre, S.D.

Sully funeral procession with riderless "Old Jim Long String".
Photo courtesy of South Dakota Historical Society, Pierre, S.D.

Lucas to Burke stage – Jack Sully was shot and buried near Lucas, S.D.

Husking Bee. 32 teams, near Lucas, South Dakota.

Jack Sully in casket on day of funeral.
Only known authenticated photo of the famous Jack.

Claude Sully holding "Old Jim Long String"
on day his father was shot by Marshall Petrie's posse.

Chief White Thunder.
Led raiding party that killed
Logan Fontenelle. Killed by
Spotted Tail Jr., in succession
fight after death of Spotted Tail.
*Photo courtesy of South Dakota
Historical Society, Pierre, S.D.*

U.S. Marshall Petrie
*Photo courtesy of South Dakota
Historical Society, Pierre, S.D.*

J.C. Harmon and wife at
Old Soldiers Home.

Spotted Tail, Jr. killed White Thunder
in succession fight after his father was shot.

"Buffalo Soldiers" stationed at Fort Randall.
Photo courtesy of South Dakota Historical Society, Pierre, S.D.

Summer picnic at Fort Randall.
Photo courtesy of South Dakota Historical Society, Pierre, S.D.

Father Eugene Buechel, S.J.
Photo courtesy of Buechel Memorial Museum, St. Francis, S.D.

Rev. John Jutz, S.J.
Photo courtesy of Buechel Memorial Museum, St. Francis, S.D.

Four of Spotted Tail's wives. (Note age of children)
Photo courtesy of South Dakota Historical Society, Pierre, S.D.

August "Kid" Rich and his first wife May Louise Narcelle.
Photo courtesy of Ernie Gottschalk

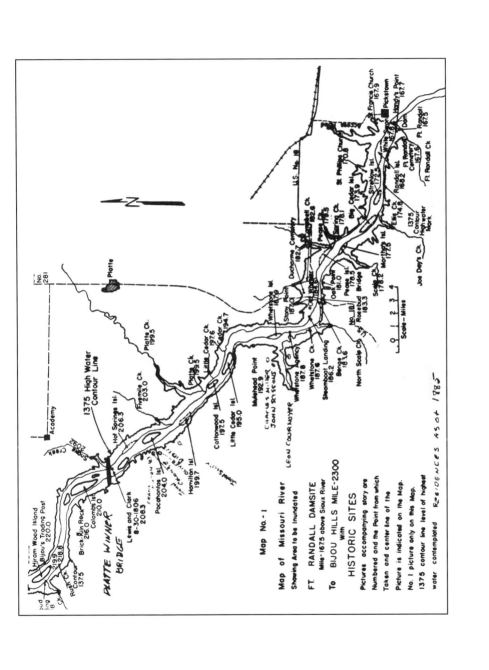

SECTION TWO

CHAPTER TEN
EARLY ADVENTURERS

Across the plains

In 1861, thirteen year old Jacob Harmon hopped a train west from Marion County, Indiana to St. Joe, Missouri. He took the ferry and was caught without any money. A well dressed man paid his ten cent charge and got him a job chopping wood for a restaurant owner for his board and room. At suppertime the landlord called him in.

"On entering there was a nice looking gentleman who asked if I could drive oxen. I answered: Yes Pap has one yoke of oxen at home, Buck and Charley-one is red and the other is white. I cut down trees in the pasture and drag them up with Buck and Charley and if you have such oxen as they are I can drive them."

"Well, Lad, I have all kinds, and you would have to drive six yoke to two wagons—do you think you could do that? 'Well I don't know', I replied. 'Where do you want me to drive them and what do you have to haul?' . . . 'Across the plains', he said."

Harmon's story

"In about three days we started loading and after loading we drove out about five miles and corralled. Then he took all the men and boys back to town and bought each a new outfit—boots, shoes, clothing to last until we crossed the plains and returned. I thought he was the best man in the world. Everything was ready to start to cross the plains."

"On Monday morning we were ordered to drive in the bulls and once in the corral we began to yoke them up and the fun commenced. Every fellow for himself. You had to take your yoke on your left shoulder and with one bow in your right hand strike out among the 1900 head of bulls to yoke up six yoke of them. The bosses would show you your wheelers, that is the two that go on the tongue of your wagon and the next are your leaders, then come the swing yokes. You take out your wheelers and put them on your wagon tongue, then go and yoke up five more yoke and drive them out and hitch them ahead of your wheelers, then you are ready to pull out and stand by your team until it comes your turn to pull and then your trouble commences. Then you are in for a half day's walk. Of course there were no bull whackers allowed to ride, not even on their own wagon tongue, you just had to walk.

Monday was our first experience in bull whacking and I wished for my part that I had not undertaken the job. I was not in the habit of swearing, but I soon got into the habit. Of course I had lots of lessons in swearing, rehearsed by older whackers than myself, and on hearing these others I was not long graduating, being a dull Missourian.

We had dinner and on we went. Night came and we corralled our yoke and began getting supper. We were cut up into messes of from ten to fifteen in each mess and one of each mess had to do the cooking and it was some cooking too, for there were none of them that knew how to cook. At last supper was ready and each whacker grabbed a tin cup and tin plate and got a cup of coffee and grabbed some "bully" and slap jacks and sneaked off to one side and sat down on the ground and went to eating.

Well I was disgusted, and thought if I were only back home I would stay there. But no, I was billed for Fort Laramie, Wyoming Territory and in the morning after a good night's rest we were awakened at four o'clock. Of course that went against my pride. Breakfast over, in came the cattle or bulls. The bulls were in the corral. Orders came from Gabe Wade, he being the 1-8 boss, to yoke up.

The fun began. There wasn't ten men in the outfit that knew what bulls to yoke up. You just took a yoke and put it on your shoulder and turned yourself loose among nineteen hundred head of bulls. It was a great mix up. One bull would hit you with his horn and about that time another bull would kick you and you wished to the good Lord that you had never been born, or at least that you had never run away from home.

Well, we were ready at last and began to pull out. When our outfit was all pulled out and ready to go we were strung along the road for a mile and a half. From the time the head wagon started, it would be one and a half hours before the hind wagon would pull out, and a soon as all were on the road the whooping, cursing, and whipping commenced. I had a fine bull whip, the lash being eighteen feet long and the stalk two feet and when I would get mad and try to split a bull open with my whip I generally got it wound around myself . . .

We gathered up the buffalo chips and within few minutes the cooks hollered "grub pile!" "Of course I sat still and the rest of the whackers jumped in and when I got there my rations were slim. But I remembered that yell "grub pile!" after that."

"Whistling Dick" taught young Harmon the following bull whacker's song:
> I am a good bull whacker and I whack the Denver line,
> And I can whip the son of bitch
> that yoked that bull of mine.
> And if he don't unyoke him you bet your boots
> I will try to floor him with my ox bow.
> ROOT, YOU HOG, OR DIE!
> When we get our loads and out upon the road
> A very awkward team and a very heavy load,
> Have to whoop, whip and holler
> and swear a little on the sly-
> Come down on them heavy, boys,

ROOT, YOU HOG, OR DIE!
Its every day at noon there's something for to do,
If nothin else a bull for to shoe,
Three ropes to throw him down and nine
men to make him lie
While we drive on the shoes, boys
ROOT, YOU HOG, OR DIE!
O' maybe you like to know what we have to eat,
A little bit of bread and a little bit of meat
and a little bit of coffee and sugar on the sly.
That's good for us bullwhackers.
ROOT, YOU HOG, OR DIE!
We arrived in Denver on the second day of June,
The people were surprised to see us there so soon,
But we are good bull whackers and we know
the road is nigh-come on them heavy boys.
ROOT, YOU HOG, OR DIE!

"At last we arrived at the Big Blue River, which flows through Nebraska and from there we crossed the prairie to the South Platte River. We struck the South Platte at old "Doby Town" east of Fort Kearney and when we got to the Platte and laid over one day and I thought I was an old man, the time had been so long since I left home.

However, I had only been away from home one month. We got a good rest and the next thing we noticed of importance was Jack Marrow's ranch which is located south of the South Platte, and about four miles above where the North Platte River empties into the South Platte. On we went. I thought we were going clear out of the world. Gabe Wade told us we would cross the river at Fremont's Orchard. We had to put eighteen yoke of bulls on one wagon to pull it across. But the water was awfully shallow. We were four days crossing. After we left the river we went on the Ash Hollow route.

At the head of Ash Hollow was where Old General William Harney had his massacre in 1859 and we were over this battlefield two years after it happened and skeletons of Indians and white men and mules and horses lay all over the ground. You can tell an Indians skeleton from that of a whiteman from the fact that the bones of an Indian are dark brown and a white man's are whiter."

They finally arrived at Fort Laramie way out in Wyoming. After unloading, the boys who were hired for the round trip started back. Harmon stayed at Fort Laramie and with his friend "Whistling Dick" drove a caravan back to Omaha for Mart Scott. Mart Scott hired Harmon and Dick to once again cross the plains and night herd the bulls west to Denver. Mart Scott was his first boss, Harry Good the second boss and Bill Dupp was the third boss.

"I got along better than I expected. I had a bunch of ponies and when one played out would get another until four o'clock in the morning when I would wake up Gabe and he would "turn out" the whackers. After about three weeks on the trail the bulls became tired and settled down. I would find an old gentle bull and would lean up against him and sleep. At last we arrived at Julesburg, where the cut off is taken to Denver. By the cut-off it is seventy miles and by the river it is ninety miles. We took the river route. We made the river route in twelve days."

They arrived in Denver and unloaded one hundred wagons and sent them and the whackers down the Platte River about 100 miles. Forty wagons loaded with flour, whisky, bacon and tobacco and went from Denver to Golden Gate and there the boys had to pay one dollar a wagon to go up "Gyn Hill" While the wagons were unloading Harmon took in the sights, including touring a gold mine. He described how the Chinese would wash over the waste that came from the mine, extracting smaller amounts of gold. Of course they made money, he stated, for "they lived on what a whiteman would starve to death on."

Harmon returned to the wagons and bulls on the Platte River and he and Bill Skinner were hired to winter the bulls on the Colorado and Nebraska prairie. "Everything was very pleasant when all of the whackers were there but in the morning when all of them pulled out we stood and watched them as far as we could see them."

Before he left Mart Scott had told them if they see any Indians they should feed them and not spare the grub for in that way they would make friends and not enemies. The first day they went looking for the bulls they hunted and chased antelope and ended up getting lost.

Before long a big Indian came in at the door of the tent and said How! How! Remembering what their boss had told them they proceeded to fix some grub and before long 10 more Indians showed up and they stayed with their camp for three days.

Shortly after the Indian visit they observed the long Mormon trains coming up the trail. The two herders made friends with them and enjoyed fresh bread that the Mormon women baked and left for them. He describes the train thus: "One would have a span of horses and a wagon and the next team a yoke of cows and the next would be a young married couple pulling a two wheeled cart with their belongings."

Within a short time Bill Skinner started to hanker after a drink of whisky and convinced Harmon that he should find a "whisky ranch" and bring back a couple of gallons of booze. After riding all day Harmon reached a "whisky ranch" about dusk. "There was a corral and I put my pony and then went to the ranch and when I entered the room old Howard was behind the bar and six thieves or gamblers were sitting there half drunk. Each of them had one or two guns strapped around their waist and of all the cursing and swearing you ever heard it was there. Pretty soon they began talking to me. Say feller what is your name, they asked? What are you doing?"

Harmon told them what he had done and that he worked for Mart Scott wintering his bulls. A fellow by the name of "Banjo Bill" started a poker game and Harmon had some drinks with them. Everything was cozy until about two in the morning. "They pulled their guns and began shooting into the ceiling of the room, so I jumped behind the bar, then behind the barrel, then I made a straight shoot for the door."

At day light he sneaked back and talked to Howard Kempton who told him old "Ephe" had got a hole in his Stetson but nothing else had happened. Harmon paid 18 dollars a gallon for two gallons and rode back to his partner, Bill Skinner. Skinner's breath was taken away twice, once when he took a swig of whisky and second when Harmon told him how much it cost.

For the remainder of the year they herded the bulls, and investigated the surrounding area including Clear Creek and the Cashladuka Rivers. When Spring came in 1862 Harmon hired on to whack to Fort Laramie, Wyoming and Fort Hallock, Utah. In 1862 Harmon quit whacking oxen and enlisted in Company D of the First Colorado Cavalry.[1]

On March 26, 1862, Jacob was wounded at the little known battle of Glorieta Pass. Later he recorded with near perfect accuracy the members of his company. He also described many Indian encounters, including the Sand Creek Massacre on November 26, 1864 and the return of the Eubanks hostages in the spring of 1865. After discharge from the Volunteers, Jacob went to work for E.W. Whitcomb, a large rancher in northeastern Colorado.[2]

Jack Sully: Scapegoat or Scoundrel

Jack Sully was shot from ambush in early May 1904 along the upper Whetstone creek in northeastern Gregory County, South Dakota. His story is related by friends, enemies, neighbors, contemporaneous newspaper stories, editorials, "true" newspaper and magazine accounts and oral recollections and memories of the Sicangu and the first white settlers. He has become a west river legend.

The census of June lst, 1885, listed Jack Sully as 35 years old and born in Virginia. He enlisted at Minneapolis, Minnesota on January 20, 1862 in the infantry and was released on October 28th of the same year. On October 29th he enlisted in Company I, 1st. Cavalry at Berlin, Maryland and was discharged on November 20, 1864 at Opequan Creek, Virginia.[3]

Jacob Harmon, then seventeen, first met Jack Sully in 1865 while rounding up E.W. Whitcomb's stock from Horseshoe Bend to the North Platte in western Nebraska. Harmon wrote: "So next morning we were on the trail early for Horseshoe Bend. We were gone four days that time and had fine luck on the trip. We returned and found everything in fine shape."

"In this camp were Chas. Elgin, Jack Sully, who worked for Bob Saunders, and Ben Claymore. There was also Chet Dubrey and William or Bill Whitcombe. Ben Claymore and Bob Saunders were squaw men, and Chas., Jack and myself were still single."[4]

Later in life, Jack Sully revisited this area. The "Iona Pioneer" reported on May 19, 1904 that "for some time after his (Sully's) escape from the Mitchell jail last spring, he hung around his old haunts on the Whetstone, about thirty miles south of here. But the scent got too close, and last fall he hit the trail for western Nebraska or Colorado, and took a lay off."[5] Jack may have been hiding out at the Bordeaux ranch located Southwest of St. Francis, South Dakota, just north of the Nebraska border. The descendants of William Kincaid relate that Sully and Kincaid would hideout there.[6] Many of Jack's friends "went north" to Canada and it is possible that he also stayed with them while things were cooling off. Other news stories of the time conjectured that Sully had "gone north" to Canada.

Stealing horses from the Utes.

Jack then enticed Jacob Harmon to help him steal some horses from a camp of Ute Indians in northeastern Colorado. Along in the fall Jack said:

"Jacob, I have found a camp of Utes in the mountains in the forks of Clear Creek about 12 miles from here and their ponies range down to Clear Creek from where they are camped. So if you are game and want a little extra money we can run them off without any danger of getting caught." Jack left Jacob to hide at the bottom while Jack stole the horses from under the Ute's noses. On Jack's signal Jacob joined him in driving the horses down the canyon and onto the plains. They kept driving the horses until they reached one of Ben Holiday's stage lines where they sold 10 head for 40 dollars and a bottle of bitters. Later, they left the stage station and ran into Bill Sherman who bought the remaining 37 head of ponies for 120 dollars.[7]

In 1867, Jacob wintered at Jack Morrow's ranch on the south side of the Platte, went broke gambling and took a job at a hotel in North Platte, Nebraska. He relates that Jack Sully, also known as John McCarthy, was there that winter. Jacob relates that Jack ran away from home in St. Paul, Minnesota in 1860 when he was 15 years old.

Jack went to St. Joseph, Missouri where he hired out to whack mules to Denver, Colorado and first received the nickname "Sully".[8] Jack Sully worked for Bill Paxton and Jack Morrow who trailed cattle to the Whetstone Agency in South Dakota in 1871 and ran the Keystone cattle company that was situated near Pine Ridge, South Dakota. Jack Morrow was known from Denver to Kearney and located his "ranch" south of the junction of the two Platte rivers and south of Fort Cottonwood.[9]

Texas Drovers

The driving of cattle to the Whetstone was described in the "Omaha Weekly Herald" of May 17, 1871 as follows:

"I have during several years experience on the western frontier, seen many startling proofs of bravery among the rough men who live there in their encounters with buffalo, etc., but pales before the actions of Morrows' herders who are constantly among the immense herds of wild Texans, who almost every day charge upon and overthrow both men and horse in their mad career." "I saw several instances of this kind while watching the efforts to get the herd across the river

(Missouri at Whetstone), and must say that I greatly prefer attempting to handle a wounded and enraged buffalo bull, rather than the Texans drove here.

"Morrow and Paxton have the men who can manage them, however, such as Jack Sally (Sully), John Kincaid and others."[10]

Great herds of Texas longhorns were driven up through Oklahoma, Kansas and Nebraska. They crossed the Platte at Kearney and swam the Missouri at Niobrara. A Mr. Mayberry and Bill Paxton of Omaha trailed many cattle north.

The herds ranged from 2,000 to 3,500, and it was a big job to crowd these wild cattle into the river. The cowhands would construct a plank fence or log pole wing into the river, and then push 200 or 300 into the water at a time. They would enlist several fellows from town who would use skiffs to keep the cattle away from the soft sandbars. Sometimes critters would drown and float down stream. Ponca Indians would then tow them to shore and butcher them.

When the cattle had been delivered to the Dakota side, the southern trail hands would stay a few days to hoop and holler. Some of the southern hands preferred to stay north. Perhaps they had good reason not to return. Some of those who stayed were Frank Aldrich, Joe Ague, Joe Allen, Jack Sully, Harper Cleveland and his brother in law, Andy Lunderman. Most all migrated into Dakota on the old Chisolm trail.[11]

EARLY POLITICS

The LaMont organization

The *Mitchell Daily Republic* of August 30, 1947 and P*eterson's 1906 Atlas of Charles Mix County* of reported that Jack Sully was elected Sheriff of Charles Mix County in 1872. One polling place was the Joe Ellis spread just north of Pickstown. Sully was a member of the LaMont organization in what is now Charles Mix County, South Dakota[12] The LaMont organization existed to see that the right Territorial delegate to Congress and the right governor were kept in office. They held elections and rotated the county officers among themselves. What votes they couldn't convince they could bribe or frighten.[13] Colin LaMont was the organizer and it was known as LaMont's county. The LaMont group lost power in 1875 and Charles Mix County was organized in 1879.[14] Some of the early settlers there were Jack Sully, Jim Somers, the Cournoyers and William Hollrough who worked for General Charles T. Campbell and ran a roadhouse on Campbell creek.[15] Hollrough was a mean man, not unlike the other road house owners and employees, when he was drunk.

The *Mitchell Daily Republic* of August 30, 1947 stated:

The famous Jack (Sully) . . . was elected Sheriff of Charles Mix County (LaMont County) in 1872 by the overwhelming majority of 61 to 1. The opponent who gar-nered the single vote was one William Holbrough (Hollrough). The record isn't immediately clear as to how long Sully served as sheriff but it is presumed to have been for two years. An intriguing phase of this 1872 election is contained in the fact that only 55 persons voted in the county." Jack was a piker. For delegate to

Congress, Moses K. Armstrong had 349 votes, G.C. Moody 30 and 39 for W.W. Brookings. The combined vote for any one other Territorial office did not exceed 200, and the number of voters casting ballots for County offices was 55.[16]

Spink and Burleigh vs. Armstrong

The LaMont organization played an important role in the election of Moses Armstrong as Territorial delegate to Congress in 1870. The abstract of votes showed that Armstrong had received 1,198, Burleigh 1,102 and Spink 1,023 votes. Burleigh and Spink filed an election contest in the House of Representatives and testimony was taken throughout the territory concerning the misdeeds of the election.

The LaMont organization hired teams, wagons and drivers to bring in voters from wherever they could be found. The wagon master was usually given $50.00 and the voters were given $1.00 or $2.00 and all they could eat and drink. Since Colin LaMont was clerk of the election, in order to get paid the voters had to cast an "open" ballot, that is they would not fold the ballot and showed it to the clerk. Many "breed" Indians from Spotted Tail's agency voted.

Both sides participated in the electioneering with Armstorng distributing whisky to the Missouri river folks while Burleigh provided milled flour to the Swedes in eastern Charles Mix and Clay county. The election was won by the LaMont organization for Armstrong. In addition to the mixed blood voters from the reservation, the Armstrong folks encouraged the "colored" at Fort Sully to vote for Armstrong.

The officers at Fort Sully had "colored" manservants, who were Davis Harrison, Henry Howard, W.H. Comer, P.T. Rodgers, Stephen Harris, Henry Cassar and John Marshall. P.T. Rodgers who was a twenty three year old servant to Lt. Thomas Traxel of the 17th U.S. Cavalry testified as follows:

"Lt. Goodlove handed me the ticket out of his vest pocket, he said "you go and vote for this man (Armstrong)-about as good a man as we can have elected in this Territory—he is the one we want." All the blacks were told that if they did not vote and vote right they would have to leave the Military reservation. (At that precinct Armstrong received 40, Spink 3 and Burleigh 1 vote.)

Armstrong carried the Joe Ellis precinct with 88 votes, Spink 1 and 11 for Burleigh. Things were different at the "Campbell ranch" precinct. Burleigh had 38, Armstrong 38 and Spink 1. There were 251 votes cast in Charles Mix County at the precincts near the Missouri River and at Fort Sully. By comparison Minnehaha County had a total of 138 votes cast, with Spink receiving the lion's share of 110 votes.[17]

Vigilante hangings

"The Dutchman" William Hollborough, of the rival Burleigh faction, ran a roadhouse about three miles southeast of the Bijou Hills. Holbrough complained to the authorities at Yankton that there were a bunch of horse thieves in the LaMont area.

Working for him at the road house was a man called Henry Hirl. Hirl had quit the gang of horse thieves and had been giving information to the Dutchman that was passed on to the Yankton authorities. As they were gathering the horses one evening they were jumped by three men and hung.

The Dutchman's wife cut him down and tried to revive him, but to no avail. His grave is located across the line on Snake Creek, but the hanging took place on the Northeast quarter of Section 31, Eagle Township, Charles Mix County. The body of Henry Hirl was left hanging until it was cut down by passersby the next day. Hirl's grave is about 80 rods south of the old Bijou Hills school. Campbell Creek flows into the upper end of Wheeler bottoms (NW1/4, Sec 8, T96 N, R67 W Charles Mix County, S.D.) It was named for Gen. Charles T. Campbell, who brought a colony from Canada and founded the town of Scotland and lived at the mouth of this creek.[18]

John Kincaid

Jack Sully and John Kincaid were among the "pioneer guard" mentioned in Peterson's Atlas of 1906. They were described as follows:

"Jack Sully is first heard of in this county when he was elected sheriff under the Lamonte organization in the early sixties. He roamed up and down the river but his chief place of abode appears to have been at the mouth of Platte creek, near Drapeau's, his father in law. His first marriage is said to have been to a Norwegian girl at White Swan. Judge Foster T. Wheeler performing the ceremony, but his bride left him within a week. He next married Drapeau's half blood daughter who died. He then married the widow of John Kincaid, also Drapeau's daughter, with whom he later moved to Sully Flat in Gregory County where he was shot a few years ago. Sully was a notorious character of whom much has been written, and who has been charged with numerous crimes, the greater number of which are probably fictions."

"John Kincaid came to this county as a soldier and first appears at first to have been a pretty decent sort of fellow. He came to Ft. Randall about 1867 and soon became identified with the Sully gang and roamed up and down the river. His chief place of abode was with or near Drapeau his father in law, at the mouth of Platte creek. He died of cancer in the seventies."[19]

Sully's neighbors

One of his closest neighbors was John Jergins, who along with the Stamer, Frank Mullen, Colombe and Dion families were among the first settlers of the Pocohontas Island area. Jergins relates in a newspaper interview that he came to "Sully Flats" before the land was opened for homestead and one of the first persons he met was Jack Sully. Jergins was a friend of Sully's until the day of his death.[20]

Sully told Jergins that he only took cattle from the big interests who ran their cattle free of charge on the reservation land. Jack told Jergins that one time when the officers were on his trail he dressed as a squaw and with a squaw sitting on either side of him started on his way home. He met the officers and they asked if the party had seen Sully. They answered they had not and proceeded home.

Jack Sully wasn't the only law breaker who escaped with the aid of a disguise. While Sully impersonated a "squaw" in his escape, "Texas Charley" Fugit fixed himself up like a black man.

He imitated the dialect and fooled the ranchers along the Keyapaha, until he made his getaway. Fugit was later shot at a dance at Buffalo Gap, South Dakota by City Marshall Archie Riordan.[21]

Sully, a great horseman, also made a daring escape while his were hands tied. A sheriff was bringing him in and Sully at the right moment managed to slip the bridle, which was tied to the sheriff's horse, off his mount and escape by guiding his horse with his legs gripping the horse and grasping the horse's mane.[22]

Jergins also relates in the article that it was not uncommon to find the bodies of dead Indians and white men hidden in the trees and gulches, having met death at the hand of some unseen enemy. Jergins also admonishes us to ignore the stories that the early cowboys were bad men. He states they were honest, though reckless of nature.[23] Not all deaths were the result of livestock rustling. One of the first deaths reported in Charles Mix County in 1879 was the murder of Jackson Camp. The murder took place at Rosebud Landing. The official records state: "Camp, Jackson, age 30 years, born in Ohio, died in April, 1879 shot sparking another man's wife."[24]

Neighbors' recollections

John Mullen, Frank Mullen's son, indicated that Sully was a good neighbor. Just days before Sully was killed, Mildred Sully delivered a letter to Mullen in which Sully explained that there were others involved in the stock stealing for which the authorities had a warrant for Sully's arrest.[25]

J.M. McMullen, who lived past 90, came to Gregory County in 1885. He was a neighbor of Jack Sully and once accused Sully of stealing 21 head of horses from him. Sully told him that he didn't steal the horses but thought he knew who did and promised to help get them back.

He returned 13 horses to McMullen's ranch with the remark, "You know, Mac, I don't steal from poor people."[26]

Jake Walker, another of Sully's neighbors, recalls that in 1881, his father broke his leg and was disabled, so the kids went to Sully's to get milk. Jack Sully gave them a fresh red milk cow to take home. Walker's mother never had an unkind word for their neighbor, Jack Sully.[27]

Harry Kelley, whose father ran a butcher shop in Castalia, Charles Mix County, South Dakota in 1890-93 knew Sully well. He had stayed with Sully just prior to Jack's killing. He and Jack slept in the attic at Mike Anderson's place and they could see the hunters' prairie moon coming up in the east.

"The moon and I are good friends," Sully mused, "we drove cattle together." Before they settled in, Sully commented that Olaf Nelson had taken his good shooting outfit, and then he sighed "I hope the time comes that I won't have to wear this."[28]

Sully was an excellent shot and the story is told that he could shoot a "hand hold" on the fringe of a can.[29]

There is evidence that Sully also lived on Cedar Creek, an Indian village, probably located in what is now the Lower Brule Reservation, just west of the mouth of the creek.[30] We know that Blakely, the Stockgrowers' hired gun, was looking for him when he lived at Cedar Creek. Richard La Roche lived in the area and knew Sully well. He indicates that early on Jack Sully lived at Cedar Creek and worked for the Indian Service.[31]

The fact that Sully may have been employed by the Indian Service when he lived at Cedar Creek is interesting for several reasons. First, it lends credence to the legend that Sully may have been working for the enforcement of "Indian" law and order and this employment would not have endeared him to the Stockgrower mentality. The fact that there is a paucity of information concerning this work for the Indian service is not surprising. Indians don't tell much to nosy white people asking questions about their friends. Such interviews are usually met with stony silence. They would not have volunteered such information to any stranger.

Life on Hamilton Island

I was never molested by any person but those who represented the state.
If you would know the flavor of huckleberries ask the cowboy or the partridge.
—Walden Pond-Thoreau

Jack's first recorded run in with the law was in the 1870s when steamboating was the most important means of transportation on the Missouri River. Wood sold for $10 a cord and save for hired help the timber cost Jack Sully nothing. Three deputies from Yankton had come up the river to arrest him for cutting wood without a government permit and he sent them all packing back to Yankton, the Territorial Capitol.

The only way to reach him was to cross the river in a skiff. Sully kept a good lookout and, when the boat was about half way across, he walked out to the end of the sand spit, leveled a gun at the intruding officer and ordered him back.

Sully meets Marshal Petrie

John R. Petrie, deputy U.S. Marshal under Seth Bullock, was aware of this and when he boarded the skiff he took along a Winchester rifle and 36 rounds of ammunition. Sure enough, his reception was quite like that afforded his predecessors.

But when Sully cried, "halt" and presented his gun, "Johnnie" Petrie noted that it was a single barreled affair and not a repeating rifle. He paid no attention to the order but kept on.

Sully was greatly puzzled and dropped the barrel of his weapon over his arm, holding it there until Petrie jumped ashore with his Winchester ready for action.

"Say, you've got your nerve along," was the timber thief's salutation.

"Nerve?" "Oh more than that, I've got a warrant for your arrest," was the cool response.

From his six foot two inches of stature, Jack looked down at little Johnny Petrie's five feet six and then laughingly "broke" the gun he held on his knee, showing that it did not contain a cartridge.

"Fooled 'em all that way" he commented as he stepped into the skiff. He was taken to Yankton and fined the sum of $500.00 for illegal timber cutting.[32]

Sully came to Dakota Territory after leaving the Hat Creek area of the Whitcomb ranch which was located near the intersection of Nebraska, Wyoming and South Dakota. He married John Kincaid's widow, Mary Goulette Brinnell Kincaid, who had three Kincaid children: Estelle (Mrs. Joe Blackbird), Emily LaRouche and Billy Kincaid. Mary and Jack Sully had eight children; Louise married Pete Waugh, Eva married Pat Bronson, Mildred was a girls advisor at the Pierre Indian school, John Jr. of Gregory, South Dakota, Frank ranched near Wood, S.D., George of Colome S.D., Sam stayed at home and Claude ranched near O'Kreek, S.D.[33]

Sully's first wife Louise, who died in childbirth in 1875 at the age of 19, is buried in the Sully cemetery located 6 miles south and 7 miles west of Platte, South Dakota.[34]

In the late 1870s Tim Burleigh's steamer, the "Black Hills", burned near Hot Springs Island. Much of the cargo was saved, but the whiskey was still aboard. Jack Sully invited John Craven to go to the burned boat for the whiskey. Both got gloriously drunk and started for home in a skiff late at night. The skiff, captained by the two drunken cowboys, capsized and Sully turned up two miles below the Island, believing that John Craven had drowned.[35]

Roadhouse manners

In the 1870s, Cuthbert Ducharme, Amiable Gallineau, Louis Bordeau, Jim Somers, McKay and other local roadhouse operators were known to take the law into their own hands and do away with trouble makers.[36] Louis Bordeau shot a man at the McKay Ranch, "Old Pap" or Ducharme was reputed to have killed more than one and Amiable Gallineau got into a drunken quarrel with a Frenchman by the name of Boquelle and "shot his head off with a shot gun". Gallineau was tried in Yankton and acquitted.[37]

Sully and Harmon meet in South Dakota

Jacob Harmon married and settled near Oacoma in Lyman County, South Dakota where he again crossed paths with his old buddy, Jack Sully.

"Henry Juliff was our county sheriff (Lyman County) and he was pretty busy up to the time Jack Sully, my old pal was killed. While Jack Sully was living the U.S. Sheriffs would be after him for rustling while somebody else would be running off the stock and Jack would get the blame for it. There is more than one man in that county who got well fixed by blaming Jack Sully there were the Nelson boys . . . who are today claimed to be the largest landowners west of the Missouri river, besides being engaged in the banking business. Olaf Nelson is now president of a Sioux City bank and Nels, Carl and Albert are now operating a prosperous ranch in Tripp, County, South Dakota."[38]

Civil law problems

Some aspects of the law were not taken lightly by the friends and family who lived with Sully on Pocahontas Island. When his stepdaughter, Estelle Kincaid married Joe Blackbird, Joe had got the marriage license at Wheeler. The law required that they be married in the county where the license was procured. They were married in a rowboat by Justice of the Peace, Baxter H. Brady, just past the middle of the channel, on the Missouri River, closer to the Wheeler shore just to make sure it was a "legal" marriage.[39]

While Sully was living at Cedar Creek he did have some trouble with the civil side of the law. In 1895 Sully bought a stallion from Marvin McNapes and gave him a promissory note for $200.00, co-signed by John Waugh.

In 1897 McNapes sued on the note for non-payment. Sully and Waugh defended the case claiming that the stallion was "not a good foal getter" and therefore was "unfit for any purpose for which the horse was purchased, to wit for breeding purposes."

McNapes recovered a verdict for the amount of the note, interest and costs of the action.[40]

Chapter Ten End Notes

1. Harmon Ms.
2. Harmon manuscript written in 1922. Ms was given to author by Morris O'Connor, Jacob Harmon's grandson with permission to use it for possible publication.
3. SDHS Archives, Pierre South Dakota. Sully file and census of 1885.(These dates are very questionable) Jack Broome, Burke S.D. great-great grandson of J.M. McMullen in reviewing this article states: "There is a discrepancy here as far as his age. I tend to feel that the paragraph, 'Jack ran away from his home in St Paul in 1860 when he was fifteen years old', is more accurate. As far as I'm concerned this is the most credible I have seen on this point"
4. Jacob Harmon Ms. Saunders, Dubrey and Whitcomb were early ranchers in the Pine Ridge-Chadron-Cheyenne area. Whitcomb would later be involved in the Johnson County war.
5. *The Iona Pioneer*, May 19, 1904. Published by E. L. Senn, an early pioneering printer. Sometimes reckless with the truth, his paper plant at Oacoma was burned to the ground. He also published papers at Kennebec and Deadwood. He was known for his aggressive and often trouble provoking style.
6.. Interview with Mary and Sonny Waln 1991, St. Francis Indian School, St Francis, SD. Waln was a descendant of John and Billy Kincaid. His ancestors were raised at the Bordeaux ranch in southwestern Todd County, S.D.
7. Harmon Ms. Stealing horses from the Utes was also the favorite pastime of the Sicangu Sioux of Spotted Tail.
8. Harmon Ms. There are many stories concerning the origin of Jack Sully. The most reliable appears to have been his roots in Virginia and move to St. Paul, Minn. He was not a product of the Lower East Side of New York as some "true" accounts have claimed.
9. The Jack Morrow ranch was known far and wide along the Platte River trail. Morrow was also known to trade liquor and guns to the Sioux. Lemmon, Ed., Boss Cowman, Bison books, University of Nebraska Press, 1974, p. 35.
10. *Omaha Weekly Herald*, May 17, 1871. The skill of these early men in handling horses and cattle was legendary. They would swim their mounts across the Missouri River, rope the wildest long horn and even herd and rope buffalo.
11. Bert Hall Collection, SD Archives. Henry Tienken notes.
12. *Mitchell Daily Republic*, August 30, 1947; Peterson's 1906 Atlas of Charles Mix County. Colin La Mont was an early settler in Charles Mix County and was active in territorial politics; SDHC Vol. 9, p.229; Vol. 10, p.435.
13. SDHC Vol. 9, p.229; Vol. 10, p.435.
14. Ibid.
15. Campbell was made a General by President Lincoln, because Lincoln believed he would soon die from his wounds. Campbell promptly recovered and became an erratic and much loved early settler. SDHC Vol. 9 p.283 Vol. 25 p.221.
16. *Peterson's Atlas of Charles Mix County.*
17. House Miscellaneous Document #47 "Papers and Testimony in the case of W. A. Burleigh v. M.K. Armstrong. US Serial Set Vol. 1525.
18. Ibid.
19. *Peterson's 1906 Atlas of Charles Mix County.*

List of the names and numbers of votes at an election held at the house of Charles T. Campbell, in Charles Mix County, Dakota Territory, on the 11th day of October, AD 1870:
W.T. McKay, J.W. Smith, Henry Cleymont, C. T. Campbell, William McKelfresh, John Wright, M.H. Summers, John Callahan, John Fairburn, W. H. Harrison, Moses Arcon, Charles Marshall, William Emery, Charles Wambole, Jos. Langlois, F. Fallas, A. LeBeau, John Bordeaux, Ed. Fletcher, J.F. Flowers, R. Rodgers, M. McDonald, C. Peacott, Leon Connoyer, F. Marshall, C. Duchann, P. La Paint, Jas. Bordeaux, Jas Pullum, W. H. Holbrough, C. Barton, B. Connoyer, A.G. Shaw, S.S. Needlet, Lester Pratt, J.H. Bridgeman, T. Randall, John Sission, C. Goodridge, C. Du Bray, John Davidson, L. Gonkee, Pier Pillisere, Jas Byrne, P. Cleymont, P.

Martin, J. Simms, J.W. Goff, A. Janis, D. Galleneau, E. Swallow, C. Bernard, L. Moran, B. Langlois, L. Archambeau, W. Baugh, O. Gegar, T. W. Packard, John Ross, Louis Archambeau, J. H. Bigelow, Joseph Preu, H.R. Taylor, D. Jones, M. Davall, W.A. Dempsey, N. Joannies, John Dion, B. Bordino, A. Wilson, Jos Volin, Jas. Mckennen. D. R. Rodgers, Wm. Houston, H. Hampton, L Rubiedu, C Joannies, C. Harvey, John T Tangress, James Jackson, William Schmidt, L. Bordeaux, William Jones, John Reymess, Batties Towitt, J.H. Mclain, Leon G. Salis, L Gangrow, E. White, A. Bordeaux, Jule Siminole, Emmanuel Romero, James Swagerman, James Donnelly, George Trimmer, Wm Joases, Foster T Wheeler, J.M. Cook, Lewis Auberchon, G.R. Sherman, M. LaMont, H. Ruban, H.W. Bryan, Lewis Drapo, J.B. Depotie.

The polls at Joseph Elise's house, in Charles Mix County, Dakota Territory opened at 9:00 O'clock A.M. whe the following named persons presented themselves and voted:
John Stafford, Ed. Fisher, Frank Genty, James G. Griffin, James W. Conklin, Thomas Griffin, John Woods, C.H. Gadge, Joe Stangramage, D.J. Stafford, John Mares, John C. Adams, John Bristee, T. Richard, Hugh Campbell, William Chalker, George Trumbo, Thomas Welsh, T. Hill, Edwin Venton, Charles K. Poor, Frank Swortz, David Desisire, Samuel Henderson, W.T. Ketchum, G.W. Argo, Alick Reed, Jacob Woodring, Alex C. Young, Peter Angan, Ole Gender, Ester Doren, John Peterson, N. B. Randall, John Egan, V.P. Thielman, H. Larson, Lewis Belson, L. Hedor, Michel Woods, J.P. Sherman, Antoine Desirsie, A.J. Fisher, Thomas Welsh, J.H. Thompson, C.E. Hamilton, Hugh Mcferfery, J.S. Fangborn, Thomas Maine, H. Waller, S.M. Campbell, James Urvine, Rank Sinclair, Lewis Gerdock, Samuel Beaded, W.J. Shepman, Ellie Shiperkins, George Chamberlain, Robert Coats, John S. Norris, Aleck Reed, John Calhoun, J.C. Robb, James A. Fitzsimmons, W.A. Pottinger, Ray Cavener, G. Barrett, William Equium, C.H. Thompson, James H. Thompson, John W. Kincaid, John M. Sawyer, C.J. Brazeau, F.H. Gilday, James Adams, J.D.Flick, Felix Le Blanc, Joseph Ellis, Colin LaMont, Joseph Mcferron, James Smith, William Dodge, Narcisse Drapo, Wm. P. Lyman, William Gay, J.H. Barker, Bill Keeler, David Johnson, Thomas Reed, A.B. Hurd, Simon Jackson, W. Wineland, Christian Braker, John Layne, C.F. Rudolph, Kerwin Wilson, E. Powers, Perrine, J. P Sherman, and Edward Deming.

20. Hall, Bert L., *Roundup Years*, p 522, State Publishing Co., Pierre SD 1954. Claus Stricker, grandson of Jergins, states that Jergins was an independent Dane who had grown up as a merchant sailor in the late 1880s. Jergins operated a ferry across the Missouri directly opposite Platte Creek. Stricker still returns to the area to hunt and fish and was interviewed during that time and also when he was called by the author in a Gregory County case to give testimony concerning the historical use of the road coming up from the ferry crossing to the Fort Randall military trail. See Gregory County Civil court records in the Matter of the Petition of Betty Jones for the establishment of a right of way.
21. Bert Hall Collections SDHS Archives, Tienken notes.
22. Conversation Pat London, Winner, S.D. 1992.
23. *Roundup Years* p. 522.
24.. SDHC Vol. 10 pp. 450-51.
25. The Mullens were neighbors of Jack Sully and related to the Colombe family. Frank Mullen, the grandson, still resides along the North Fork of the Whetstone. John Mullen, the elder Mullen's son, was bailiff at the Gregory County Courthouse would often tell the author stories of Jack Sully, including the Sully letter, when we were awaiting a jury verdict. The letter has been lost, but his son Frank, who was also a witness in testimony concerning the early military road, confirms its content and the fact that it was written. See also 1885 map of the reservation.
26. Bert Hall Collection, SD Archives. undated Mitchell Daily Republic clipping.
27. Bert Hall Collections, SD Archives, Jake Walker notes.
28. Bert Hall Collection, SD Archives, Harry Kelley notes.
29 Ibid.
30 *Roundup Years*, p 431.
31 Ibid.
32. SDHS archives. Sully file. Copy of early undated Sioux Falls Argus leader newspaper recounts Petrie's story of the arrest.
33. Gnirk, Adeline, Saga of Sully Flats, p.311. Determination of heirs, Eva Sully Estate, BIA examiner of inheritance.

34. See *Saga of Sully Flats*, infra. SDHS archives, WPA cemetery records, Charles Mix County.
35. Peterson, E. Frank, Atlas of Charles Mix County, S.D. 1906 1st edition, Huron, S.D. 1906.
36. Ibid. see also Voturba, Stanley, Upper Missouri and Charles Mix County Reminiscences.
37. See *Atlas of Charles Mix County*, SD 1906 and Upper Missouri and Charles Mix County Reminiscences, infra.
38. Harmon Ms., infra. Many stories of the life and times of the Nelson Brothers have been recounted by old timers in Tripp and Todd County S.D. One son of a hired man states that when a fireguard was being plowed around the ranch headquarters an unmarked grave was uncovered. The next day the Nelsons poured a concrete floor for a new farming building on the site. (Interview LaVern Boettcher, Winner, S.D. 1987.) Others have detailed accounts of gold coins that had been inadvertently left on the kitchen table, after they had been retrieved from a basement cache. (interview Don Boreson, Hamill, S.D. 1989.) Jack Bailey, whose father sold "pharmacy" whiskey from his drug store, indicates that the Nelsons usually paid for their "pharmacy" whisky in gold. (interview Jack Bailey, Winner, S.D. 1989.)
39. *Roundup Years*, p.380
40. Charles Mix County clerk of courts records.

CHAPTER ELEVEN
SPIRIT OF THE TIMES

U.S. and the Sicangu

In 1864 Red Cloud and his allies had defeated the United States cavalry and secured the Treaty of Fort Laramie. There were still millions of buffalo in the area that the Indians had set aside as "theirs". During their zenith there were 20 to 40 million buffalo on that range.[1] Just 26 years later at the Wounded Knee massacre in December of 1890 the last "hostiles" were massacred and the sacred buffalo, which was "their everything", clothing, food, myth, spirit and religion, was no more. Big foreign and eastern cattle companies soon filled the vacuum caused by the indiscriminate slaughter of the buffalo. By 1902, 30 to 60 thousand cattle were trespassing on the reservation, driven there by the big cattle companies, who hired the toughest guns available to enforce their own law. In the resulting wild west days of West River South Dakota, dozens of Indians were being tried and sentenced for eating the white man's buffalo.[2]

The U.S. Army's treatment of the horse herds of the Sioux compounded the problem of Indian depredation and resentment toward the white man. On the Pine Ridge Reservation the army had impounded and sold thousands of the Indians' horses. The officers and their friends stole many, just as the horses and Indian property captured at the Sand Creek Massacre were "stolen".[3]

A letter addressed to General Hugh Scott dated June 1888 describes that in addition to the theft of Indian herds they were taken away and died a cruel death. It does seem reasonable that if Washington would order the Sicangu to move from White Clay Creek to the Whetstone in the dead of winter that the horses of the Sioux would suffer the same dreadful and deadly journey.

The letter states:

". . .We took over three thousand horses from the Sioux of the Standing Rock and the Cheyenne River Resrvations in South Dakota."

". . .We received orders from Washington to drive these three thousand Indian horses to St. Paul to be sold at auction. This was in the dead of winter."

"We couldn't transport forage for the horses and we knew that it was the height of folly as well as extreme cruelty to try to take these horses in the dead of winter to St. Paul."

". . .We left a trail of dead horses clear from Dakota to St. Paul. They starved and froze to death. A mere handful of these three thousand horses finally staggered into St. Paul . . ."[4]

If the army felt sadness and remorse one can realize the feelings of anger and loss that the Sioux felt over this senseless act. Is it any wonder Jack Sully and other small operators would treat the property of the eastern moneyed interests in like manner?

The small cattlemen would keep the trespassing cattle off the reservation by shipping them to market the same way that the Wyoming and Western Stockgrower Association sold all mavericks and unclaimed strays they rounded up on "their" range.

Reservation strays

By 1900 the feud between the homesteader, small rancher and the Association over the open range and the Association's "monopoly" on the gathering of strays had reached the South Dakota legislature. The State prohibited the shipment of any cattle by anybody but the owner, unless the written consent of the owner was obtained. The act was the result of the Association's roughshod handling of stock taken in "their" roundups.

As late as 1950 Bruce Siberts was still complaining about the loss of a steer in 1893. He wrote Bert Hall, "I lost a good steer in 1893 to the Wyoming Stockgrowers branded = on the left side. It was worth $40.00 and was shipped from Orin Junction."[5]

The South Dakota Association passed a resolution partially blaming this law for the increase in rustling. Since the Association could no longer take up estrays and keep the profits when the owner couldn't prove ownership, the Association reasoned this "left mature beef animals on all portions of the range to become prey" to the rustlers.

Of course the only cowboys who would rope and brand these strays as their own were Jack Sully and company. Or so the lacey sleeved set would have you believe. Many of the early white adventurers who camped on the Pine Ridge and Rosebud Reservation were Texans who had "gone north". The two Quigley Brothers are typical. Involved in some hanging offense in Texas they came north and assumed the last name of Allen. One, "Tom Allen" became a favorite in Valentine and eventually ran the "Boiling Springs Ranch". He married a white woman teacher and their offspring became well known in Nebraska legal and political circles. His brother, William B. Quigley, married one of the Larvie sisters, whose older sister had married Crazy Horse. Calvin Quigley, one of William's Lakota descendants told me that at first the two sides of the family celebrated and mourned together. "Now", he said, "well, we're just Indians".

The Western Stockgrowers were as truthful about strays as they were about listing the correct number of cattle at tax time. By their own admission they listed about 50% of what they actually owned. They were able to work their will and soon everything that was not proven to their satisfaction to be "yours" was "theirs".[6]

In 1900 it was plain that the Association had to help themselves. They promptly appointed A.P. Long and Ed Blakely as stock detectives. Blakely had investigated and "shadowed" Sully for some time. Long was in the posse that killed him.

Range hangings and murders

Hangings, back shootings and murders, would be the unfortunate result. If the Government would not protect the Indians from the trespassing eastern cattle, they were left with only one alternative. As a result both sides would take the law into their own hands.

Jack Sully would never find a time when he could live "without wearing this six shooter." His wish would not come true. Vigilance committees of stockmen were active, especially in Keyapaha County, Nebraska, which bordered the southeastern portion of the Rosebud. One member of the Committee of '89 was asked:

"Do you have any idea of about how many rustlers were done away with and how many driven out by the committee of '89?" The vigilante member replied:

"I think there were 10 got away with (killed) and probably 30 scared out."[7]

On May 29th, 1889 John T. Newell, who was a friend to supposed rustlers, was riddled by shots and killed in his own bed. On the same night the Keyapaha county jail was broken into and A.J. Maupin was riddled with 14 shots.[8] The perpetrators, although known, were never brought to justice.

E.F. Gannon caused the following notice to be printed in the Keyapaha Press:

"May 7, 1889-Any vigilance son-of-a-bitch prowling around this place, I will foreclose the mortgage of his life, which I claim to now hold, and the result will be

"INSTANTANEOUS DEATH!!!" NOT HANGING"

E.F. Gannon, Holt Creek
K.P. Co. Neb.[9]

Racism, Fraud and Greed

You might as well raise a turkey from a snake's egg
as to raise a good citizen from a papoose
Black Hills Pioneer, June 8, 1876

In 1864 the Sioux were totally victorious. In 1890 they were defeated. Millions of buffalo in 1864. None in 1890. The oldest Larvie sister married Crazy Horse, the greatest of the Sioux warriors. A younger sister married white rancher Scotty Phillip, the first inductee in the South Dakota Cowboy Hall of Fame. Had any other people suffered such a change?

When gold was discovered in the "cote noir" it is certain that Jack Sully and his cohorts were there. The editor of the Oacoma paper had written that Jack was an intimate of "flat nosed George", Lame Johnny Webster and Jim Foster who were among notorious highwaymen of the Black Hills.[10]

The Sioux were forced to give up all claims to the Black Hills or starve to death. In 1876 Congress authorized no further funds for the Sioux until they gave up the Black Hills, which was done on Feb. 18, 1877.

Editorial attitudes

The attitude of the Western editors of the time was sanguine, sinister and "red neck" in the extreme. They stated that men who came to the Hills in 1876 should have stout hearts and strong arms. Should a conflict occur between the settlers and the natives every red should be cleaned out, and the whole country left safe for the whites.[11] Typical of the attitudes of the Black Hills whites toward the Indian was the following editorial in the Deadwood Black Hills Pioneer of June 8, 1876:

"Some pap-sucking Quaker representative of an Indian doxology mill, writes in Harper for April, about settling the Indian troubles by establishing more Sunday schools and Missions among them. He says: "The young Indians are at first sweet tempered, and seem playful and happy, and if they grow up savage, it is because their minds are dwarfed and corrupted by neglect and want of Christian influences."

"It is enough to make western men sick to read such stuff. Reason, experience and everything contradicts it. You might as well try to raise a turkey from a snake egg as to raise a good citizen from a papoose. Indians can be made good only in one way, and that is to make angels of them.

"But then, some people will advocate anything for "soft" appointments."[12]

Vigilante hanging of Indians

At Fort Yates, North Dakota, after the Supreme Court of North Dakota had granted Alex Coudet a new trial following his conviction for murder, vigilantes hung him and two of his friends before the court could retry him.

The Chamberlain Democrat of November 18 1897 reported the vigilante hanging as follows:

"At about 2:00 o'clock in the morning . . . there was a rap on the jail door . . . and no sooner had he (deputy) opened the door than a mob crowded into the corridors. All of them were masked and the leaders carried ropes purchased for the occasion. The leaders presented revolvers at the head of the deputy sheriff and demanded that he open the cells . . . .. The prisoners had been aroused from sleep by the entrance of the mob and sat up half awake and trembling with terror. Holytrack and Ireland were dragged from their beds, ropes fastened about their necks and they were dragged out on the ground after being told to prepare for death. Coudet was first to be hanged. It is reported that he was asked before he was hanged whether Black Hawk and Defender had also been concerned in the murder for which he was about to be hanged. He answered that they had been.

Holytrack and Ireland were so nearly unconscious from the effects of the dragging that they did not realize what was about to happen when the ropes about their necks were tossed over the cross beam. They were unable to stand and were slowly winched from the ground on the beef windlass until their bodies hung in the air and dangled from the windlass with the body of Coudet."[13]

Rancher scalps Indians

Incidents of white rancher brutality toward Indians who butchered some tres-passing beef were reported. John Hart, in an article in the Rapid City Journal states: "One morning two ranch hands discovered a band of several Indians skin-ning the cattle. Without hesitating the two men bore down on the surprised red-men and fired away with six shooters. Three of the Indians toppled over and the rest dashed away. So angered was the rancher after the skirmish, that he drew his hunting knife and scalped the three dead Indians and tied the trophies to his belt."[14]

White greed and Indian generosity

In the early Lyman County days, John Dillon, an early government agent, matched his racehorse against a horse owned by an Indian. The Indian horse won. Most of the wagers on the race were in the form of horses that were held in the stockyards, pending the outcome of the race. Dillon, a poor loser, let the horses loose from the stockyards. When the Indian accosted him, Dillon hit him over the head and killed him. Dillon was tried and acquitted.[15]

Many early families, especially the widows who were brave enough to home-stead, were recipients of the Indians' charitable nature for those in need. Indeed, many early homesteaders would have perished had it not been for the generosity of the Sioux.[16]

The Indians quickly learned the ways of the big ranch interests and when the government issued cattle to the Indians, the Sioux dubbed them "eat 'em right away" cattle. They knew that if they didn't eat them right away they would wander off and be claimed as part of the ranchers' trespassing herd. Ironically, in the 1930s the government branded Emergency Relief Act cattle ERA.[17]

Before the opening of the Rosebud in 1904 and in 1908 the large foreign and eastern cattle companies trespassed upon the reservation lands with impunity, paying small sums here and there or hiring Indian cowboys or "fronts" to look after their reservation interests.[18] They also usually hired the toughest guns and always were generous in seeing that some of the Indians on "their" range would get a "nice fat cow to eat". So what if it was a cancer-eyed old son-of a bitch.[19]

Here is the typical scam that was worked by many Indian agents and the white rancher. In the early 1900s a company was formed to furnish beef to the Pine Ridge agency. The firm included Stirk, Brennan (the Indian agent), Gleason and Hank Simmons. In the spring they shipped 3000 steers from New Mexico. They were old dogs, green mossy horned, 10 to 15 year old reprobates and renegades. Since Brennan was involved they had no trouble at the agency and were sold as prime cattle at great profit.[20]

Rustling

John Cournoyer, Jack Sully's longtime friend (who had been one of those who Mrs. Sully had stopped from seeking revenge on Harry Ham after the death of Jack

Sully) was brought to justice by Marshall Petrie.[21] Petrie followed Cournoyer's trail for three days and nights, finally catching him at the old Sully ranch. Cournoyer had just emerged from the house preparatory to continuing his flight when little Johnnie Petrie rounded the corner of the barn and stood guard over the rustler's saddle horse and rifle. Cournoyer made a desperate effort to get by him but surrendered when Petrie got the drop on him. Cournoyer was tried and convicted and served time at Leavenworth.[22]

Jack Sully was not the only enterprising law breaker in Oacoma. Postmaster L.L. Armstrong of Oacoma was arraigned before United States Commissioner C.D. Tidrick in May of 1904 on the charge of selling whisky in the Post Office.[23] Many other early cowboys and Indians wanted for rustling made their escape from the clutches of the law, were successful, or if caught were not shot. John Canourie (John Cournoyer) had been sprung from the Oacoma jail as well as the Somers lad who was charged with burning editor Senns' buildings. Frank or "Pete" Waugh and Bobby Burns also tried daring escapes.

"Bobby" Burns

Jesse Brown, Lyman County deputy sheriff, had received a warrant from the Indian agent at Standing Rock to have Bobby Burns arrested for a jail break from that agency. Brown went down to Sully Flats and found Burns cutting wood on an Island in the Missouri. He waited for Burns to come in for dinner and Burns demanded to know if Brown had a warrant for his arrest. Brown didn't have a warrant, but told him he was going to take him to Rosebud and let the Indian Agent settle the matter.

Brown let Burns eat his dinner. When Burns finished eating he picked up his plate and cracked it over Brown's head. One of Browns' helpers came in and subdued Burns, who was then hog-tied and taken to Rosebud.

Burns escaped from the Rosebud jail and was picked up near Valentine, Neb. The U.S. Marshall took Bobby to Deadwood to await trial where he again escaped, this time for good.

The Mitchell Gazette of May 28, 1904 stated that when Burns was taken by Marshall John Bolding from Valentine, he became unruly and it took four men to subdue him and he was placed in fetters for the trip to Deadwood.[24]

Frank Waugh jumps from train

Frank "Pete" Waugh also tried a daring escape from the law. The Fairfax Advertiser of June 14, 1904 reported the following:

"Deputy United States Marshal Lamb has just placed in the Minnehaha County jail a prisoner who gave him considerable trouble. A short time ago a warrant was placed in the hands of Marshal Lamb for the arrest of Frank Waugh on the charge of horse stealing. Waugh is a son-in-law of late Jack Sully and considered a tough customer. Deputy Lamb learned that Waugh was at a ranch near Platte and he went out after him. He arrested his man and brought him to Geddes where he had a preliminary hearing and was bound over to the next term of court. Waugh was committed to the Minnehaha County jail for safe keeping.

Lamb left Geddes with his prisoner and everything went along smoothly until the prisoner made a request to be permitted to go to the closet. As the prisoner had been on his good behavior Lamb suspected nothing and granted the request. As soon a Waugh entered the closet he slammed and locked the door and Mr. Lamb heard a window raise. He was suspicious at once and ran to the rear platform of the car just in time to see his prisoner leap from the closet window. Not to be outdone, and notwithstanding that the train was running at full speed, Lamb leaped from the train after the man. Both men were on their feet at about the same time and only a short distance apart. Waugh started to run and Lamb drew his revolver and fired one shot over his head. Waugh turned, threw up his hands and surrendered. The rear brakeman on the train witnessed the event, stopped the train to take Lamb and his prisoner aboard."[25]

"Buffalo" George

Another legendary contemporary of Jack Sully was a fellow Virginian who went by the name of William G. George aka "Buffalo George" aka Joe Cobb. "Buffalo" was born in Virginia in 1868 and came to the Crookston, Nebraska area south of St. Francis and the Rosebud Indian Reservation. While there he met Cornelius Utterbach who had married a Larvie girl and was a brother-in-law of Crazy Horse and Scotty Phillip. George was some cowboy and would help Phillip wrangle the buffalo he bought from the Dupree's ranch on the Cheyenne River.

Buffalo George's exploits were legendary. He was, like Jack Sully, a friend of Olof Nelson in Lyman County. "Buff" was shot at least three times in South Dakota while resisting arrest and also received a full load of buckshot when he high-tailed it to Montana, after serving three different stretches in the South Dakota Penitentiary.[26] He was shot and wounded by the law in 1902, 1904 and 1906 and one time stayed at Olof Nelson's ranch until he recovered.[27] The local paper reported that when he was arrested many "higher ups" were worried that he would turn state's evidence. The paper stated it would "take the Gold Dust Twins and a can of concentrated lye to remove the spots from some of the spotless characters who have posed as leaders west of the Missouri."[28] After he had been shot several times while resisting and after Sully had met his fate he put up no fight the last time he was arrested in Lyman County.

"Buff" was no dummy. When Sheriff Sheldon showed up with Olof Nelson and his brother as members of the posse, he was not going to run any Jack Sully gauntlet. "Buff" was sent to the S.D. penitentiary in 1908, 1912, and 1919. He was acquitted of several charges prior to that time. After his discharge he disappeared until Walter Prahl of Murdo S.D. published a private book outlining his life.[29]

"Jack Sully". "Jack Kincaid", "Persimon Bill", "Bobby Burns", "Lame Johnny", "Pigeon Toed Kid", "Buffalo George", "Laughing Sam", "Bunk White", "Dago Mike", "Arkansas", "Pecos Bill", "Big nosed George", "Vinegar Bill", "Rocky Mountain Tom", "Black Dick", "Slobberin Sam", "Doc Middleton", "Bunk White",

"Tom Allen", and "James Murray" had probably all taken names to escape their pasts.

They were essential in settling western South Dakota and Nebraska. They made the Rosebud and its surrounding area unique. Most would be hung, shot, serve time in prison, or "go north" to new horizons. Some like Tom Allen and James Murray would clear their names and become "spotless" citizens. The unnamed associates of Jack Sully, "Buff" George, and the hired guns of the stockgrowers who were "leaders of the west" either would return to the east or stay in the west as "spotless" leaders in their community. No prior criminal record would survive to question their impeccability. Only occasional notes and innuendoes and other clues would be left for anyone to question their past.

As Adolph Stamer wrote, in commenting on the death of Jack Sully, "only in the final date will the merits and virtues of all acts be known."

Hired guns

From 1889 to 1902 the Stockgrower Associations were busy protecting their interests in Dakota and Wyoming by both public and secret means. Bruce Siberts relates that sometime in February, 1892, Tom Horn came to see a neighbor in Stanley County, South Dakota. Horn was hiring gunslingers for W.C.Irvine and the Wyoming Stock Growers for the impending Johnson County War in Wyoming. Horn was offering $150.00 a month plus expenses and a bonus of $500.00 for each rustler killed.[30]

Tom Horn also paid a visit to Jack Sully. The Bordeaux ranch was located southwest of St. Francis, South Dakota, and it was here that Jack would often hide out when things got too rough at home. Tom Horn rapped on the window of the bunkhouse at the Bordeaux ranch and called Jack Sully outside.

Sully and Horn rode off and had a long conversation. Although Sully never revealed the subject of the talk, one may assume that Horn had either tried to enlist him as a hired gun in the Johnson County invasion and Sully had turned him down, or Horn was delivering a discreet warning from the lacey sleeved ranchers to Sully.[31]

After the defeat of the ranchers' faction in Wyoming, many of the hired guns made their way into South Dakota where the South Dakota Association hired them.[32]

The land which was untaxed, unowned, but fenced by the ranchers belonged to those who had the guts and money to hire the toughs necessary to hold it. Thus the public domain became their own private domain. As Badger Clark, the poet, says in one of his verses, it was good . . . "When all the land, without no fence or fuss, belonged to God, the Government, and us."

White depredations

The Indians' rights were never factored into the equation unless some white rancher would benefit. In 1871 the Coe-Caster cattle company fraudulently secured an affidavit, with the help of Todd Randall, signed by Spotted Tail, Two Strike, Windy, Black Crow, Rooster, Crooked Foot, and No Flesh that Spotted

Tail's band had butchered 300 of their cattle. In 1879, U.S. Attorney G.M. Lambertson successfully prosecuted the fraud. Of course the white ranchers or outlaws, "greymen" as the Indians called them, not only stole the Indians' cattle but also filed claims for every real and imagined loss they sustained.[33] On October 14, 1879 Indian Commissioner Hayt wired Spotted Tail's agency to be on the alert as they had word that a plan was afoot to steal all the Indians' stock.[34]

With the vast boom in the cattle industry their pasture was soon overgrazed. As the grass was overgrazed in this semi-arid area the foreign and eastern money interests looked with envy on the large and verdant pasturelands of the Pine Ridge and Rosebud reservations.

Early settlers

Scotty Phillip, Utterback, Craven and others all married Larvie sisters and used their Indian rights to their ranching advantage. The oldest of the seven Larvie sisters was married to Crazy Horse and two of the youngest were married to Ben Gerry and a whiteman by the name of Quigley who had traveled north from Texas with his brother and who had been traveling under the names of Tom and Joe Allen.

Jack Sully had married an enrolled Indian woman and became entitled to certain privileges on the Rosebud Reservation. With the opening of the nine million acres for settlement on February 10, 1889 the White River became the northern boundary of the Rosebud Reservation. Oacoma's location made it a focal point for whatever elements of the two battling civilizations sought adventure or revenge.

The influx of the homesteader created a condition that would de-stabilize the large open range's freewheeling cattle industry. The homeseekers took the best water and fenced their claims. In Tripp County alone 114,769 persons filed for four thousand homesteads.[35]

In the rush for free land, families who were not accustomed to hardscrabble farming and even widows with small children drew allotments and started on their great plains adventure. Some met with death and disaster as did Mat Matson on Phelps Island on the Missouri,[36] the two Somers in an uncle-nephew shoot out near Chamberlain,[37] and Albert Wood in a "bluff game" near Hamill, South Dakota.[38]

The Stockgrowers Association rounded up cattle on these ranges, even fenced the Reservation as their own, claiming their own cattle and picking up 42,952 estrays in the 10 years prior to 1902. If ownership could not be established, the money from their sale was put in the Association's rustling account.[39] The reservations had not been open to lease prior to 1902. Thereafter, Ed Lemmon paid a visit to President T.R. Roosevelt and returned with a lease of 865,529 acres of reservation land.[40]

Roosevelt roundup

The roundup of 1902 was caused by government order to remove all trespassing cattle from the reservation. It was popularly called the "Roosevelt roundup".

It was to be the world's largest cattle round up ever, 40 to 60 thousand cattle, all trespassers on Indian land. Eighteen wagons with up to eighty riders each worked the roundup.[41]

Rustlers' paradise

The 1902 report of the Association's executive committee stated: "Numerous arrests have been made in the southeast corner of the range, but as long as Lyman County is a worthy contestant for the honor (?) so long held by Johnson County, Wyo., as a rustlers' paradise, the results have been anything but satisfactory . . . . . The situation in that section is real serious, the rustling element being protected in Lyman County by the sentiment in their favor and on the Rosebud reserve by the ruling of the U.S. court, consequently, they are practically beyond the reach of the law and are fully aware of it. About 200 head of cattle were recovered by inspectors on which the brands had been worked."[42]

Dakota death list

Had the Association found it necessary to compile a "death list" as Irvine had done in Wyoming, prior to the Johnson County War? Had their losses been such that they would blame "the male Indian who won't work unless driven to it by starvation and he won't be driven in that direction as long as range beef is available" and the ever encroaching homesteader?[43]

The situation called for "secret work". The executive committee was authorized to appoint three members "to take charge of any "secret work" of this association and not be required to report until the next regular meeting." Dawson, Craig, and W.C. Irvine of Wyoming were appointed to the secret committee.[44] Who were these three men who were given the unfettered power to do the Association's "secret work" How had they used such a grant of power in the past? Who did they represent?

The secret committee

H.A. Dawson came to South Dakota as a reservation clerk for the Indian Department in 1882. In 1884 he received a license to trade with the Indians and operated a trader's store. By 1900 he was one of the largest cattle operators in South Dakota. He became the owner of the U+ and in 1910 shipped out 16,000 head of cattle. An industrious man indeed. Dawson returned to live his remaining years in Maryland, his home state, in 1911.[45]

James Craig, came to South Dakota from Scotland in 1884. In 1893 he took over the management of the VVV, a large Scottish owned ranching operation that was closely associated with the affairs of John Clay of Wyoming fame.[46] In fact, Craig and Clay had grown up as boyhood chums in Scotland.[47] When the bushwacking murder of John Tisdale of Buffalo, Wyoming was being investigated, Jim Craig was there. The State's witness, who prior to the hearing had recognized Frank Canton as being the bushwhacker, lost his memory at the hearing. Just to make things a little more solid, James Craig testified that he saw Frank Canton in Buffalo at the time the bushwacking took place, some six miles from town.[48]

Craig was part and parcel of the Wyoming stockgrowers who invaded Johnson County with their death list. He was also a member of the group that stalked the two witnesses to the murder of Ray and Campion across Wyoming and into Nebraska and helped spirit them away to the East Coast so they could not testify against the Association members who had committed the murders.[49] When the two witnesses reached the East Coast and tried to cash the checks the Association had given them, they bounced.[50]

W.C. Irvine of Wyoming was an early large cattle operator who had a reputation of being hot headed and hard case. He is considered to have been, along with John Clay, the mastermind of the Johnson County invasion. He put more faith in the bushwacking tactics of Tom Horn and Frank Canton than he did in the judicial system.

The records of the Lyman County courthouse reveal that, indeed, Lyman County was a hotbed of rustling prosecutions. They were the rustling capitol of the world

Private police

By 1904 the "secret work" called for by the Western Stockgrowers Association had begun. "Detectives" from the Association had become permanent fixtures in the area, with some, like Ed Blakely, hiring out for special work in Fairfax and Gregory, South Dakota during the land rush openings of 1904.

Blakey was no novice at gun play. He was the sheriff of Fall River County in 1889 and had as his deputy Sam Moses.[51]

He had worked for Whitcomb's Bar T ranch and was hired as a range detective by the Western South Dakota Stockgrowers Association in 1896 to replace the missing Elliot, who had been scared by survivors of the Johnson County war and fled to Alaska without picking up his last paycheck.[52]

Blakely had been shadowing and looking for Sully for some time. Lou Cagley of Oacoma, who helped run the ferry at the mouth of Five Mile Creek, states that Blakely went to Cedar Creek to try and catch Jack. On the way Blakely and Sully met face to face. Blakely asked him if he knew Jack Sully? "Why yes", he replied, "he lives just up the creek there." The officer didn't recognize him and Jack rode off.[53] The record number of people charged with rustling in Lyman County from 1901-1904 indicates that many other peoples' rustling had been laid at the foot of Jack Sully. There is no doubt that Olof Nelson and others were involved.

The availability of thousands of foreign and eastern cattle that were trespassing on reservation range was an overpowering temptation to the small operator who was treated with disdain by the lacey sleeved set. Many of the cattle belonged to such companies as the Canadian Cattle Company who bought out the Grace Howard spread and was soon delinquent in its taxes.[54]

Olof Nelson

The editor of the Oacoma Gazette Leader knew who was in cahoots with Sully but feared to tell his readers outright who he was. The paper stated: "the notorious cattle thief . . . was associated with a white man by the name of _____." [55]

The editor and his readers knew that the name that everyone would insert in that blank space was Olof Nelson. Nelson, who had been clerk of courts, was a powerful figure in Lyman County politics at the time. He had been charged with rustling on December 11, 1901. This is the case where States Attorney Bartine went to Gregory County and fought with their States Attorney over Nelson. It is the same case where all of the Gregory County records, save one, have disappeared. The powers that were behind the Lyman County States Attorney were after Nelson.

They knew they could never secure his conviction in Lyman County so they filed affidavits that the state could not get a fair trial in Lyman County and the trial judge quickly ordered the trial moved to Sanborn County and the Mitchell South Dakota courthouse.[56]

Nelson's attorneys secured a writ of habeas corpus from the South Dakota Supreme court who promptly ruled on March 19, 1902 that the State Constitution prohibited the State from changing the place of trial from the county wherein the crime is alleged to have taken place.[57]

The lacey sleeved Association set was stymied. With no state jurisdiction on the reservation proper and the residents of Lyman County in sympathy with small operators the Association appeared to be stopped in their tracks. Or were they? Would the vigilante lynching be replaced by the "44" as had happened in Wyoming and recently just across the border in Nebraska.

Certainly some "secret work" was needed.

The Cowardly murder of August "Kid" Rich

Within months of the appointment of the "secret committee" of Dawson, Craig and Irvine by the South Dakota Stockgrowers in 1903, another "Wyoming style" bushwacking murder had taken place near Cherry Creek on the Cheyenne River Reservation in South Dakota.

Kid Rich was found dead, shot in the back, on February 20th, 1903 on Red Bull Bottom on the Cheyenne River in western South Dakota.

Early times

Rich had been raised in Custer County, South Dakota. He came from pioneer stock and he and his sisters were raised by his widowed mother.[58]

Kid had a shooting scrape with Ed Blakely, the Stockgrower's hired detective, in an Oelrichs saloon in southwestern South Dakota. In this gunfight, unlike the target practice killing of Tom Milligan's partner in the early days of Custer, South Dakota, the two gunslingers, Rich and Blakely, shot it out in the saloon and no one was hit by any of the many shots that were fired. They did manage to hit several of the whisky barrels.[59]

Prior to coming to the Reservation, Kid had killed Johnson who was the nighthawk for Ed Lemmon. He was sent to the penitentiary for two and one half years. On the day he was released Lemmon hired him as nighthawk. Such a light sentence for homicide would certainly lead one to speculate that either powerful people were at work on his behalf, or Johnson's death had also been contracted by the lacey sleeved set.[60]

Who killed Kid Rich?

There were rumors that Kid had been a hired gun for the Association. There were also rumors that Narcisse Narcelle was unhappy with him. Kid Rich had married into the same Indian family and Rich had "split" from his wife who was the sister of the wife of Narcisse. Those who knew Narcisse well state that he would never have let this anger cause him to bushwhack Kid, Wyoming style. Besides, "putting away", not killing, was an accepted Indian norm.[61]

The boss cowman, Ed Lemmon, knew Kid Rich well. Of all the outlaws and lawmen Lemmon knew he considered all to be salt of the earth except his nighthawk Johnson, who was killed by Kid Rich, and Blakely, the stock detective who trailed Jack Sully.[62]

Of them all he liked Kid Rich the best. Why would Lemmon hire Rich as his new nighthawk on the very day Rich was released from prison for killing Lemmon's old nighthawk, Johnson? Why was Kid Rich bushwhacked after being sentenced to only 2 1/2 years for homicide?

Kid Rich didn't learn his manners in south Texas or back east. He was a true son of the west. Raised in southwestern South Dakota he was the region's own cantankerous, practical joking, outlaw prodigal son. Like Jack Sully, he had his troubles with the law and dealt too closely with friends who may have double crossed him, but neither he nor Sully turned tail and ran north to escape the wrath of the neighborhood.

Kid was a native son devil may care cowboy, who never believed that the man who came calling for him that night would slip a gun in his back, pull the trigger, and blow him clean out of the saddle. Was Kid Rich killed to keep him quiet as some of his friends and neighbors indicated? Why was the story fabricated that Narcisse Narcelle had killed him over some family jealousy? Was there something about the killing of Johnson and others that could have a bearing on Kid's murder?

Remember that he was killed just short of four months after money hungry Dawson, Scottish born Craig and short tempered W.C. Irvine were appointed to arrange the "secret work" of the Stockgrowers. In the words of Olof Finstad when he was asked who shot Jack Sully in the back, "Who had the most to gain by the death" of Kid and why?

Rich may have done some dirty work like Horn, Canton and others, but if one of his enemies had come for him that evening his death would not have occurred six miles down the road, but they would have had it out at the ranch. Kid Rich was set up by his "friends." In all probability they were powerful people.

Rich was different than Phelps who plotted the murder of Matson and hired a killer to do the deed just to divide the spoils. Nor was he of the same ilk as old man Kunnecke, up Fort Pierre way, who made a habit of hiring transient herders then working them until they demanded pay and murdering them to save money.

Rumors around Fort Pierre credit him with eight to ten murders. He was finally caught when he dug up one of the bodies and moved it to a new location. The law caught him in the act and he was sent to the penitentiary.[63]

The killings of "homesteaders", "nesters", "sod busters", and "honyockers" never bothered the lacey sleeved set like Moreton Frewen, John Clay, H.A. Dawson, W.C. Irvine and others. They considered it a welcome dividend when their sought after results were accomplished without having to hire a Tom Horn, Frank Canton or a rumored secret hit man from back east who was called in for special work.[64]

They were ever complaining about cow losses and "their" domain being fenced by homesteaders but they never complained about the death of any human until their own lives were threatened by sheriff Angus and a small army of citizens who had them holed up at a Wyoming ranch after they had murdered two homesteaders and started the Johnson County War.

Who did the job on Kid Rich? Was it one of the Association's hired guns? Why was there no investigation or any attempt whatsoever to find his killer? The officials and witnesses were afraid for their lives. Would they have shown such fear if the murderer had been a lone eagle looking for revenge? Perhaps their fears were made ever more real by the fact that a powerful vindictive organization had hired the killing and would hire others, if necessary. As the fella says, "it was sure their style".

The lacey sleeved cattlemen had done this work before. It was simple. It was sure. It was cold blooded, back shooting murder. It was their style. They were the only group whose power could intimidate both witness and lawman, as they had done time and again in Wyoming.[65]

The practical joker

Kid made friends easily. He was always a practical joker. One of his early friends along the Cheyenne River was a young Iowa cowboy, Bruce Siberts, who had come alone to seek his fortune in the west.

Bruce and Kid helped organize a Sunday school class. Please don't get the idea that these two boys really got religion, for their motives were far from pure, but then oft times the preachers and Christian women of the congregation weren't all that pure either.

In fact one of the congregation, Sophie Abair (Hebert) Narcelle had some very strange ideas of her own. No lacey sleeved lady, she was half French and half Indian, and when Narcisse Narcelle died she had him disemboweled, filled his body cavity with salt and kept him in her living room until some neighbors complained and the law made her bury him.[66]

Well, Kid and Bruce were not fools. Kid was elected treasurer of the Sunday school group and he and Bruce collected the money and "looked after" the receipts. The devil took hold of these two cowboys and they stole the treasury and bought several gallons of whisky. Later some would say that the school had been the idea of a bunch of sheepherders anyway, so Bruce and the Kid were admired by some for stealing from that "bunch of sons of bitches."

Bruce and the Kid took their whisky and proceeded to share the wealth by riding from place to place and drinking with all their cowboy friends. Along the way they met some Indians and Rich gave one a cup full of whisky and then told him that Mrs Abair was expecting and that she was, in gratitude, throwing a party for all the Indians of the neighborhood, at her place that evening. The Indian wives soon spread the news and that evening they all descended on Mrs Abair. You can imagine what happened when all of those uninvited Indians showed up for the party celebrating her imaginary pregnancy.

Some in the community got quite upset over Siberts and Rich buying whisky with the Sunday school money. Generally they would raise hell with Siberts, but most of them knew better that to razz the Kid. Kid got even anyway.

He started a rumor that the sheriff was on his way to the area to investigate the butchering of O.P. (other peoples') cattle. Bruce said that many a fresh killed beef was stashed in holes that were hastily chopped in the Cheyenne River ice to ditch the evidence, before the rumored sheriff could arrive.[67]

These same neighbors believed he had been murdered by someone brought in by the big ranchers to do the job. They believed that Rich had done some "secret work" for them and had been murdered to keep his mouth shut.

Plowing up Main Street

Rich's love of whisky and a practical joke were apparent right from the start. Along with his whisky barrel shooting scrape with sheriff Blakely in an Oelrich saloon, Kid and a cowboy friend literally tried to plow up Harry Oelrich's town.

In the spring of 1886 Kid Rich came to Oelrichs and proceeded to make a day of it, well a day and a night of it. He proceeded to party it up at the same local saloon where he and E.W. Blakely had their famous "whisky barrel" shoot out.

Kid "closed the bar", as any good cowboy would in those days, and met his cowboy friend out in the street. The two cowboys found a seat on a plow that was displayed in front of the local hardware store.

The Kid's friend finally decided to go home. Kid didn't want to leave so his friend roped the plow on which Kid was sitting and announced he was going to pull the Kid home.

Horse, rider, rope, plow and Kid Rich clattered up Harry Oelrich's plank sidewalk. Kid, of course, fell off and on getting up grabbed the handles of the plow and announced that "go on I'm going to plow up this goddamned field". Rich and his friend proceeded to plow Harry Oelrichs fine new plank sidewalk until at last the plow fell through and the saddle horse could pull no more. Before he collapsed in a heap to sleep it off, the kid voiced the opinion that Oelrichs should "never have brought that son of a bitching plow that far west in the first place."[68]

The murder

Soon the Kid would be found passed out near a building on the main street. A few short years later he would be shot in the back in the most cold blooded murder in the history of western South Dakota.

When they found Kid Rich on that cold February morning in 1903, he lay on the cold ground, his roan horse standing near, with both stirrups of his saddle pulled to one side of his horse where they had been pulled when he fell mortally wounded, having been shot in the back in the most cowardly manner.

The body was examined by a doctor, who removed the slug from the front of Kid Rich, pronounced him dead and stated that he "had died from bleeding to death caused by a bullet in the back." It seems that the presence of the Doctor would indicate that the law may have been more interested in a determination that Kid Rich was in fact dead more than anything else.

The only investigation was made by some local Indians who tried to follow the tracks of the lone rider who had shot Kid Rich in the back. The Indians did find a throatlatch from a bridle, but it could not be traced. The Narcisse Narcelle ranch was checked and all of the bridles were accounted for and none had missing throat latches.[69] There was no further investigation made of the death. Imagine what a hullabaloo would have been caused if a butchered steer, belonging to one of the big outfits had been found dead, killed by some homesteader rustler.

On the night of his murder, Kid Rich had been working at the Jim Cavanaugh ranch, where he and his wife were staying. The ranch was just six miles from where the murder took place. On the evening of the bushwhacking a man knocked at the ranch house door and the owner, James Cavanaugh, went to the door. Cavanaugh says that the man slipped around the corner of the house and said "I want to talk to Kid Rich."

Cavanaugh, who knew all of the ranchers and Indians in the area, said that he did not know who the man was and, "that even if I did, the less I have to say, the better it will be for me." Kid Rich's wife said that when the knock came on the door she and Rich were in bed and when Cavanaugh went to the door, he walked outside so she did not hear what was said.

Rich got out of bed and asked Cavanaugh who it was that wanted to see him. Cavanaugh told him he didn't know. Mrs. Rich went back to bed. Kid stepped out to talk, came back in and started to dress. His wife asked him who it was. Rich didn't answer her but stated that he had been sent for by the Indian chief of police. He took his revolver and left.[70]

Whoever was riding with Kid Rich that night knew him well. Kid must have had some faith or trust in them or otherwise he would not have gone. This "friend" placed his pistol in the middle of Rich's back pulled the trigger and murdered him. The blast of the pistol left a hole three inches in diameter in the back of Rich's sheeplined winter coat. Kid fell from the saddle and in one last effort grabbed the bridle of the murderer's horse pulling the throatlatch loose when he fell from the saddle.

Chapter Eleven End Notes

1. Hornady, William T, *Extermination of the American Bison*, Smithsonian report of 1887.
2. Lyman County Clerk of Courts: Criminal files.
3. SDSHA Pierre, S.D., Jordan file.
4. Ibid and see Hall, Bert L., *RoundUp Years* p.51, State Publishing Co., 1954., Sandoz, Mari, *The Cattlemen*, Bison Books, 1978.
5. *RoundUp Years* pp. 245 et. seq.
6. *Last Grass Frontier*, pp. 247 et. seq.
7. *The History of Keyapaha County*, pp. 16-21, Pine Hill Press, Freeman, S.D.

In the fall of 1883, Murphy, Old man Wade, Eph Weatherwax, and a fifth person were hung by Vigilantes in northern Holt County, Nebraska. In January of 1884 the vigilantes went north into Indian Country and killed two supposed horse thieves and returned with 16 head of horses. In the same year Kid Wade was hung by a vigilante group headed by Henry Richardson, who like Harry Ham, had much to fear if Wade would be allowed to talk.

In March of 1884, Tom Berry had two of the regular vigilante leaders indicted for stealing his horse. The editor of the Valentine Reporter reflected: "we shall hereafter look upon every one who professes to be a vigilante as a horse thief of the deepest dye." See Valentine Reporter, Nov. 22, 1883; Jan. 17th, 24th, 1884; Feb. 1, 14, 21, and 28, 1884. Ainsworth Nebraska News Dec. 20, 27, 1883; Mar. 27 and April 3, 1884. (Tom Berry's son would become a cowboy governor of South Dakota.) (Governor Berry's son, Baxter would shoot and kill Norman Little Brave, an unarmed Lakota preacher, in his corral in 1969. An all white jury acquitted Berry and the following year the jury selection for most counties on or near the reservation were obliged to follow Constitutional guidelines)

8. Ibid. In fact there were over 13 hangings or murders in the area from 1883 to 1888. Archives, Cherry County Historical Society, Valentine Nebraska.
9. Ibid.
10. *Oacoma Gazette*, June 16, 1903.
11. *Black Hills Pioneer*, June 6, 1876.
12. Ibid.
13. *Chamberlain Democrat*, November 18, 1897.
14. Hall, Bert L., *RoundUp Years*, State Publishing Co., 1954.
15. Ibid, Hall, p.251, Harmon Ms. Dillon was an early entrepreneur on the Lower Brule reservation. He secured a contract for the building of agency buildings and would often light his cigars with a five dollar bill and always "set up a round". Hall Collection, SD Archives.
16. Kolenne Newbold, student in author's history class at Sinte Gleska University, 1991 related that her grandmother was a "widow" who homesteaded and would have perished had it not been for the generosity of the Sicangu Sioux. In 1885 Solomon Morey was freighting from Valentine to the Rosebud Agency. On one trip he helped an Indian freighter "pull" the long hill just north of Valentine. Other teamsters had passed him by. Later Solomon lost his horses while camped out on the trail. By late morning a team appeared with the same Indian and his family. The Indian's boy had attended St. Francis school, so Solomon's troubles were relayed to the father. A pony was unhitched and the Indian soon returned with Solomon's horses, who had broken their hobbles during the night. Solomon and the Indian shook hands, but not a word was spoken. Gladys Morey Erickson, A Sandhills Century, Book 2, The people, Cherry County Centennial Committee, 1985 Service Press, Henderson Neb., 68371 p 357.
17. Oral history related by Vi Waln, student Sinte Gleska University, 1991.
18. White Ranchers always have had Indians front for them in order to get prime grazing units, at bargain prices. The tradition continues in every federally financed Indian improvement project to this day. South Dakota Governor William Janklow, as a young legal aid attorney on the Rosebud, after having been involved in prolonged, labrynthian case involving such fronting, filed a claim asserting

the ownership of the Indian front man, after the white "overseer" and the Indian front man had died. He sought the ownership of the cattle for the heirs of the deceased Indian. Needless to say all hell broke loose. I represented the family of the deceased white rancher. Many threats were made by the individual parties and some "reservation revenge" resulted after the case had been decided in the favor of Gov. Janklow's clients.

19. Donations of an old cow or two by white operators for pow-wows and gatherings, but most importantly near important elections, was and is, commonplace.
20. *RoundUp Years*, p.109, 183, 184.
21. Oral history: Christine Valandra, granddaughter of Jack Sully, Sinte Gleska student, 1990.
22. Hall Collections, SDSHS Archives. Sully's foreman, Ernest Towler was sentenced to 2 years in Leavenworth for rustling from J.A. Fulwider. (Fulwider and Ham were buddies and both had been arrested for rustling themselves.) Charles Mix County News, Nov. 12, 1903.
23. Lyman county court records, Kennebec, SD.
24. *Mitchell Gazette*, May 28, 1904.
25. *Fairfax Advertiser*, June 14, 1904.
26. *The Elusive Horizon*, Walter Prahl, Register-Lakota Printing, Chamberlain, S.D. 1990, p. 4,5.
27. *RoundUp Years*, p. 331.
28. *The Elusive Horizon*, p. 7.
29. *The Elusive Horizon*, Infra.
30. Siberts, Bruce, *Nothing But Prairie and Sky*, Univ of Okla. Press pp. 100-110.
31. Interview Mary and Sonny Waln, St. Francis, S.D., 1991.
32. *Fairfax Advertiser*, Feb. 25, 1904 (Ed Blakely mentioned). Bob Lee and Dick Williams, The Last Grass Frontier, pp. 196-209.
33. Letter from U.S. Attorney Lambertson, re fraudulent filing of claims against Spotted Tail and Red Cloud's people. National Regional Archive, Kansas City, Mo.
34. Telegram dated October 14, 1879. National archives K.C. Mo. (This is the same time that Carter, Tom Allen, Jim Murray, Leneaugh and other Texans who were on the lamb showed up in western Nebraska and Southwestern South Dakota. Carter started "Bodega" saloon's in Valentine, Chadron and Deadwood. Tom Allen was really James H. Quigley of Valentine Nebraska, fame. Jim Murray was James Dahlman who would later be mayor of Omaha, Nebraska. If there were any easy Indian cattle to steal, this group was in the area and would surely have been tempted.) See: Lemmon, Ed, Boss Cowman, p.147
35. SDHC Vol. 20, p.156.
36. Harmon Ms.
37. SDHC Vol. 29, pp.134-135; 8:18,9:301, 10:446-9, 24:513,13:109.
38. State v. Langan et al., Tripp County clerk of courts.
39. Bob Lee and Dick Williams, *The Last Grass Frontier*, Black Hills Publishers, Inc., Sturgis, S.D.,1984. p.225.
40. Ibid p. 223.
41. Ibid p. 224.
42. Ibid p. 220.
43. Bob Lee and Dick Williams, The Last Grass Frontier, p. 228.
44. Ibid p.217. These men had also been members of the Wyoming Stockgrowers Association who had hired secret hit men other than Tom Horn. On July 28, 1886 at Nogales in Arizona Territory John H. Smith, aka John H. Morrell was killed by George Miles, aka George Bailey. Miles was a hired gun of the Wyoming Stockgrowers Association. John Smith was being held for the legendary James L. "Whispering" Smith who was a "roving" detective for the Association. "Whispering" Smith had promised Miles $100 to: "capture and hold him (John H. Smith) until I reached there, either that or kill him and in either case I would hold myself good to him for a hundred dollars." San Francisco Chronicle, July 26, 1886 p. 3, col. 6. Wyoming Stockgrowers Association letter file, Archives of the American Heritage Center, University of Wyoming, Laramie, Wy. 1887, letter, James L Smith to Thomas Sturgis (Secretary of Association); Jan 11, 1886 (1887). On January 21, 1887 the Executive Committee minute book stated: "The Secretary read a letter from Inspector James L. Smith contain-

ing an account of the manner in which expenses claimed by him (in the killing of John Smith) were incurred. On motion duly seconded the Secretary was authorized to settle the claim above reft.to- ($100.00)-" Murray L Carrol research paper deposited with Valentine Historical Society, Valentine, Nebraska.

45. *Last Grass Frontier*, p 245 et seq.
46. Ibid pp. 106-107.
47. Ibid p.258
48. Smith, Helena Huntington, *The War on Powder River*, U. of Neb. Press, 1967. p. 172. See appendix 3.
49. Sandoz, Mari. *The Cattlemen*, U of Neb. Press, 1978. p. 393.
50. *The War on Powder River*, pp. 181, 190, 191.
51. *Fairfax Advertiser*, Feb 25, 1904. The Last Grass Frontier, pp. 209, 213.
52. *The Last Grass Frontier*, p. 209.
53. Bert Hall Collections, SD Archives, Lou Cagely (sp) notes. In 1900 a severe drought forced Dawson to move his cattle to the Westover-Keyapaha range of the Rosebud reservation. This was Jack Sully territory. His foreman traded a lump jawed steer to an Indian for some grazing at Westover and Dawson was able to secure the necessary permits to graze along the Keyapaha River in what is now Tripp County. It was shortly after the Dawson cattle were moved to this southeastern portion of the range that the Association appointed their "secret committee". See: RoundUp Years pp. 180-186. Jack Hudspeth aka "Panhandle Jack" was appointed brand inspector for the SDSGA in the winter of 1900 and stationed along the Keyapaha, no doubt to keep an eye on Dawson's cattle and Jack Sully. Nelson named "Panhandle Jack" Hudspeth as being one of the old timers who would best let bygones be bygones. See: RoundUp Years, p. 112.
54. Lyman County court records; *Roundup Years*, p. 244.
55. *Oacoma Gazette Leader*, May 19, 1904.
56. In re Nelson, 19 SD 214; 102 NW 885.
57. Ibid.
58. Hall, Bert L. *RoundUp Years*, p. 273. Ernie Gottschalk of Vale, South Dakota writes: "I have a photo of Kid Rich when he was much younger than his wedding photo and it was taken at Baraboo Wisconsin so I figured he was born in that area." Letter from Ernie Gottschalk 9-18-96
59. Lemmon, Ed, *Boss Cowman*, pp.184, 185, 187.
60. Ibid.
61. Hall, Bert L. *RoundUp Years*, p. 273. Letter of Agent Pollock to Indian Commissioner, 1879. Kansas City Archives.
62. Lemmon,Ed. *Boss Cowman*, pp. 184, 185, 187.
63. Hall, Bert L., *RoundUp Years*, p.306, Bert Hall Collections, SD Archives, Letter from warden Jamieson. Kunneke escaped in 1919 and was never apprehended.
64. Sandoz, Mari. *The Cattlemen*, p. 393. See also appendix 3.
65. Ibid. See also foot note 2 Dakota Death List?
66. *RoundUp Years*, p. 259. Ernie Gottschalk writes that the reason she removed the entrails was to allow a sister to come to the funeral. He also states that the entrails were placed in a copper boiler and buried by a ranchhand. Gottschalk letter 9-18-96 Narcelle always dealt in gold coin and buried it about his ranch. " My money in those days was always in gold. In half a dozen places around my house in 1850-1860 I had hidden 30 to 60 thousand dollars in gold." Winner Advocate October 3, 1912. On October 2, 1909, Narcelle was found dead along the trail after being thrown in apparent runaway. Those about to be robbed were known to have swallowed their gold. Local lore indicates this was a French way of outsmarting highwaymen. This is another explanation why his wife removed his entrails before burial. It is claimed that more gold has been buried in Frenchmen than exists in the rest of the world.
67. Siberts, Bruce, *Nothing But Prairie and Sky*, p. 100-110.
68. Schatz, A. H., *Opening a Cow Country*, p. 89.
69. Hall Bert L. *RoundUp Years*, p. 273.
70. Ibid p. 273.

CHAPTER TWELVE
RUSTLERS, FIGHTS AND STOCKGROWERS

Lyman County—rustling capitol of the world

The convergence of homestead honyockers, early squawmen, eastern cattle interests, 30 to 60 thousand trespassing, overpriced and over-mortgaged cattle, and starving Indians without annuities led to the inevitable.

Lyman County had over twenty six felony arrests for crimes relating to rustling in the space of a year and one half. Oacoma was, indeed, as the Stockgrowers stated: "vying with Johnson County, Wyoming as the rustling capitol of the world.[1]

Secret circle society

Jacob Harmon in his manuscript states: "A secret society or band of thieves at the forks of the White River had their headquarters there at a lonely store (Westover) that was run as a blind." Harmon relates that this was a secret "Circle Society" which included Myer Winter, his wife, Joe Demarsche and David Colomb.[2]

William Red Cloud Jordan corroborates Harmon's Story about the den of thieves. On December 25th, 1899 Myer Winter, who the Indians referred to as "Nakpatanka" or Big Ear, was charged with receiving stolen property being a steer and cow the property of Charles T. Jordan. William Red Cloud Jordan relates that John Bartine defended Winter who had been charged with 8 other rustling matters. He alleges that there was a secret "circle society of thieves" and although Winter was acquitted (for the ninth time) a message was delivered to him by the vigilance committee. Jordan also relates that Nels Nelson, brother of Olof and Carl, who had been charged with rustling was a member of the vigilance committee in Lyman County.[3]

Tom Milligan

The best evidence that Oacoma had become a bona fide cow town is shown by the February 7, 1894 notation of the Clerk of Courts that: "Tom Milligan and Frank Morgan were charged with disturbing the peace and breaking up a lawful assembly in the Hickey house (road house) and trying to shoot up the place."[4]

Milligan had come north driving Texas cattle. Mari Sandoz credits Tom Milligan and James (Murray) Dahlman for much of her knowledge about the Texas longhorn cattle which she related in her book, *The Cattlemen*. When she was a small child Milligan would stop and visit with her father, Jules.[5] Milligan also surfaces as a witness for the defense in an early horse rustling case in Tripp County, South Dakota.[6] Later he was hired as a horse thief detective by the Rosebud Sioux Agency. He was shortly discharged because he couldn't arrest his old friends. Milligan's life on the early frontier epitomizes the humor and tragedy of the west.

In March of 1876 in Custer, South Dakota, Milligan and his partner, Alex Shaw were both drunk and were taking target practice at an old bucket. Milligan missed the bucket and hit Shaw, killing him. Milligan mollified a lynch mob which had assembled by professing to be a free-mason in good standing . He was later fined $25.00 for discharging a firearm within the city limits and told to leave town.[7]

Wild cowboys

In 1882 "Jack" Foster trailed in from Texas. He and his Indian friend, "Running Water" rode into Oacoma and shot out all the gas lights. A posse was formed and came riding gallantly down the street to get Foster. He and his friend popped out from behind a building and the posse turned tail and ran.

This deeply impressed the locals and they asked him to be town marshall, but he must first whip the town bully, a half breed Mexican by the name of "Big Tony". Jack whipped him and became the town marshall.[8]

In 1894, Olof Nelson, Ole Finstead and a bunch of round up riders descended on Oacoma. The businessmen quickly closed shop. However when the cowboys arrived they had the saloon keeper open up and rode their horses into the saloon. Sheriff Putnam ordered the round up boys to throw up their hands. One drew a pistol and quieted the sheriff by shooting off the Sheriff's stetson. Two business men, Frank Martin and Jay Wellman, were ordered to pray and dance before the effects of "Fort Pierre" whisky quieted these cowboys down.[9]

The fight at George Pete's ranch

Violent fights also occurred between the Sullys, Kincaids, Colombes and others.

On a Sunday morning in 1894 an excited cowboy rode his worn out horse into Naper, Nebraska to fetch young Doctor Zimmerman to come to the George Pete ranch house on Pete's Creek in Gregory County, South Dakota.

A fight between rival groups of cowboys and Indians had taken place the night before at a dance held at the George Pete place. George Pete was married to Maggie Turgeon.

When Dr. Zimmerman arrived at the ranch it was the scene of a drunken, bloody brawl. The beds were covered with cowboys and Indians who were too seriously injured to ride away. Teresa Scissons, a young Indian girl, helped the Doctor. The first person they treated was Jesse Elleston, who was near death from knife wounds. The other mixed blood cowboys were treated and helped on their way.

For many years the mixed blood families refused to talk about the fight at Pete's ranch, referring to it as a "bloody camp".

A pretty half breed Indian girl who had recently been divorced was the cause of the battle. Her name was Emma (Shunk) Brughier and she had come to the dance with the Drapeaus, Billy Kincaid, and the Sully contingent.

Billy Kincaid had just turned 17 and was Jack Sully's step son. The Drapeaus were his first cousins and Emma Brughier had come to the dance with them.

At an earlier dance held in their territory along the Missouri, Emma had met Chris Colombe. Colombe had come to that dance alone and had fallen in love with pretty Emma.

The Missouri River boys had ganged up on Chris Colombe and had thrown him out of the dance hall, but not before he had made a date to see Emma at the George Pete dance.

Colombe invited all of his pals to go with him to the George Pete dance. The stage was set for the bloody brawl that was certain to happen. The Drapeaus were the musicians for the George Pete dance and they had brought all their salty friends from the Whetstone to Oacoma to witness the brawl.

The dance was in full swing but none of the wild bunch from the Missouri or the Rosebud bunch were dancing. They bellied up to the bar and refused to check any of their weapons.

As sure and as swift as lightning, Chris Colombe sashayed across the room and asked Emma Brughier to dance. All hell broke loose. Colombe was a big stout man and held his own, sheltering Emma behind his back. The Drapeaus laid down their instruments and merrily joined in the fray. Even young Billy Kincaid laid aside his violin and he and the Drapeaus drew their knives to join the battle. Mixed bloods fought to get inside and others fought to get outside. Colts were used as clubs and knives were slashing out in every fight. Soon the Drapeaus and Kincaid were fighting for their lives.

Frank Drapeau made a break for his horse and made his escape. Billy Kincaid found his horse but his saddle had been rigged by the "Rosebud faction" and he was knocked unconscious by a blow from the butt of a colt peace maker. When Kincaid regained consciousness he was made to return to the dance and play his fiddle with the other musicians or die.

Chris Colombe "kidnapped" Emma Brughier that night and rode off with her to his ranch.[10] At a similar dance on August 1st, Jack Sully shot his "son in law" Frank Waugh in the arm.[11]

The Somers double homicide

In early 1870s Jim Somers, Jack Sully and the Kincaids were frequent travelers along the old military trail to Chamberlain or Brule City. Somers was born in Canada and was a prominent figure in early Dakota history. He first settled in Union County in 1860. He was sergeant at arms in the first territorial legislature and was elected to the legislature from Union County.[12] Somers had a reputation as a fighter and drinker. In 1869 he stepped out of a bar in Yankton and shot a horse that was tied in front on the bar. Sheriff Black attempted to arrest Somers and for his efforts Somers shot the sheriff, crippling him for life. The sheriff was not well liked, and his enemies permitted Somers to escape and he settled in Brule City. Somers was appointed by the governor as a commissioner of Brule County and was elected to that office at the first election held in Brule county.[13]

Somers' death was a double homicide. Jim Somers' brother, Lafayette Somers, and his son Bradley were hauling wood from a piece of land he had filed on. Jim Somers had also filed on the same land and the two brothers were locked in a land claim contest which was still undecided. Lafayette had stockpiled some lumber for his house on the site and on the fatal day found that it had been taken. When he returned to the site with more supplies, Jim Somers came up to them with his rifle and shot Bradley. After he shot Bradley he pointed his rifle at his brother, at which time, Bradley, who would soon expire, fired two shots killing his uncle, Jim.[14] Brule County legend has it that Jim Somers was a 'highwayman' who worked the military road from White Swan to Brule City. It was reported that Somers, Sully, Doc Middleton, "Bobby" Burns and Jack Kincaid held up the stage in Pukwana township on the line connecting Yankton and Deadwood. One small man by the name of Black had supposedly offered to fight Somers and his agents. Somers "gave the little runt $10" to keep him quiet. Or so the story goes.[15]

Jim Somers had three wives. One and two were Indians and the third was a white woman named Christensen. He often addressed the territorial legislature on the "half breed" bill which would allow voting privileges to half breed Indians. Jim would be steadfastly in favor of the bill and would admonish his fellow legislators to go forth and multiply with the Lakota. Jim and others of the Somers family were buried at Brule city.[16]

E.W. Whitcomb's tale

Jacob Harmon's and Jack Sully's old friend E.W. Whitcomb relates one of the most bizarre fights and executions of the old west. Jennings hid in ambush, true western style, and shot Russel in the back, killing him. Jennings made his escape and hid out with the Arapahoes. An officer disguised as an Arapahoe accompanied by two Indian friends captured Jennings and brought him to Fort Halleck where he was tried and sentenced to death.

Fort Halleck didn't have any fit or proper apparatus to hang a man in the 1850s, but since they had previously killed a black orderly who had been accused of attacking a white girl, skinned him and tacked his hide to the post hospital wall-well-they sure knew how to improvise.

At the fort there was a rude scale device used for weighing heavy merchandise. It consisted of a simple forked log set in the ground with a long lodge pole used as a lever. In this instance the pole was eighty feet long and weighted at the butt by artillery log chains.

These enterprising enforcers of justice fastened a rope forty feet long to the pole and looped the end around Jennings neck.

Jennings last words were that if he had it to do over again he would still shoot the son of a bitch. He let out a cheer for Jeff Davis and the confederacy and the officer, as if on cue, gave the signal. The "sling shot'" contraption with the weighted end was set free and the heavily weighted pole sprang up with such force that Jennings body was thrown the entire length of the rope, breaking his neck.[17]

Rosebud shoot out

In the spring of 1880 the Rosebud Agency hired Jack Atkinson as chief herder and Bob Dyer, Jack Whipple, John H. Bordeaux, Dave Gallineau, Oliver Dion, James Wright and a Negro by the name of Blair as agency cowhands.[18]

In the same year they were subpoenaed to Deadwood to give testimony in Federal court.

On their return, the foreman, Atkinson, drunk and angry at being left by his crew for Deadwood came riding up, drew his pistol and tried to shoot Gallineau. After a second unsuccessful attempt, Gallineau drew his Winchester out of his scabbard and blew Atkinson out of the saddle, killing him instantly. The foreman was buried where he fell. Gallineau was taken to Deadwood, but no formal charges were made.[19]

John J. Bordeaux, the son of James Bordeaux, was named the new foreman. In a February blizzard many agency cattle drifted across the state line into Nebraska. Bordeaux took his crew to round up the cattle. They stopped at H. Casterline's "hog ranch", located just east of Fort Niobrara.

Outlaws, who had been foiled in their attempt to hold up the Army paymaster, burst into the hog ranch to rob the joint. The owner, who had already grossed $1200 for the night on "wine, women and song", grabbed a sawed off shotgun and opened up, wounding two of the three robbers. In the shoot out that followed John Bordeaux was struck in the head by a stray bullet and died.[20]

The fifth cavalry at Fort Niobrara joined in the hunt for the three desperadoes and Lt. Cherry was placed in command. During the search the unit split and Lt. Cherry was left with private Conroy and private Thomas W. Locke. Either Locke was in cahoots with the three desperadoes or he went berserk from too much drink. He wounded Conroy and shot and killed Lt. Cherry. He was later captured and sentenced to 18 years in prison.[21]

A posse of Rosebud cowboys helped in the search for the three men who had been responsible for the murder of Bordeaux. Oliver Dion, John Arcoren, Red Shirt, Swift Bird and Wizi trailed the three desperadoes to the Big White River near Westover, thence to the Presho area and finally to Ft. Pierre, SD.[22] The three outlaws were captured at Ft. Pierre and sent to Yankton for safekeeping. At Yankton they staged an escape. Private Johnson was shot and killed in the attempt. Dick Burr escaped and was never recaptured. Tedde Read was recaptured, tried, convicted and hung.[23] John Bordeaux is buried in the St Charles cemetery at St. Francis. His widow may have been the half breed daughter of General Alfred Sully.[24]

Murder on Phelps Island

There are several sources for our story. Jacob Harmon, who gave us some new insights into the history of early freighting and Indian fights also has much to say about the murder of Matt Matson. Harmon relates the following version of the murder: "There was an island located about 25 miles south of Chamberlain, on the Missouri River, which was called Phelps Island. Now, this island was covered with large cottonwood trees and among the large timber were cedars growing up which made a dense forest. This island was inhabited by Phelps and Shrader and Matt Matson and Christina Matson, a sister to Matt . . . so Phelps hired Shrader to kill Matt Matson . . . Phelps was a murderer himself. He killed a United States soldier in the mountains and broke jail and made his escape and afterwards killed a friendly Indian in Wyoming and then skulked back to the island where he was safe. He was a full blooded outlaw." Phelps and his friends used the island as a base for cattle and horse rustling.

Matt Matson was sitting in front of his cabin washing his feet at eveningtime, when shots rang out from ambush and he fell backwards into his cabin, fatally shot in the head. Christina pulled him into the house and tried to revive him. Staying with the Mattson's was a young orphan boy, George "Shorty" McDonald, about 10 years old. Little George walked 8 miles to a neighbor, Mr. Knowles, for help.[25] Phelps and Shrader were hunted down and arrested for the murder.[26] There may have been more to the murder than Harmon knew.

Perhaps Mattson was not only murdered but silenced as well. On December 23, 1893 Christina Matson had Phelps and Will Spaulding arrested for rustling.[27] Phelps was tried for the murder of Matt Matson and was found guilty. The Supreme Court of South Dakota heard the case on appeal and upheld the conviction. Phelps died in the Hanson County, South Dakota jail, while his appeal was being prosecuted.

Harmon had understated the heinousness of the crime. Henry Shrader, who testified he fired the fatal shot stated that Phelps had shot and killed persons on different occasions, giving particulars as to time, place, and circumstances and that no one had made an effort to prosecute him.

Shrader later testified Phelps made specific persistent efforts to induce him to commit the crime He offered a part of the island, a span of horses, harness and wagon if he would kill the Matsons, and made numerous assurances that no one would suspicion Shrader if he would use Phelps' gun and go right over to the house and "clean out the whole shooting match."

Phelps told Shrader, "You want to nail them-nail them. There ain't going to be any thing done to you. I am the man they will jump". Then "we can run things just to suit ourselves. We can run the Indian cattle here, the calves that they ain't branded and who the hell will know?" That night Shrader went to the west window where he saw George "Shorty" McDonald but not Christina and fired and killed Matt Matson.

The evidence disclosed that Phelps wanted all of the Matsons killed, Matt, Olin and especially Christina, who had him arrested the previous year for rustling. Imagine agreeing to kill three people for two horses, some harness, and a chance to go into partnership with Frank Phelps.

The island later became the headquarters for rustler Harry Ham. George "Shorty" McDonald, an orphan, would move to Winner and leave his property in trust for the children of Winner. McDonald field, a kids' playground, was purchased with the money from his estate.

Reservation problems

Two weeks after the Sioux "agreed" to the 1889 land session, the Secretary of the Interior ordered the beef issue at Rosebud reduced by two million and at Pine Ridge by one million pounds. All subsistence rations were also cut.

The early opening of the nine million acres in 1889 was made without survey or provision for the Indians or squawmen like Sully who were already living on the land. This caused them not only anger over the government breach of faith but also to take up whatever means available to them to live and survive. One stark difference was apparent. Sully was killed and most of the Indians charged with rustling were imprisoned. Finstad, Nelson, Ham and other whites charged with the same offense went free.

In the October 28th 1896 edition of the Chamberlain Democrat the paper reported that the former Fort Randall Reservation had been opened for settlement. The paper reported that little provision had been made for the people who already lived and made improvements on "their" land and conflicting claims would need to be settled.[29]

The liquor trade and lawlessness became so widespread along the Missouri in Charles Mix County, South Dakota that in 1875 President Grant closed the region to settlement. He, perhaps, was heeding the definition of General Sherman that an Indian Reservation was "a large group of Indians surrounded by a bunch of thieves". A commission was appointed to estimate the value of the improvements on the land that had been made by Campbell and others and to expel all the settlers, making the Indians trade exclusively with the licensees at the government forts. The Grant appointees were more scandalously corrupt than the thieves who operated the whisky ranches. Grant's order was rescinded by President Hayes on August 9, 1879.

The soldiers who were sent to keep the "whisky traders" from selling to the Indians were less than effective. They were, in fact, the "hog ranches'" best customers. M. T. McKay and Louis Obashaw operated a famous whisky ranch just above Wheeler. General Wilson, craving for a bit of the poison, crossed over the ice, got tipsy and started back toward the Fort Randall. Being more carefree and less observant he broke through the thin ice.

In peril of death the General fumbled in his coat, found the bottle of whisky and by a "dexterous throw and slide" propelled it to safety, exclaiming, "There you are safe anyway." The General was later rescued, but he put "first things first."[30]

The Chamberlain paper also reported that the large cattle companies were missing large numbers of cattle after their fall roundup. The paper stated:

"Last winter hundreds of animals belonging to the cattlemen on the White River strayed across the stream to the Rosebud and Pine Ridge Indian

Reservations, and, while many of them were recovered, there are still a large number of which no trace has thus far been found. A round up wagon is to be started out to hunt up the strays, if possible. It is probable that many of the missing cattle have fallen into the hands of "rustlers" and will never be found, while others may have been killed and eaten by Indians."[31]

No doubt the "good" ranchers who "rustled a few" survived to be admired and respected members of the community, while others were either killed, strung up or sent to the pen. Times haven't changed very much. In the 1960s, the late Judge Harold Gilchrist would relate that in Lyman County a white man and Indian lady were both charged with adultery, having participated in the same act. Needless to say the Lyman County jury found the white man innocent and convicted the Indian of adultery.

Hangings and peccadillos
agent my hed is good my heart is bad i shall di
wahacanka mani

In October of 1902, George Bear, a Lakota Indian, was charged with the murder of George Shaw, his step-son, and Edward Taylor, boss farmer, at the Ponca sub-agency near Bonesteel, South Dakota.

A quarrel over a load of hay near Bonesteel led to the death by hanging of George Bear. The newspaper report of the times reflects typical East River homestead feelings.

"The wife of Bear was formerly married to a man named Shaw. . . .. Her son, John Shaw lived on one of the quarter sections of land owned by her and when she married Bear, the latter demanded the hay raised on the place. John Shaw objected and despite Bear's protests sold several loads of hay to a liverman named Slaughter, residing at Bonesteel. Bear went to E. C. Taylor, government school teacher and assistant farmer, at Ponca sub-agency and made complaint. Taylor wrote to major McChesney, agent of the Rosebud Agency, who had the matter under consideration at the time of the murder."

"Bear, however, chafed at the delay and learning that Shaw was continuing to sell the hay, he borrowed a repeating shotgun from a man named John Kelley and at 4:00 o'clock on the afternoon of October 8, drove to Shaw's place on Ponca Creek. He found his stepson loading hay. Angered beyond all reason, Bear accosted him and wanted to know whether he intended to settle for the hay. Shaw, who was unarmed, gave an evasive answer, whereupon Bear raised his gun and shot Shaw in the back. The Indian rolled off the load of hay and lay writhing on the ground. Running around the stack Bear again fired a load of bird shot at close range, killing him. Bear then turned his gun on an Indian named Shorty Thigh, who with his wife and a son of the murdered man were near. Thigh ducked and the charge went over his head."

"The sight of blood aroused all the heredity ferocity of the Indian, and Bear immediately drove five miles to the little school house at the Ponca agency, where Taylor was engaged as teacher. Taylor had just dismissed the school for the day, and two Indian boys, John and Mato Milk, sons of a famous chief, were in the school house with him and Mrs Taylor."

Bear had met a Mr Klackner on the school grounds, who told him where Taylor was.

Bear walked into the school house and Taylor looked up and noticed the gun and said "Why hello George, been chicken hunting?" "Yes", he replied, "and here's another chicken I'll kill."

Bear shot and killed Taylor, who died instantly. Bear was arrested by United States Marshall John Petrie and brought to Sioux Falls for trial. A plea of not guilty was entered before Judge Carland. Pioneer attorney R.W. Parliman represented the defendant. Bear was tried before a jury who recommended the death penalty, which the judge imposed

Bear was incarcerated with Allen Walking Shield, who also was on death row. Shield took delight in teasing Bear. The night before Shield was hung he taunted Bear about the horrors of death by hanging.

After Walking Shield was hung, Bear made a will giving his land to his wife and requesting that on her death it be given to the John Shaw, Jr., the son of the murdered man. Bear respected John Shaw's wife. She gave Bear money to buy a suit for his hanging. George Bear was 34 years old. Old timers said he bore a remarkable resemblance to Brave Bear, the famous Indian desperado who was hanged at Yankton in the Territorial days.

Walking Shield had also made a will. A sense of his stoicism and humor are included in its provisions.

He wrote:

i am wahaxanka mani in big house at sioux falls depity he say to me wahacanka mani big cort say you die so i make wil like white man psica heraka you good man you shal hav my wagon 1 harnes and black mare i giv pejuhta duta he poor man my lotment and 1 issu cow i caff 3sters 1 white bul if he find him not 1 plow heka duta you 1 big liar and mak laff i giv you nue wagon at agency if you find him thar tasaye duta i giv you i1top bugy and white hors 40 acers land and my close wanyaninape win she was with my enemis she shal have not agent my hed is good my heart is bad i shall diwahacanka manipejuta duta if you bery me not tonoawanda shal hav lotment

R.W. Parliman petitioned President Roosevelt, asking that Bear's sentence be commuted to life imprisonment. Parliman had volunteered to fight in the Spanish American War when he was a 36 year old man with wife and children. He enlisted in "Grigsby's Cowboys". He was one of Roosevelt's "Rough Riders" and his petition for clemency was not a vain act. The request was denied, however, and in early December, 1902 Bear was scheduled to be hung.

The Mitchell Daily Republic of December 6, 1902 reported:

"Bear himself will warmly approve the action of the President, as he has steadfastly maintained since the crime was committed that he prefers to be hanged

. . . .. The action of the President will also be strongly approved by the hundreds of whites who are scattered throughout the Indian Reservations, where they occupy positions similar to that filled by Taylor and whose lives, unless the extreme penalty of the law is meted out to George Bear, would not be safe for an instance should some Indian, with an imaginary grievance . . . (seek) revenge upon those he regarded as enemies, but who really are his best friends."

"The misguided persons who attempted to have the sentence commuted have wasted their sympathy and must have overlooked the fact that Bear richly deserves hanging. . . .. His sympathizers also forget that Taylor was wantonly murdered before the eyes of his wife, who, abandoning the luxuries of civilized life for the purpose of (uplifting) the Indians. . . .."

"The bravery exhibited by Walking Shield, the Indian who was hanged here on October 24 last was surpassed by the nerve displayed by Bear. While the rope and black cap were being adjusted, Bear did not exhibit the slightest feeling or fear. Not even a quiver shook his form."

Bear was hung on the first Friday in December, 1902. At 9:16 he was officially pronounced dead. Rev. Mr. Holmes of the Episcopal church took charge of his body and accompanied it to his old home where internment was made in the Ponca Creek cemetery.

The local East River residents weren't all that civilized either.

On the day Bear was hung, George Ohruh, a local saloonkeeper, enraged at a stonemason named Bomberg chased Bomberg out of the saloon through the crowded streets with Bomberg seeking refuge in Judge Wait's courtroom. Court was in session, but Ohruh followed Bomberg into the courtroom and before the eyes of the judge and others pummeled Bomberg in true John L. Sullivan style.[32]

Judicial Murder?

Three Indians were hanged by the federal government in 1902. In addition to George Bear and Walking Shield, Two Sticks was hanged for the slaying of four cowboys on the Pine Ridge Reservation.

On February 3rd, 1893 four white cowboys were killed at a "herd camp" located six miles east of where White Clay Creek empties into the White River. So called "hostiles" from the Rosebud and Cheyenne Reservations lived there in tents. They were the families of Bull Eye and Short Bull.[33]

On February 4th the agent sent the Indian police to arrest the suspects. They fired on the camp of Two Sticks and killed his eldest son and dangerously wounded two others. Two fled but were then brought to the agency and were sent to jail in Deadwood.

Two Sticks and White Face Horse were visited by Floretine Digman, S.J. when they were recuperating from their wounds. They were not taken immediately to Deadwood, but were treated by the agency physician. Father Digman's first visit to the wounded men was on February 20, 1863.[34]

The agency physician reported that Two Sticks who had been implicated in the cowboys' murder had been brought to him and had been kept in the field hospital. White Face Horse had been shot through the knee joint and it was not deemed advisable to bring him to the agency. The physician left White Face Horse at the Indian camp under police guard.[35]

A reporter for the Black Hills Times fabricated a "confession" and Two Sticks was promptly convicted in the press.

Notwithstanding the fact that Two Sticks could not speak English and was still recovering from his wounds at Pine Ridge the reporter for the Black Hills Daily Times on Saturday, February 11, 1893 printed a front page "confession" he said he had gotten from Two Sticks. It is as follows:

"Me and friends dancing in sweat house, spirit say we white livered to allow whites to overrun us and steal our land. The spirit say-go out and drive white men off begin at beef camp. Then we put on war paint and bonnets and dance war dance"

The "confession" went on to say that the men were shot at Two Sticks' command and that they had done the Indians no harm.[36]

The "confession" was an obvious newspaper fraud.

On the 11th of February Two Sticks' son, Mark or Uses a Fight and his nephew, Nopa-Nopa were placed in the Deadwood jail.[37]

Other newspaper accounts of a different cause were squelched. The first case to be tried was of Nopa-Nopa with Judge Edgerton presiding. Newspaper reports stated that "the Indians had practically admitted to the crime". However, when witnesses were placed on the stand they offered no evidence of guilt. Judge Edgerton ordered the foreman to bring in a directed verdict of "not guilty." The jurors retired but refused to follow the court's direction. Nopa-Nopa was released on his own recognizance and returned to the reservation.

Thereafter several of the Indian suspects agreed to plead to manslaughter and testify against Two Sticks.[38]

In reporting on the conduct and attitude of the "hostiles" at Pine Ridge, just plain fabrication by the press was not uncommon. It sold papers and reporters sold stories, and besides they didn't have to leave town to "get" the story.

Following the Wounded Knee Massacre the assembled "war correspondents"-C.G. Seymour of the Chicago Herald, Mr. Roberts, St Louis Post Dispatch; W.F. Kelley, Nebraska State Journal; John Mc Donough, New York World; F.B. Clark of the Chicago Herald; G.E. Bailey of the Chicago Inter Ocean; John Burke, "Wild West"; Alf Burkholder, New York Herald; C.W. Allen of the New York Herald; Ed O'Brien of the AP; and other newspaper reporters wrote an outlandish, deceitful and despicable "novelllete" about Short Bull, the " Brigand of the Badlands". They called his band "Singing Toads", "Sniveling Curs", their women "Bad Breath" and other scurrilous and ridiculous names. The Chadron Democrat of January 15, 1891 published the novelette.

No doubt none of the reporters had ever met Short Bull or the other dancers encamped on the Pine Ridge. But the reports sold papers. It was also callous and untrue.

Sioux "uprisings" sold papers. They also sold soap. A national newspaper ad for Ivory Soap at the time jingled:

Instead of sending out a meal
Or sending agents out to steal,
I give domestic arts to teach.
A cake of ivory soap to each.
Before it flees the guilty stain
Will cease and dirt no more remain:
Twill change their nature day by day,
And wash their darkest spots away.
They'll turn their bows to fishing rods,
And bury hatchets in the sods,
In wisdom and in worth increase,
And ever smoke the pipe of peace;
For ignorance can never cope
With such a foe as Ivory Soap.

How would others desrcibe Short Bull and the Ghost Dancers? A missionary who had known Short Bull described him thus:

"Seeing the man and observing him closer I did not wonder that at the time of the Ghost Dance he had an electrifying influence over the Indians, middle sized, well built, now forty one years old, fine cut, vivacious eyes, sonorous and well sounding voice, witty, level headed, smart, amiable and social, conscious of his dignity-all qualities of a leader."[39]

That same missionary would be called upon to minister to Two Sticks during his trial and hanging at Deadwood.

Florentine Digman, S.J. like many of his contemporary Jesuits had fled from Germany and was assigned to the Pine Ridge and Rosebud Reservations. Like most, he kept a daily diary of his mission.

His diary account of the "Two Sticks" hanging, like his description of Short Bull bears telling:

The Diary

"Dec. 22-28th. Two Sticks prepared for death. . . ..Two of the suspected murderers were at once sent to Deadwood to jail and sentenced to the Penitentiary. The old man was allowed to stay on the reservation until the wound in his arm and shoulder blade, received by the Indian Police, had healed. He then was also sent to Deadwood, tried and sentenced to be hanged."

Father Digman sent a message to 'Two Sticks" via Phil Wells inquiring whether he wanted him to prepare Two Sticks for death.

"Mr. Wells, fearing that the old man might think that baptism might save him from being hanged, plainly told him: 'Blackbeard can do nothing for you, but prepare you for a happy death.'"

Digman went to Deadwood and met with Two Sticks to prepare him for baptism. The Jesuit asked Two Sticks' attorney, Mr. McLaughlin, a Catholic who had graduated from Georgetown, to speak plainly to him and tell him there was no hope that his baptism could spare his life.

On the 27th in response to a telegram from McLauglin and Digman, President Cleveland refused to commute the sentence to life imprisonment.

The diary continues:

"Two Sticks was very attentive to the instructions. As he time and again asserted his innocence, I made a point of it to impress him especially with the omnipresence and justice of God before who nothing was hidden and who would not forget anything. 'In the war with Crow Indians I have killed three men and taken their horses so among the Sioux I am a chief, but I never shot a whiteman.". . . .. His lawyer had told me that his own daughter-in-law and other Indians had made affidavits against him that brought about the verdict of the jury.". . . .. (In response) he indicated that 'I hate nobody. It was all lies, and they would be silenced, if I would get another hearing but I forgive them.'"

Digman writes "The woman asked by the judge for a long time gave no answers, chewing at her shawl, until scared by the anger of the judge she made statements fatal to Two Sticks."

That afternoon in the presence of Father Traynor of Deadwood and Mr. McLauglin he baptised Two Sticks.

"Dec 28th. Friday. Opening the door to go to Church I found on the porch the paper of the day. In large print the telegram from Washington 'THE PRESIDENT REFUSES TO INTERFERE'. . . ..Today you have to go. He took it with wanted resignation. The execution had been set for 10:00 a.m. To fill out the time left, I sang some of the hymns of the Sioux Language . . . He was in the best disposition. Whilst generally the jailbirds in their cages were noisy and loud, they were now as the word has it "mice still".

Just before 10 a.m. the jury came in and the death warrant was read. Asked whether he had anything to say he stated " My heart is not bad, but good (i.e. am not sorry but glad). I fear not to die because my heart tells me that I am innocent of a crime imputed to me. I have killed no whites; the other four have done it. I do not say so in hope to get free. I know that I have to die today. After my death the whites will know my innocence and will be shamed when hearing of it. Also my people will be ashamed and I think the Great Father himself, when hearing of it, will be ashamed. He raised his hands like to swear and began his death song (Aiciowanpi, the Sioux call it). He always had a veritable tenor voice, but on this occasions it was really pathetic. . . . (He stopped singing and then said) 'The Great Spirit has made all men alike. I have flesh and bone and a heart like whites. I love all and hate nobody . . . .. Now I want to shake hands with you the last time' He went around and shook hands with the jury and all present, last with Mr. McLaughlin and myself 'You have stood by me' he said 'to the end'. I will not forget you and coming to the Great Spirit will pray for you.'"

On the way to the gallows Two Sticks grabbed some straps and "took one of them like playing, made a loop, threw it over his head and tried to strangle himself . . . stepping to the iron cage where he tried to reach the end to the other Indians to signify that they should strangle him.

The priest and the bystanders stopped him and he was led away to the gallows.

He once more sang his death song and he was dropped down 7 and 1/2 feet and pronounced dead. Two Sticks was placed in a coffin and put on display at the mortuary. That afternoon Digman took his body to the Catholic cemetery and buried him."

Dec 31. Back to Holy Rosary Mission. The Deadwood papers were full of apprehension that the Indians were hidden in the woods and planned a raid to free Two Sticks. Was it perhaps fear of "judicial murder?[40]"

On December 28th, the Black Hills papers recounted in minute and specific detail Two Sticks' death. "At 10:37 the trap was sprung and Two Sticks body, his neck fractured, hung dangling at the end of a rope. Justice had been satisfied and the blood of four men, foully murdered, had been avenged."[41]

In an AP story of February 12, 1999 it was reported that a sacred pipe owned by Two Sticks was turned over to his descendants. The article reported that Two Sticks was executed after accepting responsibility for the deaths of four white men who were killed by members of his tribe.[42]

In fact Two Sticks proclaimed his innocence to the end. The accounts of the directed verdict in favor of Nopa-Nopa and the plea bargain given to the others charged, together with Digman's diary and the "fraudulent" confession reported in the Black Hills Times should have raised a reasonable doubt as to his guilt.

Phil Wells was one of the first persons at the scene of the four cowboys murder. Two Sticks had caused trouble for him in the past, they were not close friends.

Wells later wrote: "We found four cowboys lying dead. Two of them Roderick Royce and Bennet were employees of Ed Stenger, a well known stockman. James Bacon and William Kelly, the other two, were farm boys from Nebraska.

Snow had covered the ground the night before the murder. Four tracks, which led to the shack and back to the lodges of the murderers were visible in the snow. I am sure that Two Sticks was not present at the murder. I carefully inspected him afterwards. I found that his right leg, which was crippled, was drawn up and he had a stiff ankle, making it possible for him to step only on the tip of his toe. Had he been at the murder, I would have known it by his tracks in the snow, which were absent."[42]

Digman had it right when he noted in his diary that the execution was nothing less than "judicial murder".

Chapter Twelve End Notes

1. Lyman county court records, Kennebec, S.D.
2. Harmon Ms.
3. SDHC, *Eighty Years on the Rosebud*, Vol., 35 pp. 324-383.
4. Lyman county court records, Kennebec, S.D.
5. Sandoz, Mari, *The Cattlemen*, p.499.
6. State v Piper, Tripp County . This was an early use of the "It was the Indian that done it" defense. Piper testified that an Indian by the name of "Pettyjohn" had sold the horses to him. The Rosebud agent testified that there was no such named Indian enrolled on the reservation. Ironically, Joe Picotte of St. Francis S.D. states that his wife had a relative in the early times by the name of Peddicord or Pettyjohn, but no one knew about him as he was quite a bad character. Nebraska Senator Exon's father ran a hotel at Wheeler, South Dakota and was a witness for the prosecution.
7. *Yankton Press and Dakotan*, Mar., 24, 1876.
8. Bert Hall Collections, SD Archives. undated Mitchell Daily Republic clipping.
9. Bert Hall Collection, SD Archives, story of Mrs Crilly and Mrs Hickey.
10. The original story of the fight at the George Pete ranch was written by Eddie Herman Jr., a Native American who lived at Colome, S.D. He was a descendant of Antoine Herman who was the blacksmith at Fort Robinson and a Lakota woman. Eddie was one of Colome's great characters. In the dusty summer days of the depression Colome would come alive when the news would spread that "Eddie Herman's back in town". Something exciting was sure to happen. Eddie was related to Jake Herman and both were legendary rodeo hands and great storytellers. When Eddie's famous roping horse died he published an obituary for "Marion Nixon." Interviews with R.C. Stenson, Colome, S.D. and Pat London, Winner, S.D. 1992. The George Pete ranch is now the farm of Harlan Smizer. Much of the action took place in the barn. Jack Broome remembers dances held in the loft. The house has been moved to Burke, remodeled and is the home of Don Stevicks. The ranch is located in the Southwest 1/4 of Section 3 in Union Township, Gregory County, South Dakota, three miles east of Burke. George Pete married Maggie Turgeon. Letter from Jack Broome, Burke, South Dakota November 22, 1993
11. Court records, State v. Sully..
12. *Yankton Press and Dakotan*, Feb. 16, 1880.
13. Ibid.
14. Ibid.
15. SDHC, Vol. 10, pp. 147-149.
16. Bert Hall Collections, SD Archives, Joe Somers interview.
17. Wyoming Historical Collections, E.W. Whitcomb, Reminiscences of a Pioneer 1857-1869.
18. Bert Hall Collection, SDHS Archives, John H. Bordeau notes.
19. Ibid.
20. C.S. Reece Jr., *Murder On The Plains*, Published by the Cherry County Historical Society, Valentine Neb. undated.
21. Ibid.
22. Hall Collection, Bordeaux notes.
23. *Murder on the Plains*, infra.
24. Agnes Picotte interview, St. Francis, S.D. 1992. There appears to have been several John Bordeauxs and it is possible that Ella Deloria's mother was married to a cousin of the John Bordeaux who was killed at the Casterline hog ranch. The other John Bordeaux was an accomplished musician who had been sent to St Louis at an early age. His life was claimed by the Missouri river, when he fell through the ice in winter.
25. Harmon Ms.
26. S.D. Democrat (Chamberlain). May 5, 1893; June 1, 1893. The paper states that "Jack" Foster was one of the officers who made the arrest and that the Island is also known as Dry Island.
27. Brule County clerk of courts files.
28. Lyman County v State 69 NW 601. The Phelps case was tried in Alexandria S.D.

29. *Chamberlain Democrat*, Oct. 28, 1896.
30. *Peterson's Atlas of Charles Mix county.*
31. *Chamberlain Democrat*, Oct. 20, 1896.
32. *Mitchell Daily Republic*, December 2 and 6, 1902.
33. University of Marquette Archive. *History of St Francis Mission 1886-1922* (includes material from Holy Rosary Mission) Reverend Floretine Digman,S.J. pp 42-44
34. Ibid. Digman reported that White Face Horse was treated at the Indian Camp and that the bone splinters in his knee had been removed with bear claws.
35. Report of the Physician, Pine Ridge Agency, July 8, 1893, Sixty Second Annual Report of the Commisioner of Indian Affairs, 1893.
36. *Black Hills Daily Times*, February 11, 1893.
37. Ibid.
38. *Wakonda Monitor*, January 4,1895.
39. *History of St. Francis Mission 1886-1922* Reverend Floretine Digman,S.J. pp 49.
40. *University of Marquette Diary of Reverend Floretine Digman*, S.J. pp 49-52
41. *Custer Chronicle*, Januray 5, 1895, Wakonda Monitor January 4,1895.
42. *North Dakota History Vol. 5 No. 4*, October 1948.

CHAPTER THIRTEEN
MYTHS AND MYSTERIES

In a paper written for the South Dakota History Conference of 1980, Col. Richard Cropp relates the following legend:

Jack Sully had visitors at the Davison County jail. The only name my mother mentioned was Kincaid (Billy Kincaid, the stepson of Sully?). Sully sawed his way out of jail and went to the barber shop for a shave and a haircut. With his face buried under hot wet towels, he heard the sheriff enter with his press gang, collecting a posse to pursue his escaped Sully. He wanted everyone. Sully, well muffled by towels, begged off, saying he had just got to town after a long absence and wasn't eligible as he was not a Davison county resident. The sheriff let him off and Sully made his way to his old haunts.[1]

In the April 1947 issue of True Magazine, another amusing story of Sully's escape and hiding out from the law was told. The author of the article, Hy Downing, had met G.A. Waitt, livestock broker, at a South Dakota reunion in California. The tale that Waitt related to Downing is reflected in letters found in the Sully file at the South Dakota archives in Pierre.

Waitt states that Deputy Marshall Petrie harbored Jack Sully in his home after Sully broke jail at Mitchell. He and Jack and others played poker at the Marshall's home and Petrie impressed on him that if there was ever a Federal warrant issued he would bring him in.

A Federal warrant was issued for the arrest of Jack Sully when the agent at Crow Creek reported that Charlie Long Turkey had identified Sully as one of the persons who had run off 50 steers from that reservation. Waitt states that the posse stayed the night at the Harry Ham ranch before proceeding to Sully's.[2]

Charles L. Nelson of Academy left the following interview of his recollections of Sully's escape.

"About the time that Sully was getting a bad reputation he was in with Harry Ham and some others on the west side of the river. The sheriff of Lyman County arrested him, moved him to the Chamberlain and then the Mitchell jail."

Harry Ham and others, he claims, were supposed to look after him and go his bail, but Harry did nothing to bail Jack out. He was told that along about Christmas of 1903 a fellow stopped at Jack Boland's leading a horse with a fur coat strapped to it. A day or two later Jack was back riding that horse and wearing the fur coat. Nelson says that Ham knew which way Jack would try to escape and posted himself on that route to make sure that Jack was killed.[3]

Perhaps the most stylized and fictional story of Sully's death is found in an issue of True West magazine. The magazine mistakenly places his home as on the "head of Ponca Creek, west of Bonesteel and in the Tripp-Gregory county line area." The story also lists Jack as of French ancestry and "a product of the lower east side of New York, like Billy the Kid."

The author claimed that Sully "pillaged settlers right and left, raiding settlements, stealing whatever he could from them and the outlying lonely ranch houses", and that Jack had a 100 yard long tunnel, which was dug from his stable to some dense brush, which was used for escape.

The True article also claimed that Marshall Petrie headed up the posse and that it left from Bonesteel, and was guided by Diamond "who was a wonder for he disregarded all trails and avoided the Indian villages with their barking dogs that would have warned the dwellers at once of their approach." A wonder indeed, if they were guided to Sully's home on Ponca Creek on the Tripp County line. In fact Sully's home was located on the upper Whetstone northeast of Burke, South Dakota some 20 miles from where this "wonder" of a pathfinder had led his charges.

The intrepid author, no doubt not knowledgeable of the ribald language of the west, quotes Marshall Petrie as shouting to the fleeing Sully: "Stop, Jack Sully! Stop in the name of the law! Give yourself up peaceably and no harm shall come to you. Stop I say!"

Sully refused to stop and the author continues, "With the distance rapidly widening, when Sully raised up in the saddle Marshall Petrie took careful aim and fired. The pony stopped and Sully fell to the ground. This scene was viewed through glasses by a Mr. Fred Lee.[4]

Another legend that has arisen in his old haunts is that Sully was a distinguished college graduate and was an undercover agent for the government who was killed because he had found the "rustlers' mole" in the law officer's ranks.[5]

This legend may persist because Jack Sully at one time lived on Cedar Creek on the Lower Brule Reservation and it is reported that he had worked for the Lower Brule Tribe. Reports about Cedar Creek can be confusing since there is a Cedar Creek near Fort Randall and also a Cedar Creek near Big Bend. The early records of Lower Brule were destroyed in a fire. However, early settlers recall seeing Jack and Mrs Sully driving their rig into Ft. Pierre, so one may assume that he did live for a time at Cedar Creek on the Lower Brule reservation.

None of these accounts have much basis in fact, except for the account of Charles Nelson. They do, however, reflect the amusing mythology that has arisen about Jack Sully.

Who shot Jack Sully?

Jack Sully was shot by the only person in the posse who was not a regular lawman. Jesse Brown related to Hall that neither he or Petrie fired a shot.[6] John Boland relates that "Petrie was interested in taking Sully alive but someone in the posse evidently was interested in getting Jack out of the way and fired a long range rifle shot that ended an eventful career."[7]

So who was interested in getting Jack "out of the way!? Who and what did Jack know about when he was killed? At or prior to the death of Sully, Joe Blackbird, Joseph Fallas, Carl Nelson, Olaf Nelson and John Dillon were arrested for grand larceny of livestock.

Ole Finstad had been arrested for grand larceny of horses in 1898. Lime Somers was arrested for the arson of the Senn print shop at Iona, S.D. at about the same time.[8]

In 1948, Carl Nelson, wrote to Bert Hall about Jack Sully and the early days: "Fifty years is a long time to go back in memory. Most of the old fellows that we knew are gone, as Harry Ham, John Dillon, Lime Somers, Billy Kincaid (Sully's stepson).

"Joe Somers is still in Chamberlain, Fred is around Spearfish, Joe Blackbird went to Canada, Billy Pressler is in Wyoming, Jack Hudspeth in Sioux City, John Ham holds out at Chamberlain. Had a recent talk with Al Fulwider and we think it best not to stir up some of the old troubles of the dim past, but let the oldtimers sleep in peace."[9]

Olof Nelson and Ole Finstead were the last two persons to visit Sully prior to his escape. It appears that Olof Nelson was tried for rustling, and Finstead was involved in the "Blackbird" affair.[10]

At the turn of the century 29 head of livestock were rustled in Charles Mix County, South Dakota. Sully was instantly blamed. Only William Vincent and Cyrus House were charged with the crime. The evidence against both men was identical. On appeal the attorney for Vincent stated that the jury decided to bring in a verdict of guilty against Vincent and not guilty against House for the reason that Vincent had sufficient financial means to appeal and have the verdict set aside and that House was too poor to appeal. Accompanying the verdict was a petition from the jurors requesting that the judge inflict the lightest possible sentence.[11]

In commenting on Sully's death, the Editor of the Charles Mix County News of May 19th, 1904 stated: "He was not shot by Mr. Petrie but by another member of the posse. He was accused of many crimes some of which he was no doubt guilty of. Jack was a well known figure to the earlier settlers of the county. He used to make Castalia his trading point and in the earlier settlement of the State was not considered such a desperado as of late years."[12]

Olaf Finstead wrote to Bert Hall: "No doubt those referred to the other side on occasion included Nelson bros., John Dillon, Joe Blackbird, Jack Sully, Billie Kinkaide and others. To give a true account of past events, would mean exposing at this time, who burned Judge Bartine's law office in Oacoma; the attempted burning of the Court house at Chamberlain; why John Ham turned states evidence . . . . . Who shot Jack Sully? Who was most concerned in getting rid of him and why? . . . ..[13]"

Who did burn Bartine's law office? Why did the county officers of Lyman County physically fight over the possession of county documents? Why did Bartine fight with Gregory County States Attorney over who would have first chance to prosecute Olof Nelson?

What kind of men were John and Harry Ham, the sons of Watson Ham, an early settler in Charles Mix County? We know that John Ham had been charged with cattle rustling both before and after the killing of Jack Sully. Did they burn the Chamberlain court house? Bartine's law office? Who put the croton oil in the jurors' meat when the Hams were on trial?

In the early morning hours of June 13th, 1901 fire was discovered in the Old Rink building in Chamberlain, which was used as the Brule County court house. The building was entirely destroyed.[14] The same issue of the paper reported the case of State v. John Ham was called for trial and it was four in the afternoon when the jury was finally selected. On account of the court house burning, Judge Smith called court for the opera house, however a juror, W.A. Williams was sick and the matter was adjourned.[15] (the croton oil sickness)

The same paper reported on August 9th 1900 the following story that shows the character of the man who legend says shot Jack Sully:

"Last week Harry Ham swore out a warrant against Miss Cora Knowles of Lyman County charging the fair defendant with the crime of cattle rustling. The preliminary hearing began Saturday before Justice Barlow of Oacoma and continued four days.

"The only testimony introduced was on the part of the prosecution, and at the conclusion of the presentation of that side of the case, on motion for attorneys for the defense, the same was dismissed. In the minds of the public generally, this looks like a case of devilish persecution as everyone (who) knows the Knowles family knows very well that they are good, respectable people. Miss Knowles is a young lady of the best character, is modest, educated and refined, and is in every respect just the opposite from what a young lady guilty of rustling would likely be. She is the daughter of Charles Knowles who formerly lived near Kimball and the many friends of the family in Brule county will be glad to hear of the dismissal of the case, although they regret that the young lady should have ever been brought to court, on what appears to have been purely spite work."[16]

I.N. Auld, the former States Attorney and father in law of (later to be Attorney General and Governor of South Dakota) M. Q. Sharpe, was roasted in the press for having been the rustlers' bought and paid for mouthpiece. Offices were burned, people falsely accused, pay-offs made for witnesses to get sick or get lost.[17]

Peter Dierks, Deputy Clerk of Courts, accused States Attorney Bartine of assault. He alleged that States Attorney Bartine attempted to take certain court papers from him by force.

"(He) got a hold of both of my hands put his foot around my legs, throwed me backwards, put his knee on my chest and with one hand he choked me and with the other attempted to get the court papers." Bartine later went to Gregory County and fought with States Attorney Milner over the possession of Olof Nelson.[18]

The Pinkerton detective agency often searched the border towns of the recently opened South Dakota settlements for their most wanted fugitives. Tom Horn was known to frequent the area.[19] At Bonesteel, S.D. at the southeastern edge of Gregory County the city officials sold concession rights to gamblers, fakirs and con men to raise money for their new city. They got more than they bargained for when a vast array of dangerous underworld characters assembled there for the drawings that would open the county for homestead. By the 20th of July, 1904 (a few months after the shooting of Sully) the crooks had become so insolent that they were running the city and the folks who sold the concessions were running for cover.[20]

In the heat of the summer, all hell broke loose. On July 20th an organized effort headed by the "respectable" gamblers was organized to drive the "undesirable" gamblers from town. The two armed forces met on the main street in the "Battle of Bonesteel". Many shots were exchanged and the "bad" element was driven from town, but not before Kid English was gunned down.[21] Gambling, hard drinking, fighting, easy women, con artists, in fact all pleasurable illegal activities were rampant in the newly opened counties of Lyman and Gregory.

In 1901 Jack Sully's brother-in-law, Joe Blackbird, was charged with the crime of grand larceny in Lyman County, in that he did, take, steal, and carry away 34 steers, cows and heifers all bearing the brand OF on the left side of the value of $700.00 and which were the property of Ole Finstead (Finstad). Among the witnesses named were Nels Cleven, Wash Leedom, M.P. Covey, O.E. Finstead, Charles J. Kinsey, E.W. Blakley (the Western South Dakota Stockgrowers' top gun who previously had shot it out with Kid Rich at Hot Springs), Jack Boland (A former river boat man who had run a store at White Swan and knew Sully intimately), C.B. Abourezk, Charles Seamen, Levi Mitchell, J.B. Strong, John Foster, D.M. Church, Charles Clayton, Ed McKay, John Ham (the states evidence man), and Mary Leedom. The court records indicate that Blakely did most of the investigating.

The mortgage records of O.E. Finstead were subpoenaed for examination and they revealed that O.E. Finstead was the mortgagor and R. Becker and Deegan of Sioux City were the mortgagees. Blackbird was released on bond, his bondsmen being Olof Nelson and Harry Ham. (the same Harry Ham that legend says shot Jack Sully).[22]

Why would Ole Finstead go to Canada and many years later write that what he had done was to ensure his right to live if he had not been in complicity with others on the brand alterations? The presence of Blakely, who was a top gun for the Stockgrowers Association, indicates that the pressure of eliminating rustling in the area may have reached the point where the end might justify the means as it had in Tom Horn's Wyoming or Kid Rich's South Dakota.

Adolph Stamer, who put together the Mulehead Ranch (which included over 47,000 acres in Gregory, County) for the Jackson Brothers, wrote: "Yes I know a great deal about Jack Sully. The hospitality of the Sully home has been extended to me many times . . . .. As you know, Mr. Hall, there are two sides to all questions, and only in the final date will the merits and the virtues of all acts be known."[23] Sully's character and reputation, from the time of his birth, to his death, was such that no man could state that he was mean tempered or a physically violent man. His neighbors respected him, his wife and family. He was not known for violence or for the commission of violent crimes.

None of the "oldtimers" who knew Sully disliked him and the only words of damnation were from the big time operators like Ed Lemmon. Those who knew the facts about his death kept their mouths shut preferring to let the "oldtimers rest in peace."

The only record of his use of a firearm was against a son in law. On August 5th 1900, Sully was charged with assault with intent to kill Frank Waugh who married Sully's stepdaughter. He was arrested without incident and the charges followed the orderly process of the law. Sully was discharged and the matter was not brought to trial.[24]

The following incident aptly describes the character of the Sully family. After her husband's murder, Mrs Sully visited at the home of Harry Smith of Kennebec, South Dakota. Smith had visited Sully when he was in jail in Mitchell. When Mrs. Sully visited him she noticed a fine black horse that he used as a driving horse. Mrs. Sully stated that she had a dead mate for the horse and had it sent to Smith as a gift.[25]

The generosity of Mrs. Sully after Jack's killing was a continuation of what Sully had done for his friends and neighbors while he was alive. Ole Severson, the father of the late Harold Severson DVM of Winner, South Dakota, recalled that when he (Ole) was a child, Jack Sully had given him a pony which bore the Sully brand. Later one of Sully's children saw Ole with the branded pony, gently lifted him down and took the pony home to Jack Sully. The next day, Ole relates, the pony was returned, as directed by Jack Sully.[26]

Walter Ashley of Dixon states that Jack Sully and his partner had stolen some Indian horses up north and had driven them as far as "Red Rock" along the Missouri River, just south of Landing Creek, when Jack's horse went lame. They were being followed by five or six horsemen. They rode double to the river where they floated downstream to Cedar Island. They then made their way to the Drapeau place where they were taken care of by friends.[27]

Olaf Finstad wrote: "I do not look back on my younger days, as living the life of a criminal, but as one who took part in a battle to protect our right to live." Since most of the cattle in the White River valley were mortgaged beyond value one may infer that the 75 head for which Sully was arrested were rustled with the consent of the owners.[28]

The ever zealous editor of the "Iona Pioneer" reported on May 19th, 1904 that (Sully) and others ran off 75 steers on the Rosebud, belonging to Montgomery and Schilling, and Harry Ham, Jewell, Dillon (all cattlemen in the valley) and others. One of the gang worked a tenderfoot from Illinois to go into partnership to buy the stock and Jack brought the stock in. Federal warrants were issued for Sully and others and U.S.Marshall Petrie, Sheriff Irish of Brule County, brand inspector Long, and the Deputy Sheriff Brown of Lyman County were joined by Harry Ham at Iona, South Dakota.[29]

On the day that Sully was shot Ole Dahl brought him his mail and he was visited by a John Hudson. A neighbor, Ben Diamond, rode over to tell him that the officers were coming for him and that he should give himself up.[30] Jack was soon out saddling his favorite steed, but instead of riding out to meet the officers who were coming from the Diamond ranch, he turned his mount to the ravine to the southwest which would lead him into the Whetstone breaks. Hid in ambush were the other possemen armed with rifles. When Sully came riding by, if halt orders were given, they were not heeded. The horse was hit four times and lived and one shot fatally injured Jack in the back. Petrie, who had wanted to take Jack alive, came on the scene after the shooting had been done.[31]

If Finstad assures us that in his youth he was not a criminal and only protecting his right to live, his honor may have been restored if he had included Jack Sully within the same apology. There were other letters from Finstad that were unpublished. Might they state that there was another side to Sully's death?

Were Jack's "friends" anxious that his testimony be totally suppressed? Did the stock agents want an "example" after their many defeats in Lyman County? Perhaps the "round up" system of the open range, the branding of mavericks only by the large interests and the economics of time and place was, as some have said, "guaranteed to make outlaws out of angels."

Jay Seath, an early cowboy on the Rosebud, wrote that Becker and Deegan would sell to anybody who had a water right. They filled the White River valley from its mouth to the forks of the Little White (north of present town of White River) with mortgaged cattle. Becker and Deegan overpriced the cattle and required that all of the cattle had to be shipped to their firm when ready for sale. The cattle were of poor quality and some ranchers just let the cattle go and the company had to do quite a bit of hard gathering, perhaps using what the trade termed cowboys with "extra responsibilities" whose duty it was to round up "slicks" from any place they could.[32]

Hall, in his book *RoundUp Years*, had other correspondence relating to Sully from Olof Finstad that said there was another side to Sully's killing. Such letters would be invaluable. Unfortunately Hall did not include them in his book. He did relate, however, that such letters and interviews indicated that when the big roundups went through, some stragglers were left behind in secluded breaks with the help of those doing the rounding up (who were probably the ranchers like Finstad, Ham and others who were bringing their mortgaged cattle in at Becker and Deegan's command) and the big bunches moved on to market and the "helpers" like Finstad and Ham returning with their friend Jack Sully to rustle their own mortgaged stock. There is no doubt that the big operators treated all cattle on "their range" as their own and would round up "honyockers'" stock with impunity. The problem was that the big operators paid the stock detectives and the hired guns and the "honyockers" survived with their wits, went to the penitentiary, Canada, or took a bullet in the back. Hall's collections were given to the S.D. Archives. None of the letters from Finstead are in the file. Why are they missing?

In researching the charges that were pending against Olof Nelson in Gregory County for his involvement in the Blackbird case all that was found was a docket entry and all of the papers that were filed are missing. Why were they stolen from the courthouse? Would the missing letters and court files prove the Gregory

County legend that others were involved who did not want Sully to tell what he knew?

A neighbor, Joe Ellis, best describes Jack Sully.

"Jack was not a bad fellow; there were worse men in the country than him, but they were lucky enough to escape the law. They persecuted Jack, and because of spite, never left him alone. He was a good fighter, a game fellow and a better friend no one ever had."[33]

Contemporaneous newspaper accounts

The editor of the Oacoma-Gazette leader knew that the life and death of Jack Sully was legendary and momentous. He knew it was a big story and wrote a detailed account of the death of Sully and the "lawless" element of Lyman County.

Jack's friends, Jack Kincaid, Bobby Burns, Jim Somers, Jim Foster, Lame Johnny, Big Nosed George, had with the exception of Burns and Kincaid died violent deaths. Burns of course was a notorious escape artist, who had started life studying for the priesthood. Kincaid is reported to have died from cancer, but his grave has never been found and some have said that he turned up in Montana and worked for other ranchers who reported that he could "shoot the head off a rooster with a six gun".[34]

Sully of course was dead, shot in the back by the man who was supposed to go his bail. Jack, after his escape, "rustled" some of Ham's cattle, no doubt to pay him back for breaking his word. The editor thought that with the death of Sully Oacoma would prosper. Instead it would wither into nearly nothing. The legend of Jack Sully would live on.

The editor's minute record of the death of Sully and his precise account of the criminal cases that were tried and dismissed as a result of his death are hereafter quoted at length because they reflect the "reformer" attitude and mark the end of the era of tough trail herd cowboys who came north with a new name, seeking glory and adventure.

The OACOMA GAZETTE-LEADER of May 19th 1904 reported:

JACK SULLY GOES TO HAPPY HUNTING GROUNDS.

"Since stealing the Schilling and Ham cattle the United States have been after Jack Sully. Deputy Marshall John R. Petrie planned an expedition last week which was the means of bringing the notorious cattle rustler to terms. He associated with him Jesse Brown, Sheriff Irish of Chamberlain, and stock inspector A.P. Long and the sheriff of Davison county. It is reported that they found Sully Monday and as he did not surrender was brought to the ground after his horse had been shot from under him. The coroner has gone to that section. We will get details later."

"Later: We learn that Jack Sully was making his way into his cave when he was shot. He was too close to allow him more time, and hence the authorities were forced to shoot him. Had he succeeded in getting in the cave where he was fortified, he would doubtless have made it warm for the officers. He lived 35 minutes after he was shot, and never uttered a word to the officers. Thus he leaves no clue to evidence those associated with him in the business."

In the same issue of the paper it was reported that:

SULLY AND HIS ASSOCIATES STEAL 72 HEAD OF CATTLE.

"Schilling and Montgomery have kept cattle on the Reservation for several years under the firm name of the Canadian Cattle Co., and used the bar X brand and the DH connected. Some of these cattle have been stolen from time to time. But one of the most famous steals that have taken place recently was that one engineered by Jack Sully, the notorious cattle thief. Sully was associated with a white man by the name of _____ and a mixed blood by the name of Frank Drapo (Drapeaux). Along with the Schilling cattle Sully stole four belonging to a Mr. Diamond, a resident of the reservation. There was also some of the pitchfork cattle belong to the Ham Bros and some belonging to Teen Fenenga of Iona. There were seventy two head of these cattle taken by way of Napir (Naper) Nebraska on April 5, 1904 and there remained for some hours in a corn field. From here they were taken to the Niobra (Niobrara) river and there held until sold. Sully had associated with him a confederate who gave a note for part payment of the cattle and a new man in that county was roped into paying $1000.00 for those stolen cattle and the accessory who gave the note undoubtedly got his share of the money after the deal was closed. Sully did not do the selling himself but had his white associate do the dealing for him.

He and his breed partner went home by way of the Niobora (Niobrara) river. The stolen cattle were located by Ed Blaikey (Blakely), stock inspector for the Western Stock Growers Association at Bonesteel . . . .."

In a November 5, 1903 edition of the Lyman Co. Record (E.L. Senn, editor) it was reported that the Sheriff had taken up a bunch of 30 head of Canadian Cattle Co. cattle and was going to sell them for non payment of personal property taxes.

The Editor of the Oacoma Gazette Leader wrote a lengthy account of the life and death of Sully in the June 16th edition of his paper. The full story, which reflects the bias of the editor is included because it reflects all of the aura about Jack Sully.

"Chamberlain SD—The circumstances leading up to the tragic end of the notorious desperado, Jack Sully, who for many years has been the terror of the Rosebud country are these: A week or ten days ago Sully stole a bunch of nearly 200 cattle belonging to various neighboring ranchers. He took a bunch of seventy four down across the Nebraska line and sold them for $20 per head, receiving half cash and half paper. He cashed the paper. Soon after Brand Inspector Long got track of the cattle, and accompanied by their owners, Harry Ham and Hugo Schilling, recovered them and returned them to the home range.

"As a result of the exploit United State Commissioner Tidrick of Chamberlain, on Sunday morning sent out Deputy United States Inspector (Marshal), Brand

Inspector Long, Sheriff Irish of Brule County, Deputy Sheriff Jesse Brown of Lyman County to bring Sully in dead or alive.

"They found Sully at his home, near Blackbird Island, on Tuesday morning and attempted to make the arrest. Sully was ordered to surrender but with a defiant taunt he made a break for his horse, sprang upon its back and made a dash for liberty." "For a time a running fire was maintained between the two parties, but the pursuers speedily proved the victors. Sully's horse was hit five times and killed, while Sully received wounds from which he died within thirty five minutes."

"Sully for the past thirty five years has been known as lawless and desperate character. His most recent exploit was to break jail at Mitchell, where he was being held on a charge of cattle rustling and until Monday the officers had not set their eyes on him."

"He has for years been recognized as the head of a band of rustlers that has been the cause of endless trouble and expense to the thrifty class of people who have of late been coming into the neighborhood, and his tragic end is not likely to cause very deep mourning upon the range."

"The Sully gang has been credited with having stolen, during the past twenty years a total of about 50,000 head of cattle and several thousand head of horses, but it is reasonable to suppose that this estimate is somewhat exaggerated."

"Nevertheless, it is safe to say that several thousand head have been stolen by the thieves during that period. The gang is also said to have been responsible for the death of seven men during the long period it was carrying on its operations along the Missouri River. The victims were chiefly inoffensive settlers, who, unfortunately for them, were foolish enough to protest when some of their cattle were stolen, or who were so indiscreet at to reveal incidents connected with cattle and horse stealing raids which by chance came under their observation."

"Sully's career naturally has been filled with interesting incidents. He first made his appearance at the Northern Pacific crossing (Now Bismarck, N.D.) in 1872 and was at that time a chum of Jack Kincaid, who killed his own sister at a country dance in Missouri. Kincaid tried to kill the fellow with whom his sister was dancing, but she sprang between the two men just in time to receive in her own body the bullet which was intended for her companion."

"Only when Kincaid was on a drunk with Sully would he ever mention the killing of his sister. "Bill" Reese, another of Sully's old time chums was shot and killed in his own dance hall at Miles City, Montana by Dr. Lefcher. The men quarreled over the affections of "Dode" Reese, supposed to have been the wife of "Bill" Reese, who after the death of Reese, lived with the slayer of the man who was her husband."

"Jim Foster, a character well known on the frontier twenty years ago, was another chum of Sully's. Foster was an accomplished banjo player, and many people who yet reside in South Dakota remember the devil may care fellow, who at intervals would visit the frontier towns for the purpose of having a glorious drunk, during which he was invariably accompanied by his banjo."

"He had a remarkably fine voice. *I'll remember you, love in my prayers*, was a favorite song of his, with which he was wont to entertain such residents of the frontier town as cared to appear upon the streets when himself and his drunken companions virtually had possession of the thoroughfares and the buildings adjacent thereto."

"One of Foster's characteristics when drunk was to light his cigars with $5 or $10 bills."

"He, like many of the former friends of Sully, "died with his boots on". He was a handsome man, a veritable Adonis, and was a perfect specimen of physical manhood, yet by nature was endowed with many of the traits of the Indian, being considerable of a sneak and coward."

"While on a hunting trip to the Black Hills with several boon companions he was shot and killed. The members of the party declared that he was the victim of the accidental discharge of a gun, but there is little question that he was shot down by one of his companions who had a grudge of some kind against him, and feared that if he did not resort to assassination, Foster, himself, would assassinate him when the opportunity offered."

"Sully was also a chum of "Lame Johnny", "Big Nose George" and a man named Gray who were all noted "hold up" men during the early days of the Black Hills." Big Nosed George was hanged by a Vigilance committee at Rawlins, Wyoming; "Lame Johnny" met the same fate and Gray was terminated by a Vigilance committee in Yankton, S.D."

"The killing of the masterful rustler removes a border character for which there probably has not been a parallel in the United States for some time. He was not a blood thirsty criminal of the dime novel variety, but an honorable man in his way."

"He was true to his friends, and not given to bloodshed if it could be avoided. If allowed to prosecute his vocation of stealing without molestation, he would molest no others."

"The exact time when Sully came to South Dakota is not known, but it was at least thirty years ago. He was a tall rawboned young man, who said nothing about his past and gave a name which is known to have been assumed."

"It was not long after he came that he built his hut on a high hill on the Rosebud reservation. Here he was surrounded by a crowd of loose characters with whom he easily carried on a big rustling business. As the civilization of the country drew closer about him, a more perfect defensive organization was necessary. Sully was equal to the demand upon him. He organized a secret society which last winter was known to have a membership of 800, extending all the way from Kansas to Canada. Many of these were ranchmen and stockmen in good standing. The strength of the society lay in the fact that no one knew who were its members. A campaign against them could not progress far without someone not known to be a member, sounding the warning."

"Sully was a squaw man too, and four half-breed daughters married and lived about him and helped him. A fine white framed house took the place of their hut at his aerie, and from this he could see the approach of the enemy for four miles.

The federal officers must have approached his house under the cover of darkness and even at that it is remarkable that they escaped the attention of the many friends of Sully living about him. Numerous attempts have been made to take him, but all were ineffective."

"Only twice in the past four years has Sully been captured. The first of these was in the fall of 1901. The habit of the rustlers was to take only a part of a herd the first time. If no fuss was made the owner of the herd would not be disturbed again. But if he a noise about the theft, the rustlers would revisit his place and take the rest of the cattle."

1903-1904 criminal court docket

On July 7th 1904 the Oacoma Gazette Leader, for the purpose of serving as a reference at some future date printed the following abstract of fifty three criminal cases set for trial during the term:

A.M. Lamphere, charged with grand larceny, tried before Judge Gaffey, found guilty of grand larceny and sentenced to two years in the penitentiary.

Olof Nelson, grand larceny, dismissed by Judge Gaffey.

Nels Nelson and Carl Nelson, grand larceny, dismissed by Judge Gaffey.

Jack Sully and Nels Nelson, grand larceny, stricken off.

Jack Sully and William Kingkade, grand larceny, stricken off.

Ole Finstad, three cases, criminal, all dismissed by Judge Gaffey.

John Dillon, grand larceny, stood trial, acquitted.

Selah Fitzer and E.F. Fitzer, grand larceny, dismissed.

John Dillon, grand larceny, dismissed.

Henry Blunck, grand larceny, continued.

H.F. Briggs, grand larceny, continued.

Peter Bergland, grand larceny, dismissed.

Genert Somers, adultery, dismissed.

W.F. Phillips, grand larceny, bail forfeited for non appearance.

Jack Sully, grand larceny, three cases, all dismissed.

Peter Nelson, grand larceny, dismissed.

Fred Seymour, grand larceny dismissed

William Black Bull, grand Larceny, continued.

Harry Pipe, grand larceny, dismissed (died in Penitentiary).

Claude Eagle Pipe, grand larceny, continued.

Ed Fitzer, grand Larceny, tried, given three and a half years in the penitentiary.

Colin McBeth, continued by consent.

Myer Winter, information not filed, case dismissed.

James ? Boyd, grand larceny, bench warrant issued.

Jesse Combs, grand larceny, plead guilty, given three years in the penitentiary.

Noel Armstrong, rape, hung jury.

Lebanon B. Somers, arson. Dr. Goodrich filed affidavit that Somers had indications of typhoid fever, hence continued. (Which proves that not only is it important to have a smart lawyer but a friendly physician as well. In the 1960s Attorney

D.R. Herman of Gregory, S.D. kept a well known member of the South Dakota
Stockgrowers in a Nebraska hospital until a charge of larceny of lost or strayed cat-
tle was dismissed. Perhaps Somers' lawyer was only following the example of
Union General McClellan, who, when President Lincoln ordered him to attack the
Northern Army of Virginia, became suddenly sick with typhoid fever.)

Henry Bonser, grand larceny, tried, convicted, given three years and six months
in the penitentiary.

Mark Slow Eagle and Goggle Eyes, same charge as Bonser, found guilty of petit
larceny.

MM Charley Johnson, grand larceny, bond forfeited on account of non appearance, case continued.

Earl King, arson, (this was for the burning of the buildings of editor E.L.Senn
of Iona.) found guilty of arson in the third degree, given four years in the penitentiary (King and Somers, who had "typhoid fever," were jointly charged with this
crime.)

Turtis Offerson, grand larceny, bail forfeited on account of non appearance.

Noel Armstrong, bond for keeping the peace, dismissed.

Gus Neidner, grand larceny, stealing a shanty, bond forfeited on account of non
appearance.

E.R. Strang and H.L. Bloomfield, continued.

Albert Night Pipe, grand larceny, continued.

Andrew Night Pipe, grand larceny, continued

Carl Zwer, shot a steer, found guilty, fined $400 by the court. Fine promptly paid.

John Canoure (probably John Cournoyer). grand larceny, continued.

Olana Sanders, Jens O. Larson, Anton Syvertson, Edward West dismissed.

Editorial Comment

"Judging the term of court as whole, then, the people when called to sit as
jurors, triumphantly endorsed the policy of the present administration and forever
cleared our offices of the vindictive abuse and criticism hurled at them by some of
those who pretend to be law abiding citizens, but who inwardly are raving wolves
seeking who they may devour."

In commenting on the actions of the States Attorney, J.G. Bartine, the editor
states: "He fought when he stood almost alone, and for years was the chief target
on which the ring organ, the Leader and Gazette-Leader, at that time owned and
edited by I.N. Auld (also a lawyer and one time states attorney), hurled its vitu-
peration, venomous slime and abuse . . . .."

Peter Dierks, who had fought it out with Bartine in the court house was chastised during the term of court by Judge Gaffey.

It seems that Dierks had arranged for the complaining witness in the Lamphere
rustling case "to go north". They made the following agreement:

"W.G. Kenaston, President. S. Winters, Vice President, Peter B Dierks, Cashier.
THE CITIZEN BANK OF OACOMA. All collections receive prompt and personal
attention. Oacoma S.D. June 6th, 1903. It is agreed that whereas Phillip Nuss is to
make a trip to North Dakota on business for Peter Dierks and A. Lamphere that
the said Dierks and Lamphere will pay all expenses and other cost that may arise

out of the same whatever nature it may be. (Signed) Peter B. Dierks, A.M. Lamphere"

The court directed the State's Attorney to bring the matter of the attempt to have Nuss leave the state before Judge Smith for proper action.

The editor concluded:

"The reform ticket of two years ago has vindicated the wisdom and public spirit of those who put it in the field. No longer can one steal with impunity . . . .. Instead of being notorious, our county government is becoming famous."

"One Pete Waugh, living north of Oacoma, suffered a loss at the hands of the rustlers and made a big "beller". As a consequence another visit was made and all his stock was taken. Waugh only made a bigger racket. The rustlers were fearful and Sully and a associate named Donneran went to a dance where Waugh was to be. A row was started, but the bullet struck Waugh's elbow instead of his heart and Sully and Donneran had to flee."

"Waugh's blood was up and, with the aid of officers, gave pursuit and captured Sully. The wily old leader soon gave bond and secured his liberty."

"Sully's one weakness was his passion for whisky, and this led to his last capture. It was found out in some way that Sully was to visit Niobrara, Neb., in the interest of a spree. Sully was remarkably successful in making these underground trips, getting into a back room in various towns near his eyrie and having his drunk and getting away without any but his friends knowing of his presence."

"This time he was inveigled into a game of cards. Liquor was handed out freely to him and he became hopelessly intoxicated. He awoke in the Niobrara jail. He was taken to Mitchell. The night the Mitchell sheriff died Sully escaped, and it is said to have cost him $1500. He made his getaway on relays of horses. It was said he emigrated to Canada, but instead went to Kansas. He returned to his old haunts once too often and met his end on the very eve of the time when the incoming of settlers would have driven him away for all time."

"Additional details of the killing of Sully have been received here, how he made a desperate break to escape from the officers."

"Ben Diamond, a neighbor of Sully's, by request of the officers, went to the Sully house and informed Jack that his place was surrounded and requested him to give himself up. He refused, saying:

"Goodbye to all. With fair play I equal three of them."

"Thrusting a 44 caliber Colt's revolver into his belt and mounting his horse, "Old Jim Longstring", he made a dash for life. He was commanded to halt, but did not obey. There were thirty shots fired by the pursuing officers, of which five took effect on the horse. By this time Sully had measured a distance of 450 yards between himself and the officers when a volley of shots was fired one of which took effect in Sully's back, causing him to reel and fall from his horse. When the officers approached him he was commanded to throw up his hands and he obeyed. Recognizing Deputy United State Marshall Petrie, he shook hands with him and asked for a drink of water after which he expired."

Chapter Thirteen End Notes

1. Col. Cropp SD Historical conference paper 1980 conference.
2. True magazine article, SD Archives, Sully file.
3. SD Archives, Sully file, notes on Nelson interview.
4. True West, articles included in Sully index, Denver Public Library, Western room.
5. Gnirk, Adeline. *Saga of Sully Flats.*
6. *RoundUp Years*, p. 227.
7. SDHC Vol. 22, pp. 99-101.
8. Lyman County History, Lyman County Historical Society.
9. *RoundUp Years* p. 373.
10. *RoundUp Years* p. 256.
11. State v. Vincent Charles Mix county clerk of courts.
12. *Charles Mix County News*, May 19, 1904.
13. *RoundUp Years* p.372.
14. *Chamberlain Register*, June 13, 1901.
15. Ibid. Virgil Boyles court reporter from 1898 recalls that Jack Sully once escaped in Oacoma through a window and that croton oil had been placed in meat to make jurors sick. See: Bert Hall collections SDSA.
16. *Chamberlain Register*, August 9, 1900.
17. See contemporaneous newspaper accounts, infra.
18. Court records, Lyman county, Kennebec, S.D. County Judge Charles Milner wrote to Hall on 2-26-49. ". . . I was States Attorney of Gregory when many in Oacoma prosecuted. We had some lively tilts and I know much of the history and that they had not stolen stock, but has bought some stolen cattle at reduced prices. RoundUp Years p. 366.
19. Interview Sonny Waln, infra.
20. SDHC Vol. 3 pp. 21-22, Vol. 20, pp. 168-169.
21. Ibid.
22. State v. Finstead, Lyman county court house records, Kennebec, S.D.
23. *RoundUp Years*, p. 234.
24. State v. Sully, Gregory County Clerk of Courts office.
25. *RoundUp Years* p. 430.
26. Lyman County History, Lyman county Historical Society.
27. *RoundUp Years* p. 170.
28. Ibid.
29. *Iona Pioneer*, May 19th, 1904.
30. Ibid.
31. *RoundUp Years* p. 227; SDHC Vol. 33 p. 215.
32. *RoundUp Years*, pp. 289, 487, 488, 489.
33. Ibid pp.295-296.
34. Clyde Libolt wrote to Hall that when his uncle returned from Wyoming he had a man by the name of Jack Kincaid with him. Jack "confided" that his real names was Jones and that he had come to evade the law. Jack had a college education and was a capable cowboy. He could neck rope and we never heard from him afterward. Roundup Years p. 111.

Editorial comments are from:

Oacoma Gazette Leader, May 19, 1904; *Lyman County Record,* Nov 5, 1903; *Oacoma Gazette*

CHAPTER FOURTEEN
THE HOMESTEADER

Vast and rapid changes had taken place in the cattle industry from 1891 to 1903. Prior to 1903, "grass was king" on all the Dakota ranges. Cattle shipped from South Dakota in 1902 was valued at $9,424,067.00. All were fattened on the western prairie grasses of what was once the Great Sioux Reservation.[1] From 1892 to 1903 the Stockgrower Associations spent $11,977.57 to prosecute cattle crimes.[2] In 1902 strays valued at $503,533.02 were taken up by the Association.[3]

The homesteader and the wire fence coupled with good farm prices would soon dethrone grass as king. By 1903 good corn ground was selling for $100.00 an acre.[4] "Boys I'm telling you, the sky's the limit" the boomers would cry.

Competition for the new settlers and the state capitol was so intense that Hughes County "boomers" bought all of the produce for their exposition at the state fair in Huron in Nebraska and Kansas.[5]

Within in a decade and a half the last of millions of buffalo and thousands of Lakota Sioux would be replaced by thirty to sixty thousand trespassing cattle, which would be rounded up to be replaced by over a hundred thousand hopeful homestead applicants.[6]

Gregory, Tripp and Lyman county would be the focal debarkation point for countless dreamers who would hope to be lucky homesteaders.

The plow, which the great boomers claimed brought the rain[7] and over 115,000 homestead applicants would by great relays of trains be brought into what had recently been the land of the buffalo, Lakota, longhorn, cowboy and Jack Sully. It was one great American lottery. The State of South Dakota claimed that wealth production per capita in 1903 exceeded that of any other state in the union.[8] Go west to Dakota young man, go west.

Go west they did. Some lived lives of great expectations. Others failed to win at the homestead drawing and would go on to greater glories. Other would win a homestead and lose a life. The following accounts set forth some dreams, excitement, and dashed hopes of this vast migration.

In the late 1800s and early 1900s homestead fever had struck America. It was the nation's first and greatest lottery. The great Sioux Nation was being opened for homestead. For just $15.00 bucks and the price of a trip west for the registration and drawing any American could have land. Their own land. A new beginning. A new adventure.

Some, like my grandfather, Casper Fergen, who had migrated from Madison, Wisconsin in the 1880s to Parkston, South Dakota, staked his sons and daughters to a year's residence on whatever homesteads or relinquishments were available. A dreamer and a traveler he rode the rails to every new land opening in the west. Along the way his children homesteaded in north central Nebraska and Gregory and Meade Counties in South Dakota. Some of the homesteaded land stayed in the family for years, as in Meade County, where no buyers could be found and perhaps because the family remembered the sightings of "St. Elmo's fire" in the evenings made Grandpa believe that there was a new "richness of oil out there grandson", just lurking around waiting for somebody to grab onto it.

"For God's sake slow down, we are over the dome right now" he would shout as he would have one of my older brothers drive him to the site of his most recent oil drilling venture.

"Its gonna be a gusher, Jack for sure" he'd shout to me over the noise. Sure, Grandpa, sure I thought, another gusher–just like the last gusher–all artesian water. Somewhere, according to Grandpa all that artesian water had forced tons of oil up into a "dome" and all he had to do was find it. He never did but he had the greatest time searching, and I had the greatest time watching and listening to his stories and tales of homesteads, searching for oil, growing up with Robert Lafollete, his knowing Alexander Graham Bell (Grandpa thought he was a pure counterfeit), wild chases in the west, and wheat fields taller than my head.

When he died the local Parkston South Dakota paper headlined him as the greatest story teller in the history of the town and Hutchinson County's biggest character. Grandpa taught me that it's more important to have fun along the way than to accomplish all your dreams.

Harry S. Truman tries his luck

A Missouri farm boy who took the lottery trip to Gregory in 1911 came to the same conclusion, that the trip in itself should be something to enjoy. He wrote a book of letters to his beloved from 1910 til his death in 1959.

This one, dated October 22, 1911, describes his trip to the great Gregory, South Dakota Homestead drawing:

"Would you like to hear what we did going and coming from notorious Gregory? I am going to tell you anyway because it is on my mind and I shall have to unburden it."

"To begin with, it was just like riding a crowded street car for a day and a night. We took a sleeper to Omaha going and coming. From Omaha up, trains were running every hour or so all day Tuesday, Wednesday, and until Thursday noon. You see, the R. R. companies from one end of the country to the other give special rates on first and third Tuesdays of each month. We got to Omaha Wednesday morning at a quarter to eight and left at eight. They had to call special police to handle the crowds at Union Station. We managed to get seats in the last coach. There were 687 people on the train and nearly all were nice looking Americans. I only saw about a dozen bohuncks all the way there and back. I never got so tired at looking at yellow cars in my life. The Chicago and Northwestern uses all yellow coaches. We played pitch and seven-up all day, taking turn about at each eating station because we didn't dare leave our seats all at once. Murray Colgan's wife fixed us the finest lunch a person could want anyway, so we didn't go hungry."

"At nearly every station, we met trains coming back. People on them would yell Sucker! Sucker! at us and men on our train would do the same. One fellow hollered for us to go right on through to a very hot place. It sounded like a good place to be up there, it was so cold."

"We got to Gregory at about 10:30 p.m. Then began a chase for a place to sleep. The hotel man finally agreed to give us a cot a piece in the waiting room, which was some luxury, I tell you. There were people who sat up all night.

"After we'd cinched our rooms we went and registered at the Cow Palace, a wooden shack. It takes about one minute to so it. There were about 20 notaries inside a hollow square. I bet there was more swearing going on there than there will be in one place again. I really don't know what a Quaker would have done. They didn't ask you to swear but just filled out papers-and you were sworn before you knew what was happening. I registered for a soldier friend so that I have a chance to get 160 acres and half another. There about four hundred claims that are worth from $8,000 to $12,000 each. Of course, I'll draw one of them. There are several thousand worth from $40 to $4000 depending of course on location."

"There is an old Sioux Indian on the reservation who is 123 years old. She looks like Gagool in Rider Haggards, King Solomon's Mines. I didn't see her but I have her picture."

"I saw all of Gregory I cared to in about an hour and a half. It is strictly modern town of about 1500 . . . ..

"I am glad I went. I have a good chance to win as anyone. Even if I don't I had fun enough to pay for the going.

Most sincerely.

Harry"[9]

President Truman lost his bid for a homestead claim in Gregory County, South Dakota in 1911, but he had seen the west and he knew that the trip itself should be something to enjoy. Who would have guessed that this young farm boy from Missouri, who had participated in the great land lottery would be President of the United States?

In light of what happened to Albert Wood, who did secure a filing on a homestead, Harry S. Truman was a lucky man indeed.

Albert and Addie Wood and their five children ages 2 to 11 years came to Gregory and Tripp County, South Dakota from Fort Dodge or Boone, Iowa on May 23, 1909 to participate in the great land drawings. Albert Alfred Wood was 34 years of age. He had been a sewing machine agent in Iowa when he decided to try his luck at the homestead drawing.

Imagine the joy in the Wood family when they discovered that out of 100,000 registrants that their name had been drawn as one of the 4000 lucky winners. At last a chance to build a home of their own, no more working for others, a dream come true. They were now a part of the great American west where a man must take care of himself and be free. In the prime of their lives and with a young family they were America's manifest destiny.

The family of seven arrived on their claim, south of Roseland (renamed Hamill) South Dakota, on October 1st 1909. Within two short weeks the violence of the west would dash their dreams into a bitter and deadly harvest.

I can look out the window of my farm home, not far from where the Woods homesteaded and can imagine that in 1909 there were no roads, no electricity, just prairie, wind and sky. The only trees to be found were along small streams and would soon be harvested for fuel. Even the ancient Indian camps are found only where wood and water were in abundance. Here, these young city folks were facing a Dakota winter alone and unprovided for. No Indian in his right mind would spend the winter in the open on that vast windswept, snow swirling plain no matter what shack had been built to protect him from the howling, freezing, sneering Dakota winter blizzard. Dakota nature is sweet and sour. In the spring the clear blue skies, the fresh and fragrant west wind, the small prairie pockets of wild flowers and the rolling hills belong only to those who can see them. But death and nature's disaster leavens all.

The family built a small shelter to protect them from the fiercely fickle Dakota winter. They must also put up hay before the ground became covered with snow.

On October 9, 1909, a neighbor, Chris Pringle, ate his meal with them and helped Albert Wood mow hay. On the same day two men came on the Pringle claim and Albert Wood ordered them off the land. Later that same day Wood and Pringle rode to the Gregory Land Office to file on the claim that Wood had run the two strangers off. They were shocked to learn that the claim had already been taken. They then went to attorney McDonald's office in Gregory where they met John Langan.

John Langan was a former Scout for the United States Calvary in the Indian wars. Langan accosted Wood and stated: "Are you the one who chased my boy off?" Wood admitted he was and Langan replied, "Well, I am coming up there to build a house and you won't chase me off."

Pringle and Wood then went to the office of attorney A.J. Wilson and employed him. The following Monday Pringle left and did not return.

Mr. and Mrs. Wood mowed the "south forty" the following week and while mowing she stated that they saw someone taking hay from one of their stacks. She stated that her husband got his gun and fired over that way to scare them off.

On Saturday the 16th of October her husband saw some men near his hayrack. Albert took his gun and left. Mrs. Wood said she heard one shot and one shot only.

After waiting for him to come to breakfast she got uneasy and started to look for him. She found three men on the butte east of her claim, but could not find her husband.

After waiting a time she went to look again and her husband waved to her from the foot of the Butte. He asked her for water and told her he was "shot through the heart." Mrs. Wood stated that her husband told her that "he had fired at them, but was just trying to scare them." He also told her that all three of the men fired at him. Albert Wood died in her arms at the foot of the Butte, just east of Snow Dam. Mrs. Wood then waved to the three men, she talked to them and they sent Wood's wagon to Mr. Miller and Mr. Moss for help.

Mr. Ross, Mr. and Mrs. Kloke, a neighbor just to the south, took the widow to the Moss homestead.

Mrs. Wood indicated that her husband had an Army Springfield rifle that used 45/70 cartridges.

John Langan told Mrs. Wood that he had shot her husband. Mr. Langan told her he held up his gun and asked to talk to her husband. Langan told her that her husband would not talk but shot at him. Langan told her that after her husband shot at him he killed him.

A William F. Kloke of Spencer, Nebraska testified that he was erecting a residence on his daughter's claim on Section 15, 101-74 and had known Albert Wood prior to his death.

While shingling the roof he heard several shots and thought the shots were a "bluff game".

Later one of the Langans came and asked him to help Mrs. Wood take her husband into his home.

He found Albert Wood dead about 80 rods from his house. He saw a 45-70 single shot rifle in Woods house and several 45-70 shells in Woods pocket.

He testified that on the week previous Frank Langan and Leo Hannan had gone to Margaret Langan's claim to get hay for their horses and while there Wood had shot at them 4 times and that he saw Wood shoot.

On the following day he had heard the decedent tell Frank Langan to "stay off that place unless you want trouble." Kloke testified that at the time of both shootings the Langans were at Margaret Langan's place.

Windsor Doherty was the prosecuting attorney and he charged John Langan, Frank Langan and Leo Hannan with murder.

Oliver Lamereaux and Don A. Sinclair were the bondsmen for John Langan, who was released on $1,000.00 bond by County Judge L. B. Callender.

John Langan took the stand and testified in his own defense that he had shot in self-defense. P.J. Donohue, a pioneer lawyer of Bonesteel (father of former Attorney General Parnell J. Donohue), testified as to John Langan's good character and reputation for truth. Langan was found not guilty by the all male jury.[10]

Chapter Fourteen End Notes

1. Kingsbury, George W., *History of Dakota Territory*, S.J. Clark Publishing Co Chicago, 1915, Volume III, p. 505.
2. Ibid. p. 505.
3. Ibid. p. 506.
4. Ibid. p. 506.
5. Ibid. p. 506.
6. Ibid. p. 504.
7. D.C. Poole. *Among the Sioux of Dakota: Eighteen Months' Experience As An Indian Agent.* New York D. Van Nostrand, 1881.
8. *History of Dakota Territory*, p. 506.
9. *Dear Bess, The letters form Harry to Bess Truman 1910-1959*, Edited by Robert H. Ferrell, W.W. Norton Co., N.Y. and London, pp. 53-54.
10. State v. Langan et al, Tripp county clerks of courts file.

EPILOGUE

Jack Sully did not "conform". He never sold his talents to the big roundups or became a "stoolie" or hired gun for the powerful as did Tom Horn, Frank Canton, Kid Rich, Ed Blakely, Phil Dufran, Mike Shonsey and even his old friend, Whitcomb.

Jack Sully died in the arms of his young daughter, Eva.

That fateful day would haunt her every day for the rest of her life. To the very end of her nearly 100 years on this earth she was convinced that Harry Ham had fired the fatal shot that killed her dad. Rita Amondson, a nurse at the Gregory Nursing Home where Eva spent her last days, said that Eva relived the dreadful death of her father every day of her life.[1]

John Kincaid's son, Billy Kincaid, who was raised by Jack Sully, was also accused of rustling cattle on the Rosebud. The rustling charges against him were dismissed and Billy successfully sued his accuser for malicious prosecution.[2]

Billy Kincaid moved to the closed portion of the Rosebud Reservation, died in 1948 and was buried at St. Francis Mission cemetery at St. Francis, Todd County, South Dakota. One of his descendants, Robert Moran, was President of the Rosebud Sioux Tribe. Others, including the Waln family are respected members of the Tribe.[3]

Shortly after the big "Roosevelt roundup" in 1902 most of the foreign and eastern outfits went "belly up". With their demise, hired guns, ambushes and vigilante activity ceased. Under the headline of "BIG STOCK OUTFITS A THING OF THE PAST", the Chamberlain Democrat of October 7th, 1906 reported that big outfits of western South Dakota and Wyoming going out of business. They reported that the "3V" and the "BxB", two of the largest cattle companies in the west, had sold out their entire stock.[4]

The Madison Sentinel of March 1st, 1912 reported that Mrs. Mary Sully, widow of Jack Sully, the so called "king of the cattle rustlers" who was shot and killed some years ago during a running fight with federal officers, and her children and other descendants, by a decision handed down here by Judge James D. Elliot, of the United State District Court are awarded more than 50 quarter sections of land, aggregating more than 9,000 acres situated in the ceded portion of the Rosebud Indian reservation in Gregory County, South Dakota.

The Sentinel indicated "Mrs Sully, although a mixed blood Indian, had accumulated considerable wealth in addition to the lands awarded to her, she being the owner of horses valued at between $25,000 and $30,000.00."[5]

The Nelson brothers prospered and purchased a large ranch in southwestern Tripp county. Olof Nelson became President of a Sioux City bank that loaned money to ranching interests in early Lyman County.[6]

Olof Finstead operated a sale barn at Gregory later moved to Hondo, Alberta, Canada.

Frank Drapeau, John Cournoyer, John Waugh and Sully's foreman were sentenced to the penitentiary for larceny.

Fred Lee, the photographer who showed up just after Sully was shot, remains a mystery. Was his presence sheer happenstance or had he been sent to get the proof that the notorious "Jack" had in fact been killed?

Officers Long and Petrie retired. Ed Blakely faded into history. Neither Petrie or Long would ever tell who shot Jack Sully, except to deny that they were responsible.

Harry Ham died after falling from a hay stack near Sully Flats.

At a recent history conference I asked Harry Ham's grandson, "do you believe your grandfather shot Jack Sully?" He replied, "the neighbors all tell me that my grandfather was the only man in the posse who could shoot straight enough to hit Sully." In leaving he said, "You know Mr. Simpson, that my grandfather made peace with the Sully family before he died".

Richard Salzman, an old timer who grew up next to the Ham place, described a visit he and his father made to Harry Ham when he was in the Chamberlain hospital after the accident that resulted in his death.

"The room reeked of death", he said. Upon leaving his father mused: "Dick," he said, "his back is broken in the same place he shot Jack Sully!".

Epilogue End notes

1. Interview Rita Amondson student Sinte Gleska University 1991
2. Kincaid v. Strong, Tripp county clerk of courts.
3. Interview, Mary Waln, St. Francis, S.D. 1991.
4. Chamberlain Democrat, October 7, 1906
5. Madison Sentinel, March 1, 1912
6. Harmon Ms.,Roundup Years pp.263;331;436

Appendix One

In 1912 the Eight Circuit Court of Appeals decided the case of Sully, et al v. United States et al. 195 Federal Reporter 113.

Mary Sully and others sued for the right to select Indian allotments. In ruling in the plaintiff's favor the court made the following findings of fact which set out the lineage of Mary Sully and her descendants. From a young Indian babe born near the stockade at old Fort Pierre, to the widow of Jack Sully, Mary's life represents the hardships and changes of "West River."

Findings of Fact

(1) That prior to 1840, Scares at his Shadow, a full-blooded Yankton Indian and Wistu, a full blooded Ai or Crow Creek Indian woman, intermarried upon what was then the Great Sioux Indian reservation, and as issue of said marriage an Indian girl, who was named Goodline was born.

(2) That thereafter, when Goodline was about 14 years of age, in 1850 or 1851, Goodline. . . married a Frenchman named Goulette, on the Great Sioux reservation near old Ft. Pierre, and was a little later deserted by Goulette, and a issue of said marriage an Indian girl was born, near the old stockade at Ft. Pierre, within the Great Sioux reservation, in the now State of South Dakota, in the year 1852 named Mary Goulette (now Mary Sully), who is the above named complainant; the rest of the complainants being her descendants, as will appear from further proceedings.

(3) That in 1868 said Mary Goulette (now Mary Sully) married Henry Brindell, a white man, and an employee at the Whetstone Issue Station on the Great Sioux reservation, and they continued to reside there until 1869 when the said Henry Brindell died, and was buried near the old Whetstone-Issue Station on said reservation, and there was born to them, the issue of said marriage, a daughter named Mary Brindell (now the complainant Mary McGhee hereinafter referred to); Mary Brindell being born at her father's place east of the Missouri river just across from the Whestone agency, soon after her father's death.

(4) That in 1889 said Mary Brindell was living on the Rosebud reservation on the west side of the Missouri river on one of the islands in the Missouri river, same being a part of the reservation, and was married to Pat Gaughen, said marriage taking place on the east side of the Missouri river in Charles Mix County, where she continued to reside with her husband for a period of about six months, when she and her husband returned to the west side of the river on what was known as Pocahontas Island, where they had resided before being married, she with her mother, and he as an employee of one of her relatives.

(5) That there was born to them the issue of said marriage, five children, complainants herein, Emmet Gaughen, born in 1893; Ollie Gaughen, born in 1894;

Mollie Gaughen, born in 1896; Julia Gaughen, born in 1899; Emma Gaughen, born in 1900-all of whom were born upon the said reservation and said Pat Gaughen died and was buried on Rosebud reservation in 1900.

(6) That after the death of said Pat Gaughen his wife, Mary Brindell, married a white man, Nels McGhee in 1902. That they continued to live on the Rosebud reservation, and in 1903 there was born, the issue of said marriage, a daughter named Grace McGhee, one of the complainants herein.

(7) That subsequent to the death of Henry Brindell in 1869, and about 1871, the said Mary Brindell (now Mary Sully) married John Kinkaid, a white man, on the east side of the Missouri river in Charles Mix County, at which place there was born to them, the issue of said marriage, Amy Kinkaid (now LaRoche), who is now enrolled and allotted on the Lower Brule agency, and who is not a party to this action; the complainant William Kinkaid, born in 1874; and Estelle Kinkaid (now complainant Estelle Blackbird, born in 1875. And said John Kinkaid died in 1877.

(8) That on January 3, 1892, said Estelle Kinkaid, daughter last above named, married Joe Blackbird, a white man, on the Rosebud reservation, where they have continued to reside, and there was born to them upon said reservation, the issue of said marriage, the complainants Susie Blackbird, born in 1896; and George Blackbird, born in 1900.

(9) That subsequent to the death of John Kinkaid above named, his widow, Mary Goulette Brindell Kinkaid married John Sully, on the East Side of the Missouri River in Charles Mix County. That as the issue of said marriage between Mary and John Sully there was born to them on Pocahontas Island, within the Rosebud reservation, the following named complainants in this action: Louisa Sully (now Louisa Waugh), born in 1882, Eva Sully, born in 1884; Millie Sully, born in 1885; John Sully, born in 1887; Frank Sully, born in 1888;George Sully, born in 1890; Samuel Sully, born in 1893;and Claude Sully, born in a 1897. And said John Sully died and was buried on the Rosebud reservation in 1904.

(10) That in 1900 Louisa Sully, the oldest child above named, was married to a white man named Frank Waugh, at and upon the Rosebud reservation, and there was born to them, on said reservation, the issue of said marriage, complainants herein as follows: John Waugh, born in 1901; May Waugh born in 1903: Reanor Waugh born in 1905, in Canada, during a temporary absence from the reservation.

Judge Elliot made other findings and conclusions, which may be useful to researchers or relatives. The whole case may be found at Sully, et al v. United States et al. 195 Federal Reporter 113.

APPENDIX TWO

The following excerpts are taken from an article written by Father John J. Jutz, S.J. Father Jutz, little known to American history, helped establish Jesuit Missions at the Wind River Reservation in Wyoming and St. Francis and Holy Rosary in West River South Dakota.

Father Jutz was born October 26, 1838 near Feldkirch, Austria. He was in military service during the Franco-Prussian war (1870-1871). Kaiser Wilhelm expelled the Jesuit Order from Germany on July 4, 1872. Jutz finished his priestly studies in Holland and Britain and was sent to minister to the Indians of North America in 1880. In 1885 he was sent to Wyoming and in 1887 he started his work among the Sioux at Pine Ridge, South Dakota. He continued such work until 1896 when he was transferred to Boston and in 1910 was sent to Buffalo, N.Y. He died March 21, 1924 at 86 years of age at Buffalo, New York.

See: German Missionary Participation During The Ghost Dance of 1890, NATIVE AMERICAN STUDIES 6:1 1992, Adriana Greci Greene pp 31-34.

The Canisius Monthly

October, 1918

(The Canisius Monthly is a literary magazine published by the students of Canisius College at Buffalo, N.Y.)

Excerpts printed with permission of Office of Archives, Rev John D. Garvey, S.J., Canisius College, 2001 Main Street, Buffalo, New York, 14208-1098

Recollections of an Old Indian Missionary.

(By Rev. John Jutz, S. J.)

HISTORIC DATA ON THE CAUSES OF THE DISSATISFACTION
AMONG THE SIOUX INDIANS IN 1890.

The Ghost Dance Religion

S I was an eye witness of the episode at "Wounded Knee" and the causes which led up to it, I thought the readers of the Monthly might be interested in its story.

As is well known, the Indian Reservations were thrown open to the white man under the presidency of General Grant. At once a number of adventurers, by no means insignificant, came out to hunt down the buffalo. That animal had been up to this time one of the chief sources of sustenance to the Indians. Hundreds upon hundreds of buffalo were shot down merely for the sake of securing the hides. Buffalo meat rotted on the Prairie in abundance, and the Indians gathered together bones, and sold them in wagon loads for a few dollars. When the Indians had no more buffalo meat, and other wild game had disappeared for the most part, the Government saw itself obliged to look about for another means of sustenance, if the Indians were not to starve.

To replace the buffalo, tame cattle were purchased by the Government and kept on the Reservations. These herds were guarded by keepers, and divided amongst the Indians according to need. Storehouses were also built at all the Agencies in which supplies were hoarded, such as clothes and clothes stuffs, shoes, and all varieties of foods, as flour, sugar, coffee, salt, lard, dried meat, in fact everything that was necessary and useful to sustain life. Every Indian family received a ticket, on which was recorded the number of members in each household. These tickets had to be brought to the Agency every two weeks, and with them the Indians could procure from the storehouses whatever was necessary for their support. Each received portions according to the number of individuals composing a family, it made no difference whether the persons were small or big, young or old. Meat was distributed on the hoof. Special cards were issued for this. The names of twenty persons were inscribed on these meat tickets, who together received a head of cattle every two weeks. On appointed days a number of heads from out of the great herd were driven into so-called corrals, or strongly hedged stockades. At the entrance the Indians on their ponies waited with their rifles. The name of a ticket was called, and a head of cattle was driven out. The Indians pursued the animal and shot it down on the prairies. The respective women then came and divided the meat. Such was the custom even as late as 1887; afterwards meat was apportioned as other victuals.

So far, so good. The Government had likewise destined sufficient supplies for each individual, so that the Indians would never have become dissatisfied had they gotten what was theirs. But now a difficulty intervened. The difficulty lay in the proper administration of these supplies and their conscientious distribution. At every Indian agency an agent was appointed to direct and supervise the supply problem, and it was no mean task. To effect it, practical and conscientious men were needed. The different supplies, such as meat, flour, clothing and all other material were contracted for by the Government, and the cheapest bidder got the contract. It was the duty of the agent to see to it that contracts were rigidly fulfilled, for vast sums of money were often involved. The meat contract alone for a few thousand Indians, amounted to more than $100,000 per annum. How did the contracts fare? Before I was sent to the Pine Ridge Agency in South Dakota to begin the Holy Rosary Mission, founded by Rev. Mother ,Catherine Drexel of Philadelphia, I had been engaged in missionary work amongst the Indians of the Shoshonie Reservation in Wyoming, and it was there that I first became acquainted with the Indians and their conditions.

A man of Lander City, a town situated about twelve miles from the Indian Reservation, and with whom I was personally acquainted, told me the following facts: He was the owner of a large cattle ranch, and hence was anxious to get the contract for the meat supply for the Indians of his vicinity. The contract was awarded to him. His herd was not large enough to supply what was needed, and so he was compelled to purchase meat elsewhere. The cost was higher than what he received from the Government by contract, and yet this man told me that he made money on the deal, and quite a sum too. How was that possible? It happened this way: Before the cattle were distributed amongst the Indians, they were weighed on huge scales, large enough to weigh ten head at one time. If the man at the scales had very little or no conscience at all, it was a very easy matter to mark down eight or ten thousand pounds instead of five. The agent indorsed the statement, and the Government paid the contractor accordingly. Of course the agent and the man at the scales were not forgotten in the division of the spoils. And that is the way that most contracts were adhered to. I have heard it said by trustworthy persons at the Shoshonie Agency that whole loads of supplies were carried off by night from the Indian storehouses and sold at private places of traffic. The poor Indians had to be contented with the leavings. When I was at the Shoshonie Agency, the agent was a gentleman from Washington. This man declared in my hearing and in the presence of officers from the garrison at Fort Washekee that he spent 300 days out of the year gambling in Washington. He certainly was not the proper man to be entrusted with the office which he held. Very likely his luck at gambling was against him, and he made up his losses at the Agency. To get the position, he needed but a few friends at Washington.

At this Agency I got acquainted with a German, who had been in the Government employ before at Pine Ridge. He told me that whilst he was at Pine Ridge a new agent arrived, who carried all his earthly belongings in a carpet-bag. But the official declared that he hoped to be more prosperous when his term of office, after four years, had expired. He was agent for seven years, and I was told by a gentleman from Washington, who was well acquainted with Indian affairs, and was a staunch friend of the Indians, that when his term was over he was worth more than a million. He built himself a magnificent house in The Black Hills, and opened a bank. His brother at the time was steward of the supplies for the Indians. During his incumbency, the Indians suffered so greatly from hunger that they ate the meat of the carcasses of horses.

When we consider these facts we can readily understand the dissatisfaction of the Indians, and their destation of the dealing of the white man; this was particularly the case with the old Indians who still remembered former times.

At this period, too, a rumor began to spread amongst the Sioux Indians that there was a man in Utah who called himself the Messiah, or Redeemer, and who knew what the Indians had to do in order to get rid of the white man. The Sioux of North and South Dakota sent an embassy to him to inquire what they should have to do to rid themselves of their enemy. The Messiah taught them the so-called Ghost Dance. When the delegation returned, the Ghost Dance began in North and South Dakota. This was about September of the year 1890. What was the nature of this Ghost Dance? To be accurate, I shall try to describe it as I witnessed it. At White Clay Creek, about four miles distant from Holy Rosary Mission, there was a level plain about five to seven hundred meters square in area. About three-fourths of this plain was surrounded by low hills. At the foot of these hills about a thousand Indians in all had gathered in diverse groups. In the middle of the plain a tree had been erected about the thickness of a man's arm, and on this tree were hung objects of various kinds which the Indians held sacred. Before the dance began an Indian approached the tree, who was supposed to represent the Ghost. His face was made perfectly white, his hair hung loose, his arm hung at his side, and he wore the Ghost-shirt. The Ghost stood before the tree for about ten minutes, with head bent low, and then walked away. Every Indian wore a Ghost-shirt through which they imagined no bullet could penetrate. Figures of all kinds were painted on the shirts, such as riders on horses, buffaloes, and various wild animals. The dance began at ten o'clock in the morning. The different groups, with flags at their head, approached the middle of the alpin, forming a large circle around the tree. Men and women, young and old, stood shoulder to shoulder, no order being observed in size or age. They huddled close together, interlocking their fingers. Every group had a medicineman. They gave the signal to begin. At one end the dancers began to push one another with their shoulders, and this was passed along until finally the whole mass was set in motion. At the same time they began to sing, to wave their arms up and down, and to stamp with their feet. These gyrations became wilder and wilder, and every one yelled at the top of his voice. The song they sang was: "Ate ehe yelo, ate ehe yelo," which means: "Thus has the Father told us." Thus should they do that the Redeemer might come who would free them from the white man. After about a quarter of an hour one could see how different dancers began to distort their eyes, and how difficult it was for them to keep on their feet; yet they were still being held fast and whirled about. Finally they were thrown off, and the circle was again completed. Those who were discarded staggered either into the circle or outside of it, fell to the ground, sprang up again, made a few steps forward, fell headlong to the earth, and after rolling over a few times, lay as dead men on the ground. Thus the dance proceeded, until all were exhausted, and some dozen or more lay prostrate on the ground, dead, as the Indians said. After resting for a couple of hours, and after the dead had come back to life, the dance was resumed. Dying was an essential part of the dance, for the Indians were of the opinion that then they could hold converse with their deceased relatives and friends. During the dance I took up my position in the middle of the circle, dressed in my religious habit, and from my place of observation I could see everything that went on. I went over to those who were "resurrected from the dead" and asked them if they had spoken with their deceased friends. I offered them a dollar if they would tell me their experiences, but they would not answer me. I offered them two, three, four, five dollars, but they only looked at me and said not a word.

Then I said to them: "Do you not realize now yourselves how there is absolutely nothing in what you believe, and that you cannot speak with your dead friends, or see them?" But my words could not convert them from their folly, and they resumed the dance as soon as they were rested.

Some one may ask how this dance could have such an effect on the dancers. The answer is that there is in every man a so-called human magnetism, that can be transferred and directed from one person to another. It is well known that some persons can magnetize others. This magnetism is different in different individuals, and not all persons are equally susceptible to it. This element is excited during the Ghost Dance and brought into circulation, and passes through the entire circle like an electric current. Those who are more susceptible are so charged with it, that they lose all sense of hearing and seeing, and are even deprived of consciousness and sensation. At this dance it happened that some people lost consciousness only several hours after they had danced, as I saw with my own eyes.

Our chool children, boys and girls, were just crazy over the Ghost Dance, and as soon as they thought they were not being observed, they danced it. I was summoned one evening by the Superior of our nuns, and she said to me: "Father, I cannot make out what the matter is with some of our bigger girls; every night one or other of them is discovered in a very strange plight." I was brought into the sick room, and as soon as I saw the girl, I realized her condition, and told the Superior that her sickness was the result of the Ghost Dance, and that there was no danger. The next day I gave a conference to the girls in the school on the Ghost Dance; after that there were no more sick patients. One of our boys was affected in the same way. During his sickness, we had the honor of a casual visit from Monsignor Marty, the pious Bishop of South Dakota. I brought him into the sick room and showed him the boy.

An Indian who had a daughter at our school came to us one day and told us that he had danced for three days without being able to die; he was not going to dance any more. A woman related that she had died twenty-five times, but was still alive.

The Ghost Dance was performed at the Rosebud and the Pine Ridge Reservations, and also in North Dakota. The Indians were dancing all the time. This state of affairs was, of course, reported at Washington, and the Government sent word to the soldiers garrisoned at Fort Nebrata to go to Rosebud and break up the dance, and to send the Indians back to their camps. As soon as the Indians heard of this action, they left the dancing plain, came over with all their belongings to Pine Ridge Reservation, and pitched their camps in the so-called "Badlands." These Badlands are a wild barren stretch of land, several miles long. A ridge passes through the length of these lands, from ten to twenty feet in height, and on its crest is a large plateau. There was only one approach to this plateau, and it was there that the Rosebud Indians encamped. They could easily defend themselves on this height in case they were attacked by the soldiers.

The soldiers not finding the Indians at the Rosebud Reservation, followed them to Pine Ridge and encamped there. There was no intention on their part to fight the Indians, but only to bring them back in a friendly way to their camp. General Brock was in command of the soldiers, and had his headquarters at the house of the agent.

The question now was, what was to be done. No one hazarded to approach the Indians, and on the other hand the Indians were afraid of the soldiers. They numbered from six to seven hundred, and fear kept them from coming to the Agency. When the supplies which they had brought with them were exhausted, they stole cattle from the Pine Ridge Indians, and from the Government herds, wherever they could lay hands on them. This was the state of affairs towards the end of November.

(To be continued.)

Recollections of an Old Indian Missionary.

(By Rev. John Jutz, S. J.)

(Continued.)

The Ghost Dance and the Indians in the Badlands

HE talk everywhere was about the Ghost Dance and the Indians in the Badlands. At first I did not want to get involved in this very troublesome affair, but as I knew quite a few of the Hostiles, as these Indians were called, and was assured that they were not hostile to me, and would surely take a word of friendly advice from me, I changed my mind. I had worked amongst them for more than a year at St. Francis Mission in the Rosebud Reservation. This Mission was also established by the Rev. Mother K. M. Drexel. So I determined to make an attempt to extricate the Indians from their perilous plight. With this purpose in view I visited General Brock on the 2nd of December, and said to him: "General, I am willing to go to the Hostiles tomorrow, and I will bring back to you accurate information concerning their sentiments." The General was satisfied with the proposal, especially as he had no one to send down to them, least of all his soldiers, without shedding blood. From the General I betook myself to my friend Redcloud, whose house was within gun shot of the General's. I told Redcloud my purpose, and tried to induce him to accompany me. But the Chief excused himself, saying that he was not feeling well, that he had sore eyes, and that the weather was cold. But he said: "My son Jack can go with you." "Very well," I said, "if Jack comes along, it will be satisfactory; tell him to come to the Mission tomorrow morning early, and I will take him with me." Jack was about thirty years old, and had a daughter in our school. The next morning, it was the 3rd of December, Jack Redcloud came to the Mission around eleven o'clock. The conveyance was ready, and so we started on our journey at once. I also took a servant along, a Mexican, who was in our employ.

and who said he knew the way. It was about twelve miles to White River, and from there, again as far to reach the Indians. We halted at White River, and took refreshments at the house of the keeper who guarded the Government herds. About half-past three we continued our journey across the river. It was a cold, gloomy day. Soon it began to snow; darkness set in, and we lost our way. Whether we wished it or not, we could not go any further, for we were in danger every moment of driving into a hole, of which the Badlands had many. The ponies were unharnessed, tied to the buggy and fed, for we had brought fodder along. Jack Redcloud wrapt himself up in a blanket and threw himself on the ground, where a kind Providence soon provided him with a still warmer covering of snow. The servant and I guarded the ponies in turns. Whilst one watched the other could wrap himself up in a blanket and keep as warm as he could in the buggy. It was a long and not very pleasant night.. Two Indians had followed us, probably friends of Jack Redcloud. They rode on, for they were better acquainted in the neighborhood than we were. After a while it stopped snowing, and the sky became a little brighter. The servant went out to look for the trail, and luckily found it. The ponies were hitched up again, Redcloud crawled out of his snow white bed, and we set out upon our journey once more. About eight o'clock we arrived at the Indian camp and drove straight to the tent of the Chief. His name was "Twostrike." We alighted, and I went at once into his tent and greeted him with the customary salutation "How, How," and presented him with a little package of tobacco. He returned the greeting. In a few minutes the tent was filled with Indians, for the two Indians who had ridden ahead of us, had arrived the evening before and doubtless had made known our approach. I told the Indians that I had come to rescue them from their sorry plight, for they could not stay where they were. Besides their food suppy would soon run out, and they were not allowed to kill cattle which did not belong to them. I also told them that the soldiers had come to wage war against them, and that the General was a very kind gentleman, who would give them meat and everything else they needed. All they had to do was to come to the Agency, and from there they could quietly go back to their camp at Rosebud. They listened to me with great attention, and then one of them stood up and said: "Father, if what you say is true, lift up your right hand and swear to the Great Spirit that it is true." I stood up and lifted up my right hand. All the Indians arose and lifted up their hands as a token that they believed me. After this most solemn protestation, I said: "Very well, if you believe my word, I will take you to the General, and you will see that I have spoken the truth. Do you want to come with me at once, or when will you come??" The spokesman replied: "Father, we cannot go with you now; it is very cold, and we have many old people and children with us, but we men, we will go tomorrow." "Very well," said I, "you men come to the Mission tomorrow; you can stay over night there, and the next morning I will escort you to the General." All consented to this arrangement, and so the purpose of my mission had been attained.

We set off at once for home, which we reached before nightfall. Our slumbers that night were considerably more restful than on the previous night.

The following morning I went to General Brock, and told him of the success of my embassy, and he was very much pleased over it. Towards evening about forty Indians arrived at the Mission on their ponies. We kept them overnight, gave them hospitality, and fed their horses. But they did not seem to be in good spirits, and I asked them the cause of their discontent. They replied that they had met a man on the way who asked them whither they were going, and when they had told him that they were going to the Agency to meet the General, he had said: "Just go ahead, and the General will take you all prisoners." Hence they were uneasy. "What," said I, walking up close to them, "you know what I said to you, and if I have not told you the truth, you may shoot me." And I laid my hand over my heart. That quieted them, and after taking a good repast, they lay down to rest.

The next morning, after a good breakfast, the cavalcade started on its way to the General. I took Chief Twostrike with me in my buggy, which was drawn by two large handsome mules. Before and behind us and on either side of us rode the forty Indians. They were all well provided with good rifles and ammunition. When they came near the Agency they asked what they should do with their guns, for they were afraid that the soldiers would take them away. I told them they should not be uneasy, I would tell them what to do, and there was no reason for being afraid. They carried a white cloth on a pole, which no doubt was to represent a flag of truce. Thus we entered the Agency, heading directly for the residence of the General. Before the house, I said to the Indians: 'Now stand your guns against the wall, and when you come out take them up again." They did as I said.

There were several officers with the General when the Indians entered the room. The General sat on a raised platform, and bade me sit at his side. On the other side sat a good interpreter, whom I had recommended to the General. This man had Indian blood in him, was a good Catholic, and was conversant both with the English and Indian tongue. The General was very friendly towards the Indians, told them they had nothing to fear, that the soldiers were good friends of theirs, and had only come to tell them that they should return to their camp in the Rosebud Agency. He told them to bring their people to the Agency, where he would furnish them with supplies, and give them everything they needed, and then they could return quietly to their homes. The Indians were pleased, and after one of their number had made a few remarks expressive of their satisfaction, and a promise to come to the Agency in a body, the meeting was dissolved. The Indians took their rifles again, paid a visit to Chief Redcloud and other acquaintances, and appeared at night at the Mission where they were cared for. After they had left the General's quarters, I also started to go, but the General took me by the hand and said to me: "Father, if I should have any more trouble with the Indians in the future I shall call upon you first." The following morning the Indians returned to their camp with the best of intentions of coming to the Agency with their families, procure the necessary supplies, and then go back to Rosebud. The precarious situation seemed to be cleared up in a most satisfactory way without the shedding of one drop of blood.

When the forty Indians who had been in conference with General Brock returned to their camp in the Badlands, with the purpose of keeping their promise to the General, they were opposed in their design by an implacable medicine man. "Short Bull" was his name. He had not been one of the delegates at the conference, and he tried to alienate the other Indians from their intentions and to hold them back. When the dissatisfaction reached the ears of General Brock, he attempted to send a delegation of Pine Ridge Indians over to the Hostiles to remind them of their promise and to bring them to the Agency. But the Pine Ridge Indians did not want to undertake the mission. So I went to the General again, and offered my services a second time if he desired them, for I was convinced that I would meet with success. But the General did not fall in with my way of thinking, and gave me to understand from a telegram he had received from Washington that the authorities were not satisfied with the method of procedure. Probably the officers doubted that a simple Blackrobe could do more with the Indians than they.

Of course I did not wish to undertake the mission against the wishes of the General. No action was taken for nearly two weeks. In the meantime, Chief Bigfoot, with his braves, came from North Dakota to join forces with the Rosebud Indians in the Badlands. But they missed their way, and instead of reaching the Badlands they came to Wounded Knee Creek, and pitched their tents there. When news of this reached the Agency, the General gave orders to the soldiers to bring these people to the railroad, and have them transported back to North Dakota. The soldiers accordingly set out during the night or early morning for the Indian camp and surrounded it.

(To be continued.)

Recollections of an Old Indian Missionary.

(By Rev. John Jutz, S. J.)

(Continued.)

EV. FATHER CRAFT, who had arrived a few days previously from the Catholic Indian Mission Bureau at Washington, and who was living with Redcloud, went to the Indians with the soldiers to act as interpreter, for the soldiers could not converse with the Indians and explain to them the reason of their coming. The intention was good, and no one would have been better able to speak to the Indians than Father Craft. But as Father Craft was in civilian's dress, and did not wear his soutaine, he could not be recognized by the Indians as a priest in the heat of the conflict, nor execute his mission successfully. Unfortunately, too, a shot was fired before the conference began. Where the shot came from, from the soldiers or the Indians, no one seemed to know, and whoever did know it, had every reason for not telling it. At once a fierce battle ensued. The Indians numbered about two hundred, and almost all of them, young and old, men, women and children were killed or wounded. Twenty soldiers were buried in the cemetery at the Agency. There was a hospital full of wounded soldiers and Indians, men, women and children, whom I saw and visited more than once. During the bitter conflict Rev. Father Craft was stabbed in the back by an Indian, and lay sick abed for four weeks in consequence, in a little day school at the Agency, where he was nursed by a schoolteacher. I offered him a home at our Mission, where the Sisters would take care of him, but he preferred to remain at the Agency. If the Indians had recognized Father Craft as a priest, he certainly would have come to no harm. And if he had gone to the Indians alone, unaccompanied by soldiers, he would have accomplished the purpose of his mission. Indians cannot be governed or converted by guns and bayonets, but they can be won over by love and friendliness, and by much patience. The shooting at Wounded Knee could be heard at our Mission. An Indian of the neighborhood of the

Mission ran excitedly to our house to call my attention to it. About nine o'clock I wanted to go over to the Agency to find out what the trouble was. I took a young Indian with me in my buggy. Half way to the Agency we could see Indians riding wildly hither and thither on their ponies, dressed in full war regalia. Two of the warriors rode over us and bade us halt. They made a sign to my escort to get down from the buggy, which he straightway did. They motioned to me to turn back. I thought it more prudent to obey on this occasion, and I returned to the Mission and told the occurrence to the Sisters. The braves followed me for several hundred yards, and then turned back. Afterwards they came to the Sisters, and the nuns asked them why they had not allowed me to go to the Agency. They replied that they wished to do me no harm, but they did not want me to go. During the day several Indians passed the Mission on their way to the White River; we could see that some of them were wounded. I invited them to come to the Mission, but they proceeded on their journey. During the following night, the Indians burnt down all the houses of white men married to Indian women, and all the Government day schools along White Clay Creek. If no soldiers had been at the Agency, they would also certainly have burnt down the boarding school there. About ten o'clock a Brother came excitedly to my room and said: "Father, come and look, they are burning down the little school over yonder; what will happen to us now?" The little school was a gun's shot distance from our Mission. When I looked out I saw the school in flames, and the teacher and her husband and two children making for our Mission. Several Indians who had set fire to the school walked away quietly. I went out to them and asked them if they intended setting fire to our house, too. They answered nothing and went their way. One could see the smoke of the burning school, and everybody believed that the Mission was ablaze. At once a squadron of soldiers came up in command of the officer who had directed the battle of Wounded Knee. When the soldiers saw that the Mission was safe, they dismounted from their horses, and I invited the officer to come into the house for a moment. Whilst I was still speaking to him a few shots were heard about a mile off in the direction of White River. At once all the soldiers mounted their steeds, and rode off in gallop in the direction whence the shots were heard. Only a few minutes after they ran into the Indians, who fired on them from both sides of the road from the hills. The soldiers fired back at the Indians, but they could not pursue them. We could see the engagement from our windows. The following fact is a proof that the battle was waged near the Mission. Whilst two of the Brothers were sitting a the window and looking down at the soldiers, a rifle shot passed between them and lodged in the door on the opposite side of the room, where you can probably find it to this day. About twelve o'clock the soldiers were almost entirely surrounded, and I sent a messenger post haste to the General and told him to send assistance at once to the soldiers, for they were being hard pressed by the Indians. At once a squadron of black riders came out and rescued their comrades from their critical condition. The shooting continued until about four o'clock when it ceased suddenly. The soldiers withdrew to the Agency, and the Indians encamped about two miles from the Mission, in the direction of White River. These Indians were not from Rosebud, but from Pine Ridge, for all the Indians had become wild and warlike after the sad affair at Wounded Knee. During this engagement two wounded soldiers were brought to the Mission, and one was later found dead. We did not discover whether any of the Indians were killed or wounded. The Sisters offered their services to nurse the wounded soldiers, but they did not choose to remain at the Mission, and so returned to the Agency. The place of conflict was enshrouded in a light mist due to the shooting. The following night was a rather anxious one, for we did not know whether or not the wild and excited Indians would attack our Mission and burn it to the ground. The quiet of death reigned everywhere, and nobody came near us. Of course we were on the alert, and had our horses and cows in the stable. The following days were filled with anxious expectancy. During this time two newspaper reporters came to the Mission and asked to stay over night. We gave them hospitality, served refreshments, and let them have our best room. During those days we held services, followed by Benediction every evening in our chapel. The visitors heard the singing and the tones of the organ, for their room was not far from the chapel. They told us afterwards how the music had made an extraordinary impression upon them, and how they marveled how we could be so peaceful, lying, as we were, between two hostile camps without any protection whatever. I told them that the Indians were not hostile to us, nor the soldiers either, and so we had nothing to fear.

I mentioned above that it was commonly believed at the Agency that the Mission was afire, when the smoke of the burning school in the neighborhood was observed. This news was immediately telegraphed down to Roeschville, and from there to Buffalo, Omaha and Washington, and I received stringent orders from Buffalo to provide at once for the Sisters and to bring them into safety. Although I was not afraid, and had no doubt whatever concerning the welfare of the Sisters, I nevertheless called for the Mother Superior, and told her that I would let the Sisters be brought to the railroad if she wished it, and that I would not take the responsibility on myself to keep them at the Mission. Reverend Mother replied that she would not go away, but would ask the other Sisters what they contemplated doing. The answer came back speedily that all the Sisters would remain with their Superior, and no one wanted to leave. And so we remained unharmed at the Mission. Very soon single persons and even families came from the Indian camp to the Mission under cover of the night, for it was very cold, and they were short of provisions. We gave them food and kept them over night, so that they could return to their camp the following morning. During this time General Miles came to the Agency and took control of things. I visited him once, and found him a very noble man, but not as friendly as General Brock. General Miles sent General Brock to the rear of the Indians in the Badlands with a squadron of cavalry. But the fight was gone out of the Indians, and they willingly returned. They marched by our house for a whole day with their wagons and all their belongings. The road was close to the Mission. General Brock pitched his camp very near our station, and he came over to see us, and wrote a letter in my room. He invited me to come over to the camp whenever I had time, and confided secrets to me which he would not have exposed to his own officers. When the Hostiles came, General Miles demanded that they deliver up their guns to him. They gave him some old pieces, and he, as a prudent man, showed that he was satisfied. Then they were supplied with necessary provisions, and one band after another went back to Rosebud to their camps.

The soldiers encamped for some days in a large meadow, called "Extension," near the Agency, between Nebraska and Dakota, and then returned to civilization. It was here that I took farewell from General Brock, who invited me in a most friendly way to visit him if I ever went to Omaha. This is the real and true account of the sad episode of Wounded Knee in 1890.

[The End.]

APPENDIX THREE

Frank Canton had been charged with the bushwacking killing of John A.Tisdale on December 1, 1891 near Buffalo Wyoming in the Johnson County War.

Canton was charged with first degree murder in the Second Judicial District at Laramie and released on $30,000.00 bail. He was never brought to trial.

J. Elmer Brock was a local historian who sealed his primary evidence concerning the Johnson County War and deposited it with the Wyoming Archives of the University of Wyoming, not to be opened until 1973. The following letter was among such effects.

The powers that be treated this bushwhacking stock detective very well indeed.

J.Elmer Brock died shortly after the letter was written.

COPY

FRANK KELL, PRESIDENT JOSEPH A. KELL,
VICE PRES. C.M. CROWELL SECY-TREAS
THE TEX-MEX CATTLE COMPANY
WICHITA FALLS, TEXAS
September 20, 1936

Mr. J. Elmer Brock
Kaycee, Wyoming.

Dear Mr. Brock:

I have your favor of the 9th. I very well remember meeting you in Mr. Hollins office on the morning of August 21st and also remember seeing you in the meetings that day and the next.

The late Frank M Canton's real name was Joe Horner. A brother of Capt. Burnett married a sister of Joe Horner, and therefore, Horner became a member of one of the most important families in Texas.

All of the Burnetts were very substantial people. Capt. Burk Burnett became one of our most prominent citizens. His brothers were all prominent men and therefore, Mr. Joe Horner's brother in law was one of the leading citizens of Northwest Texas.

Joe Horner went through to Kansas with a herd of cattle in 1869. The herd having been started in Palo Pinto and Jack County, Texas. Mr. Horner at the time was probably around 18 or 19 years of age.

He and four or five cowboys came back from Kansas over the trail. The first place they struck where there was intoxicating liquor was Jacksboro, Texas, at which point there was located a Government Fort known as Fort Richardson. There was a detachment of negro soldiers quartered at Fort Richardson at that time. These cowboys, as was the custom, in those days, got "Full" and as usual "Shot up the town." The negro soldiers undertook to arrest them but failed to do so, and when the fight was over there were five dead negroes, and no cowboys under custody.

These boys decided not to go home but struck out west passing through the town of Momanche, Commanche County, Texas, where there was a small bank. They stopped at this point and robbed the bank. Young Horner seems not to have participated in the robbing of the bank, and did not know the other boys were robbing the bank, he having been left to hold the horses.

He was arrested, however, for robbery, was tried, convicted and given a sentence of around 25 years.

The rumor is that the Sheriff's daughter became interested in him and gave him his liberty, after which he seems to have gone to your country and adopted the name of Frank M. Canton.

He seems to have gotten tired of dodging anyone who might have been a Texas officer and in 1894 he came from your country to Texas, stopped at Amarillo and employed a well known and substantial lawyer by the name of Judge Plemmons and he and Judge Plemmons went to Austin asking a pardon from the Governor of Texas, who was Hon. Jim Hogg, a very forceful character.

Judge Plemmons succeeded in getting the Governor's interest in the matter but did not get a direct promise from the Governor that he would grant a pardon. He finally said to Judge Plemmons-"By Gatlins I am not going to pardon him in the bush"

This remark became famous in Texas, and is yet quoted by a great many of Governor Hogg's old friends.

(authors note: Governor Hogg had named one of his daughters Ima.)

Judge Plemmons went back to where he had Horner secreted and told him the scope of his discussion with the Governor, and told him he thought the Governor would grant him a pardon, but he might decide to hand him over to the Department of Justice, and told Horner the matter was so serious that he, Horner, would have to decide the question himself. Horner went to his grip, got out his six shooter, stuck it in his waistband and said he was going to see the Governor and if he tried to turn him over to the Department of Justice Texas will need a new Governor tomorrow.

Horner presented himself to the Governor and interested him to such an extent that he granted a pardon, and he left Texas a free man.

My own interpretation of the matter is he was entitled to a pardon and was probably not guilty of the charge of robbing the bank.

None of these cowboys seemed to have been indicted for killing the negro soldiers. At the time it was not considered a crime for a Texas citizen to kill a negro soldier.

As you probably well know, Canton, a few years after his pardon was made a United State Deputy Marshall in the Klondike country, and as such for a year or so. Later he became Cattle Inspector for the Texas Cattle Raiser's Association, securing this appointment through the influence of the Burnett family. He served in this capacity in Northern Oklahoma, chiefly in the Osage country and was occupying this position when Statehood came to Oklahoma in 1907.

The first Governor of Oklahoma, Hon. J.M. Haskell appointed Frank M. Canton, Adj. General. He served in this capacity four years and it was while serving in this position that I had my first personal acquaintance with him.

He has a niece living in Wichita Falls, who is the wife of one of our prominent citizens. For the last many years Canton was a frequent visitor here calling on his niece, her husband and their family.

You probably know he died only two years ago, at his home in Edmond, Oklahoma, a small town north of Oklahoma City, where he had lived for the last many years.

Trusting that this short sketch may be of service to you and with kindest regards,

Yours Truly

Signed Frank Kell

INDEX